Cry of Wonder

Cry of Wonder

Our Own Real Identity

Gerard W. Hughes

B L O O M S B U R Y
LONDON • NEW DELHI • NEW YORK • SYDNEY

First published in Great Britain 2014

Copyright © Gerard W. Hughes, 2014

The moral right of the author has been asserted

A Continuum book

Bloomsbury Publishing Plc
50 Bedford Square
London WC1B 3DP

www.bloomsbury.com

Bloomsbury is a trademark of Bloomsbury Publishing Plc

Bloomsbury Publishing, London, New Delhi, New York and Sydney

A CIP record for this book is available from the British Library.

ISBN: 978-1-4729-1040-0

10 9 8 7

Typeset by Fakenham Prepress Solutions, Fakenham, Norfolk NR21 8NN

Printed and bound in Great Britain by CPI Group (UK) Ltd, Croydon CR0 4YY

Contents

Part Two Peace 139

Part Three Holiness 247

Foreword

Beginning this book, I find myself in conflict. The conflict is in my own mind. The conflicting elements are my desire to write, on the one hand, and the voice of common sense on the other. By 'common sense', I mean ways of thinking and expressing myself, of acting and relating, which are generally accepted as safeguarding us from our own folly. Comon Sense, in my imagination, is a faultless, respectable figure, unquestionably right in all things, thoroughly reliable, not given to frivolity in any form. My desire to write comes from 'me', a mysterious entity which I cannot begin to describe, not because I am afraid of revealing myself, but because 'me' has nothing of the clarity, solidity, reasonable persuasiveness of Common Sense, yet for me this mysterious entity has become steadily more real with the passing of time. This inner conflict, translated into conversational terms, runs something like this:

Common Sense: What kind of delusion is this that makes you think you can have anything useful to contribute to the vast subjects of Unity, Peace and Holiness, which are your proposed topics for *Cry of Wonder*?

Me: For millennia the human race has been writhing under the pain of human oppression and violence. Today we are witnessing wars and oppression on an unprecedented scale. We are becoming more aware of the threats to all human life, to the future of all life on our planet as the result of the violence we have done, and are still doing to each other, to our environment and to ourselves.

Common Sense: Your desire to write on peace is commendable, but you lack the expertise, the intelligence, the experience to do anything useful in this regard. Why not be sensible, accept the facts of your ageing state gracefully, and find some more pleasant occupation, better suited to your rapidly deteriorating condition, removing a useless burden from yourself and from those with whom you live and who may not share your views and enthusiasms.

Me: I recognize your voice, Common Sense, having heard it down the decades of my years. It is not a cruel, threatening voice: it is seductive. It does contain elements of truth and has enormous power over me. I know it well, it can easily overwhelm me. There is, however, something in me which I do not properly understand, but which cannot totally accept you, Common Sense, in spite of all your useful, helpful maxims.

I have experienced glimpses of this something in my life. I cannot and do not want to resist it. Therefore I shall persevere with this writing and allow the process to lead me further into the mystery, in which all humankind and all creation has its being.

Preamble

This book is a series of reflections after 70 years as a Jesuit member of the British Province of the Society of Jesus. I write for anyone who is interested in the 'why' questions of human life.

The book is based on my own experience, but it is not an autobiography. It is written to encourage readers to reflect on and value their own experience, the only reliable source on which any of us can draw when asking the all-important 'why' questions of human life.

This emphasis on reflection on our own experience is not a twentieth-century fad: it is very ancient and always very new. In our own day it is counter-cultural, considered subversive of law and order, and anarchic. This truth is not usually stated in words, but becomes manifest in our decisions and actions. There is a deepening split developing between our words and the truth of things. This is not a recent phenomenon. The Hebrew prophets, thousands of years ago, were well aware of it: they called it idolatry. What is new today is the breadth and the depth of the split, so vast and deeply ingrained in us that we are no longer aware of it.

We live in the age of the expert. We have made extraordinary technological discoveries in recent times, including an information technology that can provide torrents of new information to the majority of people living in what we call 'the developed countries'. This flow of information and its availability is a wonderful gift but, like us, it has its dark side. These wonderful gifts can blind our long-distance vision; we become so overloaded with information, so preoccupied with the complex details of modern life, that we no longer have the energy, or the inclination, to consider wider questions about the meaning of it all. We hand over those questions to 'the experts', who can provide instant wisdom on the click of a button, instant relief from pain and a great variety of ways of anaesthetizing ourselves against our own worries and anxieties.

If we can learn to reflect on our own experience, we can begin to see that the remedies for all our ills, proposed by the 'experts', do not lead us to untrammelled peace, but often aggravate and intensify the problems we intend to solve. One striking example of this is in our understanding of peace – something for which everyone professes to long, especially the arms dealers and arms manufacturers! 'To ensure peace, prepare for war' was a policy of the founders of the Roman Empire, a policy supported by most developed countries today. The very means used to endorse this policy result in the multiplication of violence. In the promotion of peace we now have an abundance of nuclear weaponry designed not for defence, but to be used as first-strike weapons, and the number of nations now possessing these weapons has increased and is likely to increase further. Ancient wisdom that violence breeds violence is being ignored, imperilling the future of humanity on our planet.

In *Cry of Wonder* I reflect on three themes which have held my interest and attention in the last 60 years and still continue to do so. The themes are 'Unity', 'Peace' and 'Holiness'. At first, I approached all three topics with my own Catholic upbringing. Later, I had the good fortune to be able to meet and work with people of different Christian traditions, with different faiths, and with people of no professed faith allegiance. Without realizing what they were doing, these people taught me new ways of looking at life and religion, the sacred and the secular, God and me. They taught me to appreciate the fifth-century St Augustine's prayer, 'that I may know you: that I may know myself'.

It was through reflection on these experiences that I began to see and appreciate my own Catholic tradition in a new way. Slowly and very painfully I began to glimpse new ways of understanding and interpreting my own experience, my ideas about God, the Church, human life. The understanding still continues, absorbs my attention, gives me hope and peace in the mess and chaos I experience both outwith, but especially within my own experience.

I write about this in order to encourage the reader to value and cherish their own experience. The book offers many different ways in which you can do this gently with yourself and at the end of each chapter there are simple exercises offered which are designed to enable you to help yourself to discover the treasure, the pearl of great price, which is on offer to you, not because of your religious affiliation, your successes and achievements, but simply because you are a human being, called to play a unique role in creation and to be at one with that power which Dante writes of, the power 'that moves the sun and other stars', the power of Love. This power is nearer to each one of us than we are to ourselves.

If we can be still and listen to our hearts, we shall discover that we are not alone. As a help for this I include here some ways of coming to stillness and some ways of praying. There are as many ways of praying as there are human beings.

I have placed this section here as its contents belong to all three themes: Unity, Peace, Holiness. Much of it is repeated in Part 3 of this book, Holiness.

'Be still' is a teaching in all major world religions and among many who profess to have no religion. Here is one simple way of being still:

- Sit with your feet flat on the ground, your back straight but not rigid, your body relaxed.

- Concentrate your attention on what you can feel in your body. *(Don't think, just focus your attention on what you can feel in your body. If you get no further than your big toe, you are doing well!)*

- If you feel an itch or discomfort, hear noises or have interesting thoughts, acknowledge what is happening but return to your physical feelings.

- Once you feel more relaxed – but do not be in any hurry – you might like to turn this exercise into more explicit prayer, repeating slowly to yourself, for example: 'In God I live and move and have my being'. This is a way of meeting God in our awareness of our own body, in our own surroundings.

- It is good to begin prayer with a stillness exercise, however short. If you never move on from stillness you are still praying well. In Christian belief it is God's Spirit who prays in us. Through stillness we can become more aware of this truth and join ourselves more wholeheartedly with God.

Praying from scripture

Lectio Divina

This way of praying is very ancient. It began in early monasteries when the majority of the monks were unable to read. Lectio Divina *(Divine Reading) is commonly used to describe this simple method.*

- It is good to begin all prayer periods with this phrase: 'God, let my whole being be directed totally to your service and praise'.

- Choose a very short passage that appeals to you.

- Imagine these words of Scripture being spoken to you personally by God and coming from deep within you. God of the Scripture is the God now holding you in being, continuing God's own story in you now.

- Petition. Pray for whatever you desire. This is important: it focuses your heart.

- Read the passage over several times, pausing to relish and reflect on any word or phrase which stands out for you. Let that word or phrase hover over your present preoccupations, your hopes and fears, worries and anxieties, your relationships. Talk with God as a friend to a friend, simply and honestly. Don't be afraid to grumble. God can take our tantrums!

- End with the Our Father, or some other short prayer.

Imaginative prayer from Scripture scenes, especially the Gospels

- Read over the passage slowly until it is familiar to you.

- Imagine the scene is happening now and you are in it. If you find visual imagination difficult, imagine you are describing it to a child, as vividly as possible.

- Pray for what you desire.

- Who is in the scene? What are they doing, what are they saying?

- If distractions come, acknowledge them and, if they do not lead you away from the passage you are praying, let them enter the scene; they may draw you deeper into it.

- Talk with the characters in the scene, with Jesus, God.

However strange the pictures that imagination presents may seem to you, as long as you can pray with them, stay with them.

Reflection after prayer and repetition

After your period of prayer, spend a few minutes in reflection. Notice, especially, any felt reaction you may have experienced, whether it was pleasant or painful, and notice what gave rise to the feeling. Next time you pray, begin by going back to those words or phrases, images or thoughts and stay with them as long as you can. This process is called 'repetition', which can be a misleading word. A more accurate word is 'continuation'. Most of the exercises Ignatius Loyola presents in his book of the Exercises are continuations and lead us deeper into the mystery of God and the mystery of ourselves.

Review of the Day

This is a method of prayer at the end of the day. The subject matter of the prayer is the events of your day, for that is where God is for you. Other people can tell you about God, but for you God can only be found in your experience. This kind of prayer can be called 'earthing our prayer', because it is earthed in our own daily experience and God is in every moment of it.

- Be still and ask God: 'Let my whole being be directed to your service and praise'.

- Recall the day, looking first at what you have enjoyed, appreciated and valued during the day. Relive those moments and thank God for them. These are God's gifts to you, signs of God's love. Avoid any moralizing, any self-approval or disapproval. Just give thanks for whatever you are grateful for.

- Pray for enlightenment. Recall your own predominant moods and feelings during the day, but without judging them. Moods and feelings, in themselves, are neither right nor wrong, true or false, but they are very intelligent, valuable and important signals. When our desires are satisfied, we are content. When they are not satisfied we become irritated. Here we are praying to know the desires and attitudes that underlie our moods and feelings. Are my desires all centred on me and my kingdom, my comfort, my success, my status, my wanting all creation to praise, reverence and serve me, or are they directed to God's kingdom, to letting God be the God of love, compassion, peace and forgiveness to me and through me, for all peoples and for all creation?

- Talk over the day with God, giving thanks for all the gifts given to you freely out of love for you, tokens of God's wanting you to share in God's own life. Acknowledge your fears before God, who always turns your acknowledged failures into strength for you and for others.

- Ask God's guidance for tomorrow and entrust yourself to God's goodness, 'like a child in its mother's arms' (Psalm 131).

We are related with everything and everyone in the rest of creation, and we can hear the message coming from the depths out of which we came to be, assuring us with these words, 'Do not be afraid, I am with you always', and evoking from you, your heartfelt 'Cry of Wonder'!

Part One

Unity

Wonder, inviting us through fear to freedom

'Wonder' is a theme which pervades this book. It is a gift which is more appreciated today as we become more aware of the mystery of our own planet, a tiny particle in an expanding Universe which not only surrounds us, but is also within us.

This book is about facing into our fears, acknowledging them and, in this way, breaking through them into a cry of wonder, a cry of delight as we begin to recognize the truth. What we had thought to be our fears of annihilation are, in fact, invitations to transformation. The invitation is not to some fantasy world of our own making. It is an invitation to recognize the reality of 'The Now'. This transformation is not an escape from our present or future trials in life: it is the beginning of a pilgrimage into the truth of things.

There is an ancient Rabbinic saying: 'Do, and you will understand'. This book is not offered as a magic remedy for all our ills. It contains recommended exercises at the end of each chapter. Reading the book may while away the time; doing the exercises can change your life and continue to change it long after you have forgotten the book's content. The exercises can enable you to get on the track of your own unique experience. It is in your own unique experience that your treasure lies. The exercises are simple: do them, and you will begin to discover your inner wealth.

The psychologist Carl Jung (1875–1961) once wrote: 'All change in human life begins in an individual, or it does not begin at all.' Most of us, in our younger days, dream of changing things. Sooner or later, we realize with increasing clarity that there are very few things we can change. We cannot change our past, our ancestry, our genes, our DNA; we cannot change the future because it does not yet exist. We can change lots of things in the present – that is how we fill our days. But for all our efforts, the changes we effect fail to be effective or lasting. A useful modern phrase, which expresses this trap of ineffectiveness in which we seem to be caught, is 'It is like changing around the deckchairs on the *Titanic*'! What we cannot do is rid the polar regions of icebergs without submerging our coastal lands in sea water. In fact, today we are in danger of doing precisely this, not through deliberate destruction of icebergs, but through the effect our way of living is having on climate change – a danger we shall be looking at later.

More obdurate than icebergs, and much more threatening to life, are personal attitudes we may have to ourselves, to other people and to creation. These personal attitudes can become dearer to us than life itself, not only to our own lives but to the lives of all other people, attitudes which threaten all organic life on earth. It is only in very recent times, through the amazing advances in technology, that we have become conscious of these cosmic dangers. These dangers are not mental fantasies: they are plain, obdurate facts, from which no amount of cleverness can shield us.

What is already destroying us are our fears. When we fail to acknowledge our fears, we react blindly and are lured into creating the very dangers we most fear.

Our human tendency to run from our fears is not a recent development in human history. The most common phrase in the Hebrew Scriptures and the Christian New Testament which is recorded of God is the phrase, 'Do not be afraid'. I am told it recurs 365 times! The second most common phrase is 'I am with you', a phrase which usually follows on 'Don't be afraid'.

If your immediate reaction to this last paragraph is 'But I don't believe in God', the statement I have made is not asking you to believe in God. The statement is offered as a fact, as a piece of information, to show that the phrase 'Don't be afraid' has been around for many millennia. It is a statement worth noting, because it is addressed to all human beings; it is not reserved for a particular group of religious believers.

In this chapter, I mention briefly some of the facts of our lives which we prefer to ignore.

An obvious fact with which to start, and which none of us can avoid, is the fact of our death. What is extraordinary is how ingeniously we try to avoid this truth within ourselves and between ourselves.

Many years ago, I worked for a six-week period in a parish in the Bronx, New York. At the time, I was chaplain to Catholic students at Glasgow University. My work included giving Medical Ethics lectures to the Catholic students, and to any others who were interested. I had gone to the Bronx because there was a large hospital within the parish, where I hoped to learn from the patients, nurses and doctors. I had much to learn, but soon realized that death itself was not their favourite topic of conversation, an aversion shared universally. Doctors and nurses tended to see death as a sign of failure: an unfortunate fact of life, which should not be seen in hospitals. Dying patients had curtains around their beds; doctors and nurses tended to rush by, having more urgent matters to attend to. The dying were often moved to places specially reserved for them, lest their presence should upset the other terminally ill patients. The main street near the hospital had a large number of funeral parlours, where the deceased lay in state, immaculately dressed in their favourite clothes, their faces carefully made up as though they were in perfect health, some holding their favourite newspaper in their hands, the room bedecked with bouquets of fresh flowers. At the many burial services, which I attended daily, because my arrival coincided with the ending of a prolonged grave-diggers' strike, there was usually a strip of artificial grass laid upon the earth-filled grave, suggesting that all was back in order and life could now continue.

Death is one of the fears which beset us and from which we all try to escape. I have had the good fortune to be at the deathbeds of people who had learned to befriend death. One of them was a woman suffering from her third bout of cancer. Visiting her a few weeks before her death through terminal cancer, I asked her: 'Are you really at peace?' She answered indignantly: 'I am not only at peace. I know I am healed.' She then continued: 'Don't let them put "May she rest in peace" on my tombstone. I have no intention of resting in peace.' 'What do you intend doing?' I asked. 'I want to be with others, who are dying and afraid, to accompany them on the next stage of their journey.' So I asked her to remember me when the time comes – and she promised to do so!

The point of telling this story is to illustrate the truth that what damages and destroys us are not the facts we encounter in life, but the way we interpret them and how we react to them. The lady, whose death I have described, had suffered severely in life. Very painful events had forced her to ask continually: 'What is the point of life?' The questioning lifted her out of her past conditioning and into a vision of life which was welcoming, not threatening, life-giving, not life-destroying for herself or for those around her.

Today we can become much more aware of the dangers threatening all life on earth than was possible for previous generations. One of these dangers is climate change, change which we can precipitate through our misuse of our finite global resources. These changes can affect every aspect of human life, including the air we breathe, the food we eat. This fact is not acceptable to sections of the population, especially those who profit enormously from this misuse of resources.

Famine has been a fear for all human beings since human life began. More people than ever in our human history die of hunger every year. The number is reckoned to be about one billion, the majority of them being in the developing countries. What is new today is not only the extent of the problem, but its analysis. We live in an age of unparalleled prosperity. The problem is not primarily shortage of food, but the mal-distribution of the supplies that we have. Food shortages can be artificially created by withholding supplies to raise the price. The poorest and the weakest are forced to pay with their lives; the owners increase their profits and those of their shareholders. Landowners can drive peasants off the land on which they grew their own subsistence crops, turning the land into luxury crops for export to the wealthy of developed countries, raising their own profits and pleasing their impoverished governments by improving the national economy. This can win them great national prestige, awards and tax relief.

Another besetting fear, presently afflicting both developed and developing countries, is the financial crisis. For clarity's sake I mention these crises one by one, as though they are all separate and independent of each other. In fact, they are all very closely interconnected. Failing to recognize the interconnections can lead to failure to remedy any one of them. Recognizing connections is another theme which runs through this book.

As the world has become richer in the last century, the gap between the rich and poor has widened alarmingly. This gap has accelerated in the last 30 years – a diminishing number of the super-rich controlling, through the power that wealth confers, a growing number of economically deprived, who find themselves inescapably entrapped in worsening poverty. The people of wealth and power are able to influence and so to control the politicians, both local and national, while they themselves consider themselves free from any responsibility beyond ensuring their own dominating position. They can also control the media, encouraging those sections which support them in their retention and accumulation of wealth, withdrawing their favours from those who endanger it. As I write this, I hear and see this subject daily in the media. We are absorbed in 'how' questions: remarkably silent on 'why'. That is why connections are so important.

We are very easily conditioned into believing that financial issues, which affect all of us in every aspect of our lives, belong to the science of economics, a science of discovery of the eternal truths which lie behind all financial matters. This simple faith in economics is not dented by the revelation that most financial advisers, bankers, brokers and insurers, not to mention chancellors in charge of national finances, seem to be unaware of these eternal truths, admitting their bafflement over the causes and the remedies for our present worldwide financial crises.

Economics is not a science like mathematics, an exact science based on unchangeable principles; economics is a human system devised by men and women, to ensure against all forms of financial fraud and abuse. This is an honourable and a necessary pursuit, but it is devised by those who are relatively secure financially; few will have experienced the poverty which cripples human development.

The only point I am trying to make here is that there is at present a worldwide financial crisis. The split between rich and poor is widening rapidly and alarmingly. The effect of this disparity is already having very practical consequences: civil unrest, rising numbers dying of starvation, rising unemployment, increasing human violence, family breakdown. These crises are discussed endlessly in the media, but the discussions do not alleviate the devastating violence.

One of the examples of our unwillingness to face the fears that haunt us, and of the global destructiveness which follows because of our blind reaction to this fear, is revealed in our attitude to and understanding of Peace.

It is very unlikely that if the general question were put to a large audience, 'Are you in favour of Peace?', anyone would declare 'Certainly not!' before stomping out in indignation at such a ridiculous question. Arms dealers themselves would claim to be working for peace, deterring

stronger countries from attacking the weaker by supplying the weaker
with arms to defend themselves. In Britain, for example, no political party
with any serious hope of forming a future government could oppose our
national nuclear defence policy, as Labour learned to its cost when beaten
at the polls in 1979, followed by eighteen years in opposition to the
triumphant Tory party. Labour no longer opposes nuclear defence. The
Liberal party, at present in a joint Conservative-Liberal government, are
themselves against a nuclear defence policy, but they voted recently with
their Conservative colleagues for a renewal of our nuclear submarine
fleet, at enormous cost, in a time of stringent financial restrictions in
government spending – a move which met with little opposition from
State or Church. What was their motive in voting against their own
principles? Was it political – to avoid the destruction of the present joint
government? If it was a political decision, what questions does this raise
about the thought parameters of political decisions? Must party loyalty
always have priority over every other decision? The government decision
to renew our Trident nuclear submarine defence system met with
opposition from many individuals, but with a terrifying silence from
most Church authorities. This silence is the most alarming manifestation
of the destructive power of fear, a power which can threaten the future
of all human life and of all organic life on our planet. Fear, if not faced,
can so overwhelm us that we begin to act blindly, and leads us to defend
ourselves with measures which not only fail to defend us, but can lead
to the annihilation of all life on our planet! As far as we know at present,
we are the only planet in the vast Universe which can sustain human life.

A most revealing example of this human refusal to face the fears
that haunt us is clear in the behaviour of those countries which already
possess nuclear weaponry, and of the many countries which are allied
with nuclear defence countries. I shall be elaborating on this point in
Part 2 of the book, which examines the meaning of Peace, a word which
throws light on the web of connections which sustain all of us in life,
and affects every aspect of it.

Our attitude and understanding of self-defence betrays our
unawareness of the nature of life. We are essentially connected with
each other, a truth which 'primitive' peoples understood but we have
forgotten. What we do to the other, whoever the other may be, we are
also doing to ourselves. Jesus' central teaching, 'Love your neighbour
as yourself', has profound implications, not only for every detail of
human life, but for all organic life in our planet.

I shall be returning constantly to this subject of our
face the fears that haunt us, an attitude which leads us t
things that we most fear. The point of the repetition is not
utterly corrupt and twisted we are; it is to help us to catch a glimpse
of the wonder of our being, the wonder of this pilgrimage through life
in which we are all engaged, whatever our religion or lack of it. And
we never make this pilgrimage alone, however lonely we may feel; we
make it for the sake of every other pilgrim through life, whoever they
may be.

Thank God the spirit of the prophets and the seers of old is still
living in our lands. One prophet of our time was the American,
Dorothy Day (1897–1980). She was born into a non-practising Jewish
family, journalists, Marxist and atheist. Dorothy became a Catholic,
left the man with whom she lived and still loved till the end of her life,
taking with her, with his agreement, her beloved daughter. She lived
very simply in New York during the Depression, wrote a daily news-
sheet, which she gave to the hungry to sell at one cent a copy. She also
fed the hungry who came to her door. The core theme of Christianity
which inspired her daily writings and her way of life was St Paul's
doctrine of the Body of Christ. With this understanding, she met the
Risen Christ in all her encounters with others, in the poor, the hungry,
the oppressed, the hopeless, the neglected and rejected.

Dorothy loved the Catholic liturgy, but she had a very 'earthed'
spirituality, expressing her love of God in feeding the hungry, housing
the homeless, giving hope to the despairing. She eventually founded a
movement called the 'Catholic Worker', buying properties and farms
for the homeless, where they could work on the land, feeding daily
hundreds of hungry people. In all this work, apart from the little
she could earn by her writing, she depended on voluntary contribu-
tions. She never accepted official charitable status, which, she knew,
could restrict her freedom in doing the work she felt drawn to do. She
was also a pacifist, in years when pacifism was considered cowardly
disloyalty, and she was frequently gaoled for her public protests
for peace. On one occasion during the Cold War with Russia and
Communist countries in the 1950s, there was a compulsory exercise in
air-raid precautions in Central Park, New York, when inhabitants were
to assemble in specially built nuclear shelters. It was at the time of the
Cuban missile crisis, when Cuba had received nuclear missiles from
Russia, capable of destroying US cities. Dorothy refused to comply

with the order and deliberately sat in the open park, preferring it to the protection of the nuclear shelters provided. She was later arrested and imprisoned. Her pacifist attitude was not approved of by the Catholic hierarchy. Although she was always respectful of the hierarchy, she never hesitated to speak her mind both in words and action.

I quote here just one question on nuclear defence from Dorothy Day: 'What is the difference between throwing innocent people into ovens, and throwing ovens at innocent people?' I have yet to hear an answer. It is a question for every individual.

Our nuclear weapons are not defence weapons. They are deliberately and ingeniously constructed to be first-strike weapons, capable of striking the enemy's launching pads before they have fired a missile. They are, therefore, attack missiles, which can be fired by pressing a button thousands of miles away from their targets. Those who fire the weapons do not know the destination of the missiles. Such knowledge could be very upsetting to the button-pusher – it might even cause them to hesitate! In all her campaigning on global issues, Dorothy Day knew that the root of all our human destruction does not come from external agencies. It lies in our hearts, and until we acknowledge our responsibility, our efforts to protect ourselves become the means of our destruction.

Another phenomenon of our modern world is especially noticeable in our 'developed world', the world which possesses the nuclear weaponry. The phenomenon is the massive exodus which has taken place from the more established Christian Churches in the developed world. The fact of this exodus is not disputed: exact statistics vary. In the UK, for example, I read a prognosis for Britain which stated that if the present rate of secession from churchgoing during the last ten years were to continue, almost all churches would be empty by the end of the twenty-first century. Others now reckon the closing date for all churches can be brought forward to the year 2050!

I have been a Jesuit for 70 years. I belong to a Religious Order, within the Roman Catholic Church, which was founded in the sixteenth century by a group of students and graduates of Paris University, inspired by a Basque nobleman called Ignatius of Loyola. I have lived through decades of rapid change in society in general, and in Christianity in particular. Today, Christianity is undergoing the greatest crisis in its history. Previous crises – the split between the Eastern and the Western Churches in the eleventh century, the sixteenth-century Reformation when the Western Church was split between Catholics and Protestants, the splitting into denominations and sects which has continued ever since – all these were splits within Christianity, whereas today's crisis is much more fundamental: it is an attack on the very idea of God, an attack, too, on the meaning and value of human life.

This crisis has been developing over many centuries. What is sudden today is the breadth and the length of it and its implications for our survival as a human race.

This book is a reflection on my own reactions to this rapid change. It has forced me to keep questioning my own certainties, thrown me into painful doubts. I still believe in God, the Christian Church, but my understanding of God, of Church and of its creeds, of priesthood, of my own Jesuit religious life, is changing in ways I could never have foreseen. God has become more mysterious, yet more real, familiar and more attractive; the Scriptures are no longer time-bound, but speak to the present, a message which is not reserved to a chosen few, because God's Covenant is offered to every human being.

Looking back on my 70 years of Jesuit life, I become aware of connections which, at the time, did not seem significant. These connections affect every experience of my life and my understanding of them. They broaden my horizons and awareness that I am caught up in something much greater than I: something mysterious, yet very attractive, something which does not give the neat answers I am looking for; but this something gradually changes the way I see myself and reality around me, leaving me very happy to be taken along this mysterious path – a journey I share with every other human being and with all creation.

About ten years ago, the BBC, in conjunction with the Gallup Poll, an organization in Britain and the USA for predicting the political voting behaviour of populations, was invited to explore 'The Soul of Britain'. It was at a time when the media gave the general impression that God was dead. The organizers, the researchers and the interpreters of the poll were amazed at the results obtained. In 'Post-Christian Britain', 75 per cent of those interviewed claimed to have had some kind of spiritual/religious experience that was still affecting them today. 'Still affecting them today' is the all-important phrase for interpreting the significance of the poll's findings. Only 7 per cent of those interviewed were still regular churchgoers.

This inquiry prompted further inquiry, including one question put to all who had experiences that were still affecting them today: 'Did you ever disclose this experience to anyone?' The vast majority had never made any such disclosure and their reason was fear of how the disclosure would be interpreted, leading to their being considered odd, unbalanced, religious fanatics, and possibly dangerous.

I am very grateful to have lived through and to be living through decades of such rapid change. I have been taught, through apparently random circumstances, to recognize something overwhelmingly attractive. I now see these circumstances not as a threat, but as an invitation into a life which goes beyond anything I can think, or imagine.

Rudolf Otto (1869–1937) wrote a classical study of mysticism, in which he summed up the mystical experience in the Latin term 'Tremendum et fascinans'. It means that the mystical experience both shakes us severely (*tremendum*), yet inexorably attracts us (*fascinans*). I believe all human beings are continuously being invited to become mystics. What do I mean by this? I mean to become people whose lives are based on our own convictions which have developed in us through our own experience, rather than people who have renounced personal responsibility, preferring conformity to the views of others. The true mystic is a resister against all those powers which treat other people as things, but their resistance is always non-violent and they delight in a life of loving resistance.

'God became a human being', wrote Athanasius in the third century, 'so that human beings might become God.' A human being, in Christian understanding, is what God could become. This human being, the historical man, Jesus of Nazareth, prayed on the night before he was sentenced to death as a criminal: 'May they all become one, as Thou, Father, are in me and I am in you, may they also become one in us.'

This God has called every one of us into the oneness that is God's very self, a God who is all-inclusive, whose compassion pervades all creation, whose forgiveness is never withheld from anyone, unless they themselves reject it. There is no depth of human despair, no intensity of human suffering where God is not, no sense of alienation, rejection or estrangement, which can prevent God from being, to quote St Augustine again, 'nearer to us than we are to ourselves'.

In the crises of our days, God calls on us in our fears, in our helplessness, self-deception, cowardly inhumanity to ourselves and to others: 'Come, I have called you by your name, you are mine. You are honoured and I love you' (Isa. 43.1-4).

Exercise

- Make a note of any predominant feeling you experienced after reading this chapter.
- Can you see any connection between the word/phrase which evoked your felt reaction and the predominant desire in your life?

2

Welcome invitations; beware 'oughts'

Recurring memories from early childhood are like precious treasures. Noticing them and reflecting on them is a most profitable occupation: they can become the starting point of a remembering process which reveals connections between past and present events of which we were previously unaware. The process is not idle navel-gazing. It can have very practical consequences, opening up for us totally new ways of seeing and understanding our present situation. The only way any of us can effectively change anything is by learning to expand the horizons of our thought, of our way of perceiving the reality in which we find ourselves.

This experience of recalling our childhood memories leads to a further question: could it be that the most far-seeing and intelligent part of us lies in our subconscious/unconscious? If that is true, how are we to be more in touch now with this all-important part?

When I was first encouraged to look at recurring childhood memories, my first reaction was to ignore the advice because this was something I had never deliberately done before! When I leaped over this lifelong obstacle a vivid memory did come back to me, but it seemed too trivial to be worthy of attention. The memory kept recurring. Years later, I began to recognize its importance.

I was probably about three years old when this event happened. I was being put to bed by my older sister, Marie. When she had gone, I remember sitting on the edge of the bed, looking out of the window and saying 'God'. I remember clearly why I said it. I wanted to see what would happen. Nothing happened, and I went back to sleep. It was a trivial incident in itself, hardly worth remembering, but to me now, many decades later, it speaks volumes. This memory indicates a

theme which has run through my life and is still with me: the search
for God and God's reply – silence! The search is like a long, mysterious
journey, sometimes dark and threatening, sometimes very lonely and
frightening, but when I look back in old age, I am grateful still to be on
this search. This silent God does not give me the neat answers and the
clear explanations I look for, but this God is near and I cannot escape
God's presence. I find it all unbelievable at times and want to escape,
but I can't.

As I now look back, I am most grateful for this silence and for the
frustration I have experienced. I have now, many decades later, begun
to get the message. What is much more important than my search for
God is the truth that God is continuously searching for me. I now want
to focus on this truth, live it, enjoy it, share it with others, because this
is something which is offered to every human being, no matter who
they are. You are closer to each of us, God, than we are to ourselves. I
keep repeating this phrase, and shall keep repeating it throughout this
book. It can reduce us to silence, to wonder, and enable us to glimpse
the loving reality in which all of us are held. If we can focus on this
truth that God is continuously searching for each of us, not because
of our merits, virtue, achievements, status, but simply because we are,
then slowly and gradually everything in us and around us begins to
change. The change is not in the facts which surround us: the change is
in the way we begin to see and interpret these facts.

I know our memories of past events can be very unreliable and that
we cannot always distinguish the real event from what we have injected
into the event from later experience, but what we can know as real is
the emotional effect the memory is having on us now. That emotional
reaction is like a signpost. It does not give us an answer: it points us
in a direction. The direction is all-important: it introduces us to a new
way of seeing, a transforming way of seeing, which brings life to us and
to those around us.

In general, my memories of the first five years of my life are all
happy, trouble-free, memories of good times, of eating, playing, family
gatherings, receiving presents. The Russian novelist Dostoevsky once
wrote: 'The greatest gifts that parents can give their children are happy
memories.' We were a family of eight: six children – three girls, three
boys – our mother and father. We lived in what I remember as a large
house, called 'Mount View', with a large garden, in a village called
Skelmorlie in Ayrshire, Scotland. The village stretched from the hilltop

where we lived, sloping steeply down to the Firth of Clyde, overlooking the isles of Bute and Arran to the west and the mountains, including Ben Lomond, to the north. At the age of five, owing to my father's illness, we had to move to the city of Glasgow, about 30 miles away, where we lived in a tenement building without any garden. This sudden change from country to city did not appeal at the age of five, but it has left me with an abiding love of open country, of scenic views of rivers, of mountains and of the sea.

Another recurring memory from childhood is very closely connected with what I am doing at the moment, writing on Unity. I am not sure whether this event took place while we were still living in Skelmorlie or whether it was at a later period, because we frequently returned from Glasgow to Skelmorlie for holidays.

The memory is of a Sunday morning when we were returning from Mass, celebrated at Wemyss Bay, on the coast, about a mile from our house. As we were climbing up the Station Hill for home, we used to meet the other villagers, predominantly Protestant, on their way to their church on the coast. Skelmorlie, in my memory, was always a very friendly place, where everyone normally greeted everyone else by name. On a Sunday morning, however, the cheerful greetings were replaced by stiff bows exchanged across four centuries! I also used to feel very inferior because the Protestant children had large bibles with tassels, while I clutched a diminutive *Garden of the Soul* which had no tassels!

This was a very trivial memory in itself, but for me, recalling it after decades, the memory draws together years of interest and involvement in the question of Church unity.

For a year, before leaving Skelmorlie, I attended the village school. There was no separate Catholic school in the village. That was the only year of my life when I was in a non-denominational school. My first experience of non-denominational teaching came 22 years later, when I spent four years at Oxford!

I have no memory of any specifically religious education at Skelmorlie school. I do remember being taught my prayers at home and always saying them with my mother or older sisters before being put to bed at night. I enjoyed learning set prayers because I was trained with what in Scotland we called 'tablet': the English called it 'fudge', a very tasty sweet. I found the 'Our Father' difficult to learn, but appreciated and remembered the 'fudge' reward for getting it right.

If, at this point, you are feeling bewildered and dissatisfied with this emphasis on 'felt' reactions, don't worry. Your reaction is very healthy!

In Glasgow, I had what would have been described as 'a good solid Catholic education'. I had two years, from five to seven, at a convent school, followed by six years' education at the Jesuit school, St Aloysius College, both schools about a 100 yards from home. At the age of 13, I moved to another Jesuit school, a boarding school near Sheffield called Mount St Mary's, where I remained for five years. In these 13 years I had a surfeit of religious education, found it very boring most of the time, heavily doctrinal, providing us with answers to questions we had never asked, nor were interested in asking. I emerged from all this with what I considered to be a strong faith in God and in the Catholic Church. It is easy to be scathing about the education we received. In general, although I now see lots of defects in my education, I am grateful for it and to those who had the patience to teach me. Despite very occasional minor exceptions, it is the kindness and tolerance of teachers which remain in memory.

At the age of 16, I had a gentle kind of religious conversion – nothing dramatic, no visions, levitations, miraculous happenings, but the effect of it is still with me. At Mount St Mary's there was a scholarship offered to one candidate about to begin his advanced level subjects. The scholarship would pay the school fees for the next two years. I applied for this scholarship and studied hard for it. To give my efforts a little topspin, I thought I might try some extra prayer. At this stage of my life, prayer consisted of reciting set prayers, like the Our Father and Hail Mary of happy tablet memory. After some months of this, I began to find the prayer attractive, especially when I stopped saying the set prayers and began having conversations with this myste- rious God! I failed to win the scholarship, but the prayer experience has never left me, not even when I have neglected it, being too busy with other more important things! It was as though the decision to pray had taken up residence in part of my psyche, where it had lived independently of my conscious mind and was influencing me far more than I realized.

About the time of my 'conversion' in 1940, aged 16 years, having passed what was then called the 'School Certificate' exam, we had to decide whether we wanted to proceed with further education for the next two years. If so, we then had to choose whether to specialize in scientific or humanities subjects. I chose chemistry and physics as the main subjects. The reason was because I wanted to study medicine. It was during these two years that I first found myself, to my surprise, thinking about the possibility of becoming a priest. We were in the first year of World War II. I also felt attracted to joining the Royal Air Force. In fact, the Air Force was the more attractive option.

I can remember how I thought my way through this at the time. I told Marie that I could not decide between becoming a priest and joining the Air Force. Her reply was that if I opted for the Air Force, I might be killed. To which I replied: 'That does not matter, because I shall go to heaven.' I had been well educated! To risk one's life in war was to offer one's life '*Pro Deo et Patria*' – for God and Country! I shall be returning to this point in greater detail in Part 2 on Peace.

The reason for including this experience of decision-making here is to illustrate how God appears to work on us, in spite of the rigidity of our understanding. At this time, my understanding of God, and of everything else, was very rigid. I realize now, many decades later, that God works through our rigidities and gradually and gently enlightens us. This information is not only about God: it is also about ourselves, and it raises some very fundamental questions for all of us, whether we classify ourselves as religious or as atheist. How am I to become more aware of my own rigidity of thought? How am I to react when I encounter this rigidity in others? These are very practical, down-to-earth questions.

My decision to apply to join the Jesuits came to me one summer's evening when I was looking out of the window in the holiday flat we had in Skelmorlie in 1941. I was sitting by the window on a beautiful summer's evening, watching the sun setting in a blaze of colour over the mountain ranges to the west, while a large convoy of cargo ships with protecting Royal Navy vessels was coming into port at Greenock, a few miles to the east. It was while gawking at this sight that I discovered the decision to become a priest had already been taken. There was nothing dramatic in the moment of discovery: at the time it felt very ordinary and obvious.

The decision felt right; I was at peace, although not elated, and I never doubted it until many years later. When I look back now on this decision, I see connections which have very practical consequences for today's crises, in society in general, and in the Church in particular.

I no longer have the faith certainty now which I had at the age of 17. I am now very glad that I see God, the nature of the Church, the meaning of Faith very differently, but the God I believe in today is the same God who guided me in those decisions of 70 years ago. A conclusion from this experience is that the reality of God is not dependent, thank God, on my current theology. God's love and providential care do not cease when my theology is awry! God is a God who lets us be, a God of infinite patience, who works on us gently, never violently.

In making these decisions at the age of 17 – decisions which were to determine my future – I still believe I was right to follow my inner convictions, even although I am now aware that my understanding of God, of Faith and of Church were dangerously narrow. My faith then was more dedicated to a system, to doctrinal belief, than to the living God, but I had no idea of this at the time.

The practical conclusion from this exercise in discernment at the age of 17 is that we must always, in all our decisions and doings, follow our own deepest inner promptings even though, in so doing, we realize that we may be mistaken. What is the alternative? The alternative is to take the path that leads to lifelong slavery, a betrayal of our true selves and a betrayal of others. This conclusion has huge implications, not only for our own individual selves, but for every other person as well. At the heart of the matter is the unity of God. We are only at the beginning of our questions and discoveries!

A further question which arises from this exploration is: 'Whom do I trust?' In all our present crises, which are ultimately about our survival as a human race, there are as many answers as there are human beings. One answer, rarely heard, is 'the problem is me'. Could that be the fundamental question for each of us and all of us? Well, it could be, but what on earth does it mean? Here I shall become dogmatic: later I shall explain why. The dogmatic statement is this: we must face into our fears, our doubts, into all those things we prefer to avoid. By 'face into', I mean acknowledge that I have them, look at them, 'gawk' at them, but do not pretend they do not exist. Pretending they do not exist is the most effective way of ensuring that fear gradually takes over our life, restricting us within the prison bars of our own fears. The fears thrive on being ignored and exact a terrible vengeance. I learned this very practical lesson through long-distance walking. Care of the feet is all-important. If you ignore the pain in your feet, trusting that if you 'bash on regardless' all will be well, you will soon suffer from your neglect. The neglected feet show their resentment mercilessly! Neglected feelings tend to react in the same way as neglected feet.

Feeling fearful, experiencing doubt is not a sign of weakness or of failure; it is an essential part of human experience. Refusing to face the question does not make it disappear – it magnifies the problem.

Another conclusion from coping with our fears and doubts is on the importance of prayer. This point will be considered much more fully in Part 3. In most Christian circles, whenever the importance of prayer is emphasized, heads nod in agreement, but we do not waste time in examining what we mean by these lofty reminders: we have more urgent business to engage our attention! I have been amazed at the very large number of committed elderly Christians I have encountered who tell me that they have never in their lives been given any instruction in prayer beyond learning a few prayers by heart as children. When they have heard sermons on prayer, they conclude that they are unable to pray and decide that their own inability must be a punishment from God because of their sinfulness. This neglect of prayer is widespread and includes seminaries and theological colleges.

We can become so accustomed to this state of affairs that we are no longer aware of the massive contradiction in our lives. We have neglected 'the heart of the matter', our call to be at one with the Lord of all creation, who holds each of us in being every moment of our lives. We replace God with a system of beliefs and practices which have little or nothing to do with any other aspect of life other than the narrowly ecclesiastical. If this conclusion is true, would it not explain how it is that so many millions of people can renounce church membership in such vast numbers in recent years, without much apparent inner disturbance, like casting off clothing which no longer fits?

I shall now reflect briefly on my own experience of the spiritual training I received. I write this because I believe every single human being is being called, each in their own unique way and unique circumstances, into a new way of being, into a transformation into the truth of things. This call has already begun in us. The present crises that we experience are not threats, but invitations to move into the very unity of Godself, along with every other human being and with all creation. My point in writing this is to encourage you to discover for yourself the marvel of your being. No one can tell you the way. Your teacher is within you. My point in writing is to encourage you to find your own unique way – a discovery which will benefit not only you, but from which we shall all benefit. We can never be alone. We live enfolded within the goodness of God. We are inextricably linked to everything else in the Universe.

Here is a very brief account of my spiritual training as a Jesuit from 1942 until 1960, when I completed my final year of Jesuit training. On reflection, 70 years after becoming a Jesuit, although I am, in general, very grateful for what I received in those years, I am also very aware of the defects of the training. I mention these defects because I know they have important lessons for us now in our present crises. Jesuit life was presented to us as though spirituality could be explained to us very simply: 'Keep the rules and regulations of Jesuit life faithfully and unquestioningly and the rule will keep you.' I did try to do this and kept trying to do it in spite of constant failures, but having a resilient temperament and basic belief in God's love and goodness, I did not have any troubling thoughts about Christian faith or my vocation as a Jesuit.

My first troubling experience came ten years after joining the Jesuits. I was studying at Campion Hall, Oxford, the Jesuit house of study, where most of us were undergraduates. During vacations we were not allowed to remain in Oxford, but had to go to some other Jesuit house, where we were left free to get on with our studies. I was walking in the garden of Beaumont College, a Jesuit school near Windsor, when suddenly and totally unexpectedly, the question came to me: 'What if all that I have been taught about God, the Church, the Christian creed is false, a fiction?'

Before going to Campion Hall, I had spent three years studying philosophy at Heythrop, the Jesuit house of studies for philosophy and theology near Chipping Norton, about 16 miles away from Oxford. There I had been introduced, via the teaching of the thirteenth-century St Thomas Aquinas, to many arguments against the existence of God and to Aquinas' 'Five Ways' of refuting them. I was not at all disturbed by the atheist arguments, so certain I was in my own beliefs. The moment of questioning, years later at Beaumont, was a very different experience. The questions now came like heavy punches aimed at my inmost being. I interpreted this experience as a temptation of the evil one, tried to ignore it and prayed to be rid of it. The doubting continued in spite of my prayers. After some weeks I mentioned this temptation to an older Jesuit, who was the spiritual director for the younger Jesuits at Campion Hall. His reaction to this revelation was to strike his forehead with the palm of his hand while appealing to God aloud with an 'O my God'! He also advised me to pay no attention to these doubts and to pray for a deepening faith. I followed this advice and the shock lessened, but the doubts did not disappear.

It was only many years later that I began to understand that these doubts were not a temptation against faith, but an invitation to deepen it. I began to see that my real difficulties were not with God, but with my image of God. This was a most valuable discovery, which has never left me. I do not mean that I now have a 'correct' image of God, with no room left for improvement: the God I now know is always mystery, always greater than anything I can think or imagine, but my heart begins to know that this God is both the reality in whom all creation lives and moves and has its being, and is also nearer to each one of us than we are to ourselves. It is this belief which sustains me when I become a little more aware of some of the crises that are facing humankind today. The question for all of us is: 'How are we to respond to this God now, this God who is present in all the circumstances of life and in our own hearts?' The invaluable lesson I eventually began to learn from this 'temptation against faith' of over 50 years ago is that it is in facing into our fears and apprehensions, acknowledging them and presenting them to God in prayer, that a measure of peace and enlightenment follows.

I can now see, more clearly than I did at the time, the origin of these visceral and terrifying doubts which assailed me suddenly during that peaceful evening walk. At Oxford I was being introduced to an unfamiliar world. I was being taught by men who were not Roman Catholic, and their kindliness, intelligence, tolerance and interest made me wonder why they were not, with one exception, Roman Catholic! I was also being plunged into reading Greek and Latin classical texts. This lasted for five terms. In the next seven terms I was introduced to Greek and Roman history, to classical Greek philosophy, and also to modern philosophy. I became fascinated by this ancient world, as I became more familiar with Latin and Greek. The method of teaching was also unfamiliar. Previous to Oxford, my education had been almost entirely instructional; success depended on a retentive memory and the ability to reproduce the relevant information to the questions set by examiners. Original thinking was not encouraged, a restriction which did not irk me at the time, but Oxford made me aware of it. Our tutors did not insist on our attending lectures, but they did insist on our doing original work and insisted on the weekly individual tutorial lasting one hour, when we had to produce Latin and Greek prose translations from English passages, or weekly essays on Greek and Roman history, and also a weekly philosophy essay. It was a method which encouraged us to think for ourselves. It was years later, when I did some study on Ignatius Loyola, founder of the Jesuits, that I realized the method of teaching I experienced in Oxford bore more resemblance to the essence of Ignatius' spiritual teaching than did the years I spent studying theology and philosophy in Jesuit houses. I know teaching methods in Jesuit houses have improved greatly in recent years; what I have described was Jesuit teaching in Britain and in Germany in the 1950s.

One of the Latin writers who attracted me was Lucretius, who lived from 96–55BC. His major work was called *De Rerum Natura*, 'On the Nature of Things', a poem in six books. It was only many years later that I began to see the connection between my attraction to Lucretius and the sudden 'temptation against faith' which assailed me. Lucretius was a man with a strong sense of vocation in life. His vocation was to set people free from their fears, because he was very aware of the damage we do to ourselves and to others when we allow fear to become dictator of our lives. For Lucretius, religious belief was the source of our fear, not only of what might befall us in this life, but also in the life to come, when the offended God/gods could exact vengeance on us for our sinfulness in this life.

His method of liberating his readers was to introduce them to the thinking of the Greek philosopher Epicurus (341–270BC), who held that the world and everything and everyone within it can be explained through the fortuitous combination of atoms – atoms being the Greek name for the ultimate constituents of matter. (The Greek word '*atom*' means, literally, that which cannot be cut.) When the combination of atoms that constitutes me changes, then I cease to be and there is no me left to worry about anything! The highest good for the human being, according to Epicurus, is pleasure.

There was a particular story in Lucretius which kept coming back to me and a particular line which, in Latin, read '*Tantum religio potuit suadere malorum*' and can be translated 'O religion, what crimes can be committed in your name'. The story was of Agamemnon, the Greek king of Mycenae, who led the Greek fleet to Troy in order to rescue the beautiful Helen, who had been abducted from Greece by the Trojan Paris. Agamemnon's fleet was becalmed at the isle of Aulis. Agamemnon consulted his holy man, who accompanied him on the trip. The holy man declared that in order to obtain suitable winds for the remainder of the voyage, he must sacrifice his daughter Iphigenia to the winds. Lucretius describes the death of this innocent girl, ending with the thunderous lines '*Tantum religio potuit suadere malorum*'.

It was only years later that I began to understand the significance of my strange attraction to those lines. It is as though our mind has an intelligence of its own, not necessarily immediately shared with our conscious minds. When I first began to think this might be true, I hesitated to admit it, even to myself. It sounded too vague, too unusual, and irresponsible, too, like the utterances of those convinced of the reality of UFOs (Unidentified Flying Objects). I no longer have this hesitation. I now have innumerable examples in my life of events experienced in the past whose significance escaped me at the time, but later became very enlightening, enabling me to appreciate and delight in what previously might have felt like a threat and something to be avoided.

I believe this gift is on offer to everyone, but fear can blind us to the gift of wonder and the gift of appreciating the miracle of our present life. When I first began to reach this conclusion about the miracle of our present life I felt apprehensive, in case I was being subtly drawn into disbelief in life after death. Now, when I face into this apprehension and bring it into prayer, I no longer feel afraid, because I know I am not denying life after death. I know that I don't have a clue as to what it will be like. All I do know with certainty is that whatever form our life after death may take, there will have to be a continuity of some kind with our life now, otherwise the concept of an afterlife becomes meaningless. The God who is holding us continuously and miraculously in being at this moment is the God who will be holding us after death: 'That they all may be one, as Thou, Father art in me, and as I am in you' (Jn 17.21). The practical conclusion from all this is to keep focusing our attention on the God of the present moment, as Père de Caussade advised centuries ago, and as Jesus taught in his own lifetime: 'The Kingdom of God is among you' (Mk 1.15).

What had shaken me and what I, at the time, interpreted as a destructive temptation against Christian Faith, as I then understood it, revealed itself, years later, to be an invitation to see faith very differently. Briefly expressed, my earlier understanding of faith was so focused on Christian doctrine, was so cerebral, channelling me into a life of rules and regulations, that I was unconsciously losing touch with imagination, with feelings and affections. I was able to do this for many years and had, as I thought, everything well under control. When the troublesome doubts afflicted me, they began to break down the securities I had built around me. The process took years and it is still going on, but it no longer threatens me. What I had interpreted as a temptation of faith was, in fact, an invitation to deepen it. The answers to these massive questions about the meaning of life lie within us, and we have the ability to discover them. The way to this enlightenment is not through theory; the enlightenment comes through living and serving others. In the doing we find the living God who is love and welcomingly mysterious.

One statement which I came across years after my initial temptation was an assertion, which I found unacceptable at first, but later discovered to be very helpful and enlightening as I reflected on it. The quotation was from Martin Buber, the Jewish thinker. (Buber did not want to be described as a philosopher, or theologian. He claimed not to be interested in ideas, but only in personal experience. He could not discuss God, but only relationship with God.) His book, written first in 1923, was called *Ich und Du*, translated into English both as *I and Thou* and *I and You*. The book deals with many issues, including religious consciousness, the concept of evil, and education, but the core of the book is his understanding of human life as an encounter, a relationship. As human beings, we do not exist as isolated monads: we are essentially related with all that is around us. We become who we are in and through our relationships, not independently of them. According to Buber, this relationship can be one of dialogue (*Ich–Du*) and of monologue (*Ich–Es*, meaning 'I-it'). In *Ich–Du* relationships we meet the other directly, an encounter which always includes an element of surprise, because neither of us can be represented simply by words. In every human encounter, mystery meets mystery: it is not like bumping into a table, or any other object. We can, of course, treat the other as a thing. Here lies the mystery of human violence. Success in war is only possible insofar as the aggressors see their enemies as things. Military training includes training in this attitude. We shall be considering this point in more detail in Part 2 on Peace. Here I just want to mention a phrase I came across in *I and Thou*, which I found unacceptable at first. The phrase was 'Nothing so masks the face of God as religion'. Buber was a most religious man: what did he mean by that statement? It took me years before I began to grasp what I thought he was saying. Then the phrase became an enlightening one, not threatening.

God is always greater than anything or anyone we can think or imagine. God cannot adequately be defined by words. Struggle with my own doubts had eventually made this truth obvious to me. Definitions, use of our reason are necessary, useful, helpful in life, but there comes a stage when we begin to see clearly the essential inadequacy of any philosophical/theological system which purports to give adequate explanations of anything.

Another memory from my time in Oxford led me to a decision which was to influence the direction of my life in the future and is the reason why I am now struggling at this moment with the question of Church Unity. What does the phrase 'Church Unity' mean for us today? In my mid-twenties, I had no problem with that question. Church Unity meant for me that the whole of humankind had to become Roman Catholic. This was not a private opinion: it was the official teaching of the Roman Catholic Church in the 1950s. The Latin term expressing this truth was '*Extra Ecclesiam nulla Salus*', 'Outside the Church (meaning the Roman Catholic Church) there is no Salvation'.

There was a group of undergraduates at Oxford in the early 1950s who had been educated in Jesuit schools and who used to meet at Campion Hall regularly for prayer, Scripture reading and reflection for one hour every week. One week the subject for discussion was the meaning of the phrase in the 'Our Father': 'Thy Kingdom Come'. Unanimously, myself included, we concluded that it meant working for the conversion of the whole world to become Roman Catholic! I felt uneasy about this. In Oxford, for the first time in my life, I was living with, socializing with, playing games and being taught by people who were not Roman Catholic. At first, I wondered why such intelligent, kind and friendly people were not Catholic! It was this question which led me, when I began studying theology, to focus on what was then spelled as 'Oekumenism' – a strange word of Greek origin which could be translated as 'homeliness', because the root of the word is *oikia*, meaning house/home. I love that derivation, for it points to something very basic and very treasured by all humankind: to have a place which I can call home and in which I feel at home.

My change from thinking the Kingdom of God means full membership of the Roman Catholic Church by all humanity to seeing it as a continuous process of evolution affecting all humanity and all creation was a huge leap. This process is drawing all of us into a unity of love and compassion in our relationships to one another, in our relationships and understanding of ourselves, the dream rooted in our trust in God, in whom all of us are held in being now. This unity is characterized by its variety, not by imposed uniformity. Could it be that

God abhors uniformity? As the prophet Jeremiah wrote, 'God's ways are not our ways and God's thoughts are not our thoughts'.

To identify the unity of God with the conformity of members of the Church to a system of belief and behaviour is clearly a contradiction. Why is it that every cell of our body – and each of us has trillions of them – are all distinct from all other human cells by their DNA? We have unique fingerprints, unique voice prints, unique eye patterns. To our conditioned way of thinking, this variety does seem excessive!

On leaving Oxford in summer 1955 to begin studying theology for the next four years at Heythrop College, 16 miles north of Oxford, I knew that the subject that interested me most was Church Unity. Six weeks before my final exams at Oxford, my mother became seriously ill. She was then living in a village called Galston, in a remote part of Ayrshire, with my two older sisters and my young brother, Joe. All three were working in Glasgow itself, so I was allowed to be with her and to do my exam preparation at home. As I look back now 57 years later, I am very grateful for those weeks at home with my dying mother. I was a troublesome child, considering her far too strict and constricting, with little or no thought of the strain she was under in having to bring up and educate a family of six on her own. I was 16 years old before I discovered my mother's and my own love of conversation with each other and her ability to listen. In her last illness, in the few hours she had each day when she was awake and free of pain, we continued our conversations, or I would read to her. She was a born worrier, but in her illness she was remarkably peaceful, loved listening to passages from St John's Gospel and the psalms and showed no sign of worry. Her health deteriorated; the doctor, whom she had known most of her life, kept erratic hours and was averse to using drugs to relieve her pain with every breath she drew. Eventually she agreed to go into hospital, recovered well at first, and I returned to Oxford. A few days later she became critically ill. I returned home, visited her in hospital, where she was very weak, but fully conscious, smiling and at peace. She died early the following morning. I returned to Oxford immediately after the funeral and my final exams began the following morning.

I mention my mother's death here because now, nearly 60 years later, I see clear connections between her death and my life, connections of which I was only vaguely aware at the time. One immediate effect of her illness was the change it wrought in my life priorities. Success in my final exams at Oxford was very important to me. Faced with my mother's terminal illness and death, worry about examination success lessened and was never a major worry in the many exams to follow in four years of theology. For this I am very grateful. I also came to realize the value of those hours of conversation I was able to have with her in my later teens, especially in the last weeks of her life. They mattered to me and have influenced me more than any examination success could ever have done. Finally, the event did, over time, effect a change in my understanding of God.

I did see that my mother had been over-strict when I was very young, that her faith was very unquestioning, lacking the critical element. I also began to appreciate other sides of her which far outweighed those defects: her practical care of all of us children, her ability to forgive and forget, her ability to laugh. My mother's defects did not embitter me or cause resentment, because the experience of her love, generosity and forgiveness was far more important, significant and life-giving to me than any brooding on her inadequacies.

Her influence affected the way I thought of God. Is God really concerned about our theological stance, our ranking in the league tables of orthodoxy, whether others approve of us or not? The questions made me much more attentive to the Gospels and also to my own experience and God became far more attractive to me. The experience of my mother's final illness and death affected the way I began my study of theology and it still affects me.

Exercise

- Begin to write a list of your own recurring memories from childhood. You will probably find that, having started on this, forgotten memories come back to you. Just make a note – but keep going back to the emerging memories, without attempting any analysis.

- Have you spotted any connections between those memories and the pattern of your life today? Don't force anything, just gawk, then make a brief note.

3

'Being at home' wherever we are

The object of this chapter is to review briefly the final years of my Jesuit training from 1955 to 1960 and the way they were later to broaden and deepen my understanding of the Unity of God and its relationship to every detail of human life.

Briefly, the four years in theology made me more aware of the fundamental importance of Ecumenism/Unity in Christian life. Unity has to do with every aspect of Christian life, its relationship to the life of all humankind and with every aspect of our relation, as human beings, to all creation. At the end of all my Jesuit training, my real knowledge of Ecumenism/Unity was still largely theoretical. My real learning began when I started working across the Christian denominations, with people of other faiths and with people of no faith.

One of the reasons for the massive reduction in churchgoing in recent years in the developed countries is because people no longer see any clear connection between the act of churchgoing and the way we live our everyday lives. Consequently, for many, abandoning church-going does not appear to make any significant difference in their lives; in fact, it comes as a relief from a tiresome and unnecessary duty. The behaviour of those who abandon churchgoing is very understandable, and it raises a much more important and fundamental series of questions, which we are so accustomed to ignoring that we no longer consider them worthy of attention. These questions, if addressed, can begin to uncover the many layers of destructive self-deception, which lock us into our present crises both in Church and State.

The questions concern not only the existence and nature of God, they raise the question of the meaning of our own lives. Is our true identity to be found in our identity cards, in our vital statistics? Does that information tell us the significance of our life and the value of it? Does it energize us and make us laugh? Does it enable us to discover what we basically long for from life? Does it expand our awareness of our utter dependence, not only on other human beings, but on all the organic and inorganic life around us? Does the information on my identity card so fill me with delight that I want to share it with those I meet, because it is wonderful news for them, too? What I begin to discover through these questions is something I cannot keep to myself, because the discovery is not unique to me: it is for everyone without exception.

If any one of us can answer, without hesitation, 'These questions are of no concern to me', then we are in desperate need of an introduction to ourselves, both for our own sake and for the sake of all who are within range of us!

For the Christian, churchgoing is an important activity. Corporate worship of some kind is to be found in all major world religions; it can take place in enclosed buildings, it can take place in the open air. Churchgoing in itself does not, however, express the essence of Christianity. In the early days of Christianity, when it was spreading so rapidly throughout the known world, the home was the place of worship – a lesson the Jews had learned in their years of exile from Israel, far from Jerusalem. Consequently, when the Jerusalem Temple was razed to the ground in the year 75AD the dispersed people had been prepared by the Pharisees to survive, spread and flourish, using their homes as their meeting places for worship.

The danger of identifying our relationship with God with church-going is not a modern problem. It was a problem spotted by the Hebrew prophets centuries before the Bible was written. It is a problem today in our post-Christian, postmodern society, a problem for all religions, but it is not generally acknowledged and discussion of it is sedulously avoided.

Here are a few examples from the Hebrew prophets' insights: they called the problem 'idolatry', a word which runs through all the Hebrew Scriptures and also through the New Testament. In my younger days, I was familiar with these frequent warnings against idolatry and the dreadful punishments that would befall the idolator, but I considered the practice to be something which afflicted very primitive peoples, leading them to create and build golden calves, round which they would later dance in worship. It was not a temptation for me and I had never, in my younger days, seen anyone daring to dance in Church.

Here is one example, written by the prophet Isaiah, probably around 735BC, when Jerusalem was under siege. It was Isaiah's mission to announce the fall of Israel and of Judah as punishment for the whole nation's unfaithfulness. This first part of the prophecy contains the first 39 chapters of Isaiah's prophecy. The prophecies, in this part, show Isaiah as a man of vision, who can see further than Jerusalem's present crisis in the face of Assyrian might. He sees a coming age when a remnant of the Jewish people will survive to rebuild peace and justice under a future descendant of the powerful King David. The second part of the Isaiah prophecy, from Chapters 40 to 55, are written by a different author towards the end of Israel's 40 years of exile in Babylon. They are called the 'Book of the Consolation of Israel' and include four 'Songs of the Servant of Yahweh', who suffers to atone for the sins of his people.

Here are a few excerpts from Isaiah, Chapter 1. Given our present crises in Church and State, the message of almost 3,000 years ago has a very contemporary ring!

'What are your endless sacrifices to me?
Says Yahweh.
I am sick of holocausts of rams
And the fat of calves.
The blood of bulls and of goats revolts me ...

Bring me your worthless offerings no more,
The smoke of them fills me with disgust.
New Moons, sabbaths, assemblies –
I cannot endure festival and solemnity.
Your New Moons and your pilgrimages
I hate with all my soul ...
You may multiply your prayers,
I shall not listen.
Your hands are covered with blood,
wash, make yourselves clean.
'Take your wrongdoing out of my sight!
Cease to do evil,
Learn to do good,
search for justice,
help the oppressed,
be just to the orphan,

plead for the widow.

'Come now, let us talk this over,'
Says Yahweh,
'though your sins are like scarlet,
they shall be as white as snow;
though they are red as crimson,
they shall be like wool.' (Isa. 1.11-18)

This quotation from Isaiah is not a tirade by the prophet against all forms of worship, of liturgy and of prayer. Whenever I read it now, or hear it read, I imagine a solemn High Mass in a beautiful, ancient cathedral, the sun streaming in through the stained glass windows, showing the billowing smoke of incense ascending like prayer to the apse of the Gothic columns, then from the rafters comes this booming voice declaring 'I cannot endure festival and solemnity – When you stretch out your hands in prayer, I turn my eyes away'. There is consternation down below. The Vergers are summoned to remove this blasphemer! The miscreant is beyond their reach. The police are called to protect the congregation.

The prophetic utterances expressed here by Isaiah are not tirades against liturgy and prayer. They are far more fundamental than that: they touch on the essential meaning of all liturgy and of its relationship with every aspect of human life in every human individual, whether religious believer or not. The prophet's tirade is about the destructive split we have created between our worship of God on the one hand and our treatment of one another, of ourselves, and of creation in which we are all held and nurtured. Our future survival as a human race depends upon our relationship with the earth which sustains us. As far as we know, in spite of the phenomenal progress in our knowledge of the expanding Universe, we are the only one of the trillions of planets which is supporting human life.

It is not an exaggeration to say that the crises in our post-Christian, postmodern world are not petty squabbles which could easily be rectified by reformed and strengthened political, social and economic structures, ensuring law and order in all these areas of life – yet that is the presumption which underlies almost all solutions offered in our modern crises. This is superficial thinking. The assumption is that a strong and effective regime of law and order will produce the desired effect. This is an assumption which we are not keen on examining:

it is safer to keep it hidden. Close examination only causes unrest, conflict, and can threaten us with chaos. It is far more sensible to ignore the question and just learn to be politically correct and be nice to each other! Underlying the smooth and reassuring words are layers of meaning that are not at all nice. They are based on contempt for human nature in general, on fear of anarchy and chaos, and they rely on the power of law and order to keep the irresponsible masses under control. The assumed power of law and order includes power over language, so that words, disconnected from our reality, mean what the powers decree they should mean. We are all capable of sleepwalking into tyranny and into self-imprisonment.

Truth is an indestructible power, which no amount of human ingenuity can ultimately destroy. Truth reveals the facts: it also reveals all forms of falsehood. It is for us human beings to decide how we are going to react in face of truth, whether to acknowledge it and cooperate or ignore/deny it. But truth is not malleable; it does not change in obedience to any human power. Truth has an utterly inexorable and indestructible quality. Jesus, in St John's Gospel, says of himself, 'I am the Way, the Truth and the Life' (Jn 14.6). Gandhi wrote 'God is truth'; he also wrote 'Truth is God'. Rejecting the very concept of God, religion and spirituality is the most destructive thing we can do: it can bring about the omnicide we all fear. Our way of protecting ourselves, the way we refuse to face into our worst fears becomes, in fact, a way of creating our own worst nightmares. As I write this, an image comes to mind. It is the image that appears in Matthew and Luke as well, but it is most vividly portrayed in Mark.

Jesus has retired with his disciples to a lonely part of the Sea of Galilee to have some peace from the crowds. No sooner has he landed than a disturbed man comes towards Jesus. Mark describes the event thus:

> The man lived in the tombs and no-one could secure him anymore, even with a chain, because he had often been secured with fetters and chains but he had snapped the chains and broken the fetters, and no-one had the strength to control him. All night and all day, among the tombs and in the mountains, he would howl and gash himself with stones. Catching sight of Jesus from a distance, he ran up and fell at his feet and shouted at the top of his voice, 'What do you want with me, Jesus of Nazareth, son of the Most High God? Swear by God you will not torture me!' – For Jesus had been saying

to him, 'Come out of the man, unclean spirit'. What is your name?, Jesus asked. 'My name is legion', he answered, 'because there are many of us.' And he begged him not to send him out of the district. Now there was there on the mountainside a great herd of pigs feeding, and the unclean spirits begged him, 'Send us into the pigs, let us go into them.' So he gave them leave. With that the unclean spirits came out and went into the pigs, and the herd of about two thousand pigs charged down the cliff and into the lake, and there they were drowned.

This is a most graphic and powerful picture. We shall be returning to it frequently. I mention it here because it illustrates our modern tendency to avoid painful situations with soothing words.

When I began my theology studies, Ecumenism/Unity, which had already attracted me, played a very minor part in our studies. We were much more intent on learning how to disprove the arguments of other Christian denominations who disagreed with our claims to be the one and only true Church. Having dismissed their objections, we then learned how to present the truth of the Roman Catholic Church to our heretical neighbours.

I also noticed that almost all the books on Ecumenism which appeared in our library were written in German, so I asked if I might spend six weeks of the summer vacation learning German. The Jesuit in charge of our theological studies, Fr Bruno Brinkman, suggested that instead of six weeks learning German, I should do the remaining three years of theology in Germany at Sankt Georgen, Frankfurt/Main, where there were lecturers who were actively engaged in Ecumenical work. In July 1956, I left Heythrop in Oxfordshire to continue theology in Germany for the next three years.

As I now look back on those three years, I am most grateful for having had that experience, although I found it very difficult at the time. The difficulty was partly linguistic, but the much greater difficulty was with the teaching method, almost entirely by way of lectures, most of them in Latin, with little or no opportunity for discussion or questioning. The teaching was mostly instructional, with little or no recognition, as far as I could understand, of the importance of the critical element in religion. On reflection on those years, I discovered that my education in Ecumenism/Unity came mainly through later events which, at first sight, did not seem to have any connection with Ecumenism as I understood it at that time.

The Nazis came into power in Germany in 1933. At first, they were remarkably popular in general, among all classes of people, including Christians of all denominations. They were also welcomed by the working classes, the wealthy and the powerful in Church and State. The personality of Adolf Hitler, founder and leader of the party, acted like a powerful magnet on a nation which was still smarting from the humiliation of defeat in World War I of 1914–18 and from the harsh financial, territorial and political conditions imposed on it by the Allied Forces at the Treaty of Versailles in 1919.

Germany saw itself caught in a permanent poverty trap from which there was no means of escape. She was also in a very anti-Semitic mood. This was not something new; it had been smouldering for centuries. The Jews were blamed for Germany's defeat in the First World War. Hitler, despite his not infrequent hysterical outbursts, was a skilled orator. He knew how to touch into the bitterness of his audience, how to inflame their hatred by reminding them of the injustices being done to them. He also encouraged them to dream of their past greatness and inspired them to fulfil their destiny as the master race.

Within 18 months of taking power as German Chancellor in 1933, Hitler had reduced unemployment by five million and Germany had the healthiest economy in Europe. He also brought in many social changes which alleviated the plight of the poor, promoted the health and strength of German youth, provided full employment, and began to show his political skills in acting boldly by forcibly recovering former German territories from the Allies. His methods, already in these early years of his rule, showed clear and ominous signs of his ruthlessness in eliminating those who opposed his plans. Already there were plans to overthrow him by groups within the military, but there was no group, either in Church or State, strong enough to oppose him effectively because of his general popularity among the people of all classes, including many Church leaders.

The Nazi threat tested the Christian churches in Germany and showed up fundamental weaknesses within and among the Christian denominations, weaknesses from which all of us Christians still have much to learn today. In showing up these weaknesses, Nazism also forced the churches to ask themselves very fundamental questions about the nature of Christian Faith. That is why Germany was years ahead of other European nations at the time of the Second Vatican

Council (1962–5) and was able to contribute so valuably to the very radical changes which the Council instigated.

Ecumenism was no longer concerned primarily with the power and influence of the Catholic Church. It was a movement in search of the unity of all humankind, a movement of love and encouragement for all, renouncing domination, replacing it with love and service. This movement towards unity abhors all forms of coercion. It is as central to Christian faith as Justice.

The years in Germany taught me a lesson which I am still learning and hope to continue learning to the end of my days, a lesson which is essential in all our work for the unity of humankind: the lesson is about the nature of prejudice. It is a learning process which slowly reveals some of the many layers of prejudice we have inherited through our upbringing and strengthened later by our own consent. We become so at home with our prejudices that we no longer recognize them in ourselves. But the prejudices do not ignore us. These deep-set patterns of thought, of action and reaction, influence all our decisions in every aspect of our lives as we struggle to survive in a competitive world, our methods creating new divisions within us and around us. We all need the help of others to begin to understand ourselves.

I was 15 years old when the Second World War broke out in September 1939. In the prewar and postwar years I knew Germany only as 'the enemy', who were intent on subjecting Britain and our allies to their tyrannical rule. Suddenly 11 years after the war ended, I found myself living with over 100 theology students, mostly German. They did not live up to my expectations, were not all militant, unquestioningly obedient, worshippers of uniformity, devoid of humour and lacking in common sense. I found them to be as varied in character as any other nation I had encountered and to be of a very inquiring disposition. They also had a good sense of humour, which varied, as in most countries, from region to region.

Having lived for periods in Scotland, Wales, England and Ireland, I began to see, for the first time, points of similarity. I was also beginning to see that 'different' does not mean 'defective' – an obvious truth, a platitude, but I have to keep reminding myself of this.

Difference is a blessing, not a threat. This platitude, if we could really assent to it, would revolutionize our approach to immigration problems, enabling both native peoples and immigrants to appreciate their mutual giftedness and to set free both parties from the narrowness of their conditioning.

Learning to recognize our own deeply ingrained prejudices and to free ourselves from them is a lengthy and usually a painful process, but it is a process that sets us free, liberates us from the prison of the conditioning which narrows our vision to ever-shrinking circles, contentedly ignoring the plight of those who are outside our range – the majority of humankind.

The three years in Germany helped me to understand Ecumenism in a new and exciting way. It is not a subject of interest only to religious people: it is a movement towards unity in every aspect of human life. This includes all our international relationships, our relationships within our own nation, the unity of every organization within our nation in every aspect of its activity. This vast range of topics necessarily leads us into speculation. Our overall aim, namely to facilitate/ invent better ways of communicating, can easily be forgotten as we focus our attention on practical details. Soon, we find ourselves at odds with those with whom we are meant to be collaborating.

The lesson I now have to keep remembering from this German experience – a lesson which subsequent experience has always confirmed – is that for any person who engages in movements to promote unity and reconciliation where there is division, we must be prepared to start the movement by giving attention to our own inner conflicts. Without this preliminary step our efforts will not lead to unity, but nurture disunity, worsening the situation, deepening the division. The reasoning behind these statements will, I hope, become more apparent in the course of this book. Here, I am relating my own experience. At this stage, it is enough for the reader to note whether anything I write corresponds in any way with your own felt experience.

I mention this German experience here and the conviction it eventually implanted in me about the nature of Ecumenism/Unity, because it is a truth which is almost entirely ignored both by secular and religious authorities when they address current crises of Church or State. For these authorities the blame always lies elsewhere, never in themselves, and the solution, they believe, can only be found in further planning, reorganization, renewal of structures. They are attempts to keep order and control over the wayward. Do these observations correspond, in any way, to your own experience?

Those who are in positions of authority, whether in State or Church, and whose decisions have precipitated the crises which affect millions of people politically, socially, psychologically, spiritually and religiously, are very rarely penalized. The less privileged are the least protected in our society and are likely to suffer most from decisions made without reflection by those in authority.

It is only by facing the destructive conflict in itself – whether personal or public conflict – that we can become aware of our own dividedness. In some mysterious way, it is the wound which heals, the wounded one who can become the healer for others. We need the help of our enemies to achieve inner wholeness. If these remarks are true, how could they be put into practice in, for example, sex abuse cases? Do you know of any examples of this practice having been tried and with what results? The principles behind these practices can be applied to any other type of offence: details of application will obviously differ.

In modern society, political correctness has, in very recent years, become a dogma of correct behaviour. I am not denying the value of political correctness, but indicating some of the serious injustices that can follow from its unreflective application, fostering an attitude of avoidance, of pretence, of denial of anything likely to ruffle feathers, reveal dissent, give offence.

It is precisely this exaggerated and unreflective dedication to political correctness that sows the seeds of violence in our society. The very measures which are taken to nurture political correctness are the measures which are most destructive. Political correctness is full of unexamined assumptions. We do not want to look at these assumptions, because they are likely to disrupt what we are pleased to call 'our peace'. But the truth is that our peace can only come to us in and through our honest acknowledgement of our own fears and apprehensions. There is wisdom in our fears. Our fears are not problem-solvers; their wisdom lies in the directions in life they can give if we have the courage to look at them. If we ignore our fears, they may disappear temporarily from our conscious minds, perhaps for years, but our unfaced fears, like atoms, are indestructible, obdurate, are not cowed by human pronouncements, no matter how solemnly stated, nor by whom.

My reflections so far have led to the surprising conclusion that unity cannot be imposed from without upon divisions in society, whatever they may be and wherever they occur. This statement is not generally accepted; in fact, it is ruthlessly and violently rejected by the majority of both secular and religious authorities.

My second reflection goes further than the first. Not only are we unable to impose unity in conflict situations, we can only reduce the conflict by acknowledging its existence, facing into it. To ignore the conflict, pretend it does not exist, does not make it disappear. We may succeed in pushing it out of our conscious minds, bringing us a measure of relief for a time, but the facts in which we live are obdurate, they do not disappear at our command, they are still working on us, influencing our decisions, affecting our behaviour. The signals we can receive of this disorder register in our moods, our feelings, above all in our fears, upsetting our sense of wellbeing. Our human psyche has a very strong defence system. In itself this is a great gift, enabling us to defend ourselves against the assaults of our fears and panics, our inner darkness and our dreads, so that we can resolutely pursue what we believe to be the true course, the honest way, the loving response. But there is a dark side to this gift; our inner moods and feelings, especially fear, can so overwhelm us that we act on the spur of the moment, without reflection, destructively for ourselves and for those around us.

This second reflection also leads to the conclusion that in any conflict situation we must face into the facts of the situation honestly, acknowledge the conflict and our fear of it and beg for enlightenment. What does that mean? It means looking at, as distinct from trying to analyse, whatever it is that is frightening us, acknowledging our own confusion and bewilderment, sense of helplessness and hopelessness. In doing this, we are not forcing anything, not pretending, not trying to change anything; we are simply acknowledging the truth of our own immediate experience. 'Enlightenment' is what follows when we expose ourselves to the 'isness' of a situation: we are not trying to change it, nor pretending it does not exist – we are 'letting it be'. Another way of describing this process is to say we are being contemplative – that is, we are observing the situation without trying to change it. Here is one way of distinguishing contemplating a situation from observing a situation – an example I have already given in another context, but there is no harm in repetition!

Imagine you are standing on the midpoint of a bridge spanning a broad river. There are many barges passing by in different directions, some very attractive-looking, others looking ready for the scrapyard. You observe, but you do not jump off the bridge into the barges; you are being contemplative, observing the 'isness' of things, letting the scene be. In this way you are allowing the scene to teach you; you are not mentally reordering the scene to suit you. In this way you have taken a most profound leap into a new way of observing your surroundings. You have stumbled into the truth of things by 'gawking', that beautiful Scottish word, which is probably related to the word 'gape', meaning to stare in wonder, in amazement, which is one of the most valuable activities any of us can engage in. In our very busy modern world, 'gawking' is not recognized as a 'useful' occupation, so a 'gawker' – even in Scotland, I am ashamed to say – has come to mean a stupid, boorish person. Could this misuse be a reflection on our age? Are we losing our humanity in our desire to have everything controlled and ordered in order to suit the whims of our rulers?

Briefly, the conclusion I suggest is that the search for human unity within an individual and for unity for all peoples must begin with individual readiness to face and to acknowledge our own inner fears, dreads and darkness. Facing them does not mean overcoming them; it means acknowledging their existence in our own lives. It is from that inner acknowledgement that the transformation process can begin within us and around us. There is no other option. This truth will slowly become clearer to us; it does not happen overnight and there are no magic solutions available for the super-wealthy – we are all subject to the 'isness' of things. As this truth begins to dawn on us, we begin to become aware of the attractiveness of the process. It opens up the horizons of our perceptions, helps us to recognize more clearly the bonds which restrict our freedom – bonds imposed on us through our upbringing, bonds which we have imposed on ourselves through our unwillingness to accept change in our own lives, to risk unpopularity from our peers or from people in authority by saying or doing what we really want to say or do.

In facing into our fears and doubts we can begin to see them not as threats, but as invitations to be transformed, encouragements from within us to enter into a new way of seeing the reality in which we find ourselves, a reality full of attractive possibilities. We begin to see that this new way of seeing is not something we have created for ourselves; it is something which has been there all the time and which we are now beginning to recognize. We may have been brought up religiously, be familiar with creeds, the sacred writings of whatever faith we hold and we may declare ourselves to be Christian, Jewish, Muslim, Hindu, Sikh,

Pentecostal, have studied religious teachings extensively, but the realization of a presence in the midst of our terrors is a new kind of revelation.

It is like a light in the darkness, a stillness at the heart of our turmoil, a deep reassurance, in spite of the continuing chaos around and within us, that I am not alone, that I am being held in being by a power greater than my conscious mind can grasp, a power in which I live and move and have my being. The 'isness of things', an expression that sounds so strange and inhuman, turns out to be friendly, welcoming, reassuring and encouraging.

This awareness may come as a momentary flash, the felt experience quickly forgotten, but it can make an indelible impression. It is something which has not come from outside, something we have received from another; it seems to have come from something deep within us, something which we know we have not consciously fashioned in any way. It is like a presence which is a present: it is not a reward, not an achievement.

Exercise

- After reading this chapter, did any word, phrase, thought give rise to any FELT reaction, whether pleasant or unpleasant? Make a list.

- Have you spotted any connection between your felt reaction and your life since that memory? Make a note but avoid analysis at this stage. And don't try too hard!

In all this reading and in doing these exercises, the all-important thing is your giving attention to your felt reactions. As you become more aware of their existence, they will begin to teach you.

4

The indestructible call to unity changes everything

The Roman historian Tacitus, who lived around the years 55–120AD, was a Latin stylist, renowned for his pithy phrases, as well as being a historian. One of his phrases is '*solvitur ambulando*' ('the problem is solved by walking'). In walking, I often find, quite unexpectedly, the answer to something which has been puzzling me. When I did crossword puzzles, this happened frequently. But I have discovered the phrase is also true if I change the word '*ambulando*' to '*scribendo*', meaning 'the problem is solved by writing'. It is as though the act of writing becomes like the action of a dredger, which plunges into our subconscious, into our forgotten memories, and produces something we recognize as the answer to some query that has been nagging at us. I find this process at work in me now as I try to write on 'Unity'. Memories pop up unexpectedly and, if I have the patience to look at them, they sometimes clarify what I am struggling to express. I am also aware that my 'dredger' works much more slowly than in earlier years and produces more and thicker mud! Perhaps I am becoming more aware of the chaos, which is the substratum of all created things!

This chapter is an attempt to embody the conclusions I have reached in Chapter 3 – conclusions that we have to face into our fears and apprehensions if we are to discover enlightenment, a new way of seeing the reality in which we find ourselves. The wonderful discovery is in beginning to see that what we most fear is also what we most long for. It is in facing our fears that the dredger begins to reveal the treasure within us and among us. Just stating this, or reading about it without reflection, may provide some information, but the process in itself is as useless as presenting someone who has never used a telephone in their lives, and has no intention of doing so, with a fat telephone directory. We are not created to become encyclopaedias: we are created to engage in life. One of the dangers of too much study is that we can forget this most obvious truth and begin to assess ourselves and others in terms of our ability to retain knowledge and deliver it on request.

When I now, in old age, reflect on my past life, I know that what I really longed for was not to amass knowledge, but to engage with life. One direction in life which has enabled me to keep on track of this engagement is an interest in Ecumenism/Unity. It is no longer, for me, a process: it is a most attractive way of being and is constantly surprising me, because it keeps revealing connections in life of which I was previously unaware. I write about this now because I know this engagement is open to everyone; it is not just revealing something fascinating and attractive, it has a transforming effect. It is something freely given, not a reward for our virtue or our good deeds. It costs, however, not less than everything, but it becomes a price we long to pay with every fibre of our being.

How was it that Germany – such a large, talented, intelligent and resourceful country with its strongly Christian tradition, its gifted theologians and very influential church organizations – could be taken in by Nazism and, in general, become supporters of Hitler, even in the bleak years after the fall of Germany in 1918? This support began to change after he became the German Chancellor in 1933: it turned into ineffective opposition. He had become such a popular leader in earlier years and used this popular support so craftily that when, in the immediate events which led up to the outbreak of war in September 1939, people in power, in the army especially, became increasingly worried at the unpredictability of his decisions and the brutality with which he executed them, yet no group in Germany was united and powerful enough to oppose him with any reasonable hope of success. In this situation there were many individual Germans, both religious and lay, men and women of outstanding courage and insight, who kept hoping when everything seemed hopeless. Many of them were executed by the Nazis before the collapse of Germany in 1945, but their message has lived on in human hearts and so enabled Germany to rise again, not to dominate, but to contribute to peace, stability and hope in Europe and beyond.

In spite of Germany's inability to depose Hitler, the brutality of both the regime and the mass bombing by the Allies of German cities was forcing Germans of all Christian denominations, and of none, to face fundamental questions about the nature of Christian faith, as well as very practical questions about places of worship. Thousands of churches had been destroyed. People of different Christian denominations began to share their churches for worship, congregations met one another after centuries of religious apartheid, strangers became friends. That is why postwar Germany was light years ahead of other European countries ecumenically.

After I was ordained priest in Frankfurt in July 1958, I asked my German superior whether I might return to Scotland for two weeks with my family. My superior's first question was 'Why do you want to go home?', to which I replied 'Because it is home'. This answer did not satisfy him. 'You must have an academic reason' was his reply, and my answer to this request was 'I am very interested in Scottish theology and I would like to make contact with the Church of Scotland and clergy of other Christian denominations'. 'In that case you may go' was the welcome reply.

After one week in Scotland, I had still made no contact with any Anglican or Scottish clergy. The one Jesuit in Glasgow who was reported to have some contact with other denominations was away for two weeks. As no other Jesuit in the Glasgow community could help, I went to the headquarters of the Church of Scotland in the city and asked if I might consult their clerical directory. On receiving it, I opened it at random and found a page headed Glasgow University, Theology Department. The various departments included one called, 'Systematic Theology', a category that was unfamiliar to me at the time, but it sounded general enough. Among those listed was a lecturer, John MacQuarrie, unknown to me, but the name suggested someone solid, not only down-to-earth but delving beneath the surface to something more solid. I phoned him later that evening. He had a reassuring, homely voice and invited me to his house on a Saturday evening. I spent three hours with him on that first visit, finishing our session in the kitchen, where his wife had prepared supper for the three of us. At the end of the evening, he invited me back for another session before I had to return to Frankfurt. In this second session he, an Episcopalian, spoke very openly of his own difficulties with the Anglican Thirty Nine Articles, the Anglican sixteenth-century creed. He also presented me with Calvin's *Catechism of the Eucharist*, which I read with great interest on the train back to Frankfurt.

This encounter with John MacQuarrie was to influence my understanding of Ecumenism far more than I realized at the time. I was
immediately impressed by the breadth of his knowledge. He was
currently translating some of Heidegger's work, had read extensively
in Catholic theology and was interested in other faiths. He had a
wonderful gift of enthusiasm and an obvious desire to share what
attracted him with anyone who would listen. There was no trace of
the preacher or the instructor in him. At the end of this second visit
he told me that I was the first Roman Catholic priest with whom he
had ever had a conversation. Before lecturing at Glasgow University,
John MacQuarrie had spent many years in parish ministry in Glasgow.
At that time, there were hundreds of Catholic priests working in
Glasgow but, in general, there was a strict apartheid among the clergy.
This extraordinary fact confirmed my desire to work for the unity of
Christians, especially in Scotland.

The encounter also made me aware, although only vaguely, of the
enormity of the task. Through centuries of division, we have become
so accustomed to our divided state that we fear work for unity. Our
divided Christian state has so become the norm that we begin to
suspect the orthodoxy of anyone who shows signs of ecumenical
interest. The loyalty of an individual is measured by their degree of
exclusivity and intolerance of those who differ in any way from what
they consider to be orthodoxy. My vague discomfort about the nature
of Ecumenism/Unity and the magnitude of the task of working for
reconciliation was soon to become much less vague and far more
uncomfortable.

One other incident from my time in Germany, which illustrates both
the centrality of Ecumenism/Unity in Christian faith and the destructiveness of its absence, came to me very strongly towards the end of my
three years there. My final theology exam would be finished in early
June 1959. I would then be free to return to the UK to do pastoral work
until my final year training, called the 'tertianship', which was due to
begin in mid-September at St Beuno's, North Wales, where I had lived
from 1942 to 1946. I wanted to have some experience of Ecumenism
in practice in Germany before returning to the UK in early July. The
Jesuit Provincial agreed. In that final year I had been reading about
and attending public lectures between different Christian denominations on very fundamental theological questions on the nature of the
Church, the place of the Eucharist in Christian life, the meaning of

'Justification by Faith Alone', 'The Nature of Church Authority' – events which I had never experienced in the UK.

I was invited to join a Dutch priest in what was called a '*Kapellenwagen* Mission' in 'the Diaspora', areas of postwar Germany now inhabited by refugees from German Sudetenland, which had been given over to Czechoslovakia after the war. Many of these refugees were Catholics, but they were living in Protestant areas of Germany where there were no Catholic churches or resident priests. The Dutchman was a Roman Catholic diocesan priest who spoke fluent German and spent his life ministering to refugees. A *Kapellenwagen* was a bus carrying a large tent and all the necessary equipment for turning it into a church, with tables and chairs, altar and room for over 100 people. I was invited to join him for two weeks, one week in each area. We received hospitality, beds and meals, going to different families every day.

I delighted in doing this active ministry after eight years of study. I was not overworked. Apart from the practical work of setting up the tent and arranging its sparse furnishings, I was asked to give a ten-minute homily at Mass each day, to hear confessions and be around to chat with anyone interested.

Our congregations in both places had been living for years far from a church and without the sacrament of reconciliation (what used to be called 'Confession') and without the Eucharist. Most of them spoke with a strange accent which I could barely understand. Consequently, my priestly ministry had to be reduced to utter simplicity. What a gift that was! I was especially moved by the numbers who came to Confession. We used one corner of the large tent for this purpose, two folding chairs on as level a patch of grass as we could find. Some of the more elderly penitents preferred to kneel, using my knee as a support both to get down and up again to and from the kneeling position. With one heavy penitent I ended up flat on the grass as he staggered to his feet. Most penitents were mercifully brief, simply saying their last confession was so many years ago and that they were sorry for all their sins. I was unable to understand those who began on more detailed accounts of their spiritual wellbeing, so I handed them over to God who, as the Book of Wisdom so beautifully expresses it, 'overlooks our sins so that we can repent' (Wis. 11.24).

The hospitality we received in both places and the generosity of the people spoke more eloquently than any words and I am still very grateful every time I remember the *Kapellenwagen* Mission. In the second Diaspora village, the Protestant community invited us to celebrate Mass in their pre-Reformation church and attended the service in large numbers. It was the first time, they told us, that Mass had been celebrated in the church for four centuries. The people we met in both villages where we held the Mission had arrived after the war from Sudetenland, carrying all their possessions on their backs, mostly farming and carpentry tools. One family had arrived with a piano strapped on the husband's back, a piano still in daily use ten years later! They were now content, at peace and relatively prosperous. Those two weeks were a very privileged time, a glimpse into lives of great heroism, of strong community bonds, forged through years of mutual support in shared hardship. Their depth of faith enabled them not only to survive years of hardship, but to recover.

After the two weeks with the Mission, I spent some time visiting people actively engaged in ecumenical work and to whom I had been referred. One place was an ecumenical centre in Paderborn, where the director, a Dr Brandenburg, invited me to stay. Quite unexpectedly, when I told him that I was hoping to do some further study in Ecumenism, he offered to have me for doctoral studies in Paderborn, where he would be happy to supervise me. I also received an invitation to attend the '*Kirchentag*'. This is a lay Protestant initiative, begun in 1949 in Hanover by Reinhold von Thadden-Trieglaff and a few friends. It was to become a week-long meeting to be held every two years in some German city, its object being to provide a forum for debate and discussion on present-day concerns. It was to be open to all who might be interested, of all Christian denominations and none. The movement celebrated its sixtieth anniversary in 2009. It now gathers about 100,000 visitors annually and has 30,000 active participants, attracting people from all over Germany and internationally. Many initiatives have come from these meetings which have affected not only Germany, but the worldwide Church. In 1961, for example, it started a dialogue between Christians and Jews. In the 1970s, it initiated new forms of worship, encouraging people to discover more of the height and depth, length and breadth of their faith. In the 1980s, the *Kirchentag*'s discussions on peace, justice and the integrity of creation influenced German national policy at home and abroad. A final invitation was to attend a two-week meeting with Lutheran pastors in the Bavarian Alps to discuss the Eucharist.

When I asked my Jesuit Provincial in the UK if I might extend my stay in Germany for another four weeks to attend these invitations, I received a curt reply from his Jesuit secretary telling me that I seemed to be unaware of the apostolic needs in the British Jesuit Province and that I must return immediately to England to work in a Jesuit parish in Preston, Lancashire for a month before proceeding to my final year of training, the 'tertianship'.

I arrived in Preston, where it was raining, after a scorching summer in Germany, and eventually reached my new destination in a soaking state. The parish priest greeted me with, 'Oh, you must be Hughes. I don't know what we are going to do with you for the next six weeks, but you will be needed for Mass on Sundays and for Confessions during the week.' This was my introduction to active ministry after 16 years of preparation! I did not know whether to laugh or cry. At the time, I just concentrated on each day as it came and, in general, appreciated the month in Preston and the little active ministry it provided. Now, over 50 years later, when I reflect on this incident, I begin to see it differently and, I believe, more clearly. That incident encapsulated a question which has stayed with me ever since, but I have only in recent years begun to recognize it and express it more clearly. It concerns the split nature of our spirituality – the gulf between our religious language and the reality in which we live. It is the question which has been and still is very painful, but it is also the question which opens up a new way of understanding faith, the nature of the Church, the nature of God, human nature, the nature of all creation and our place, as human beings, within it.

This question has come to me slowly, gradually and painfully, but it is also a treasure beyond price; it leaves me genuinely grateful for my past and for all those who have been part of it, friends and enemies. This is not to deny my own wrongdoing and failures, or other people's; it is about seeing both facts in a wider perspective. Our sinfulness is never the end of the Christian story; it is a part of it, the part that God is constantly inviting us to collaborate in transforming.

I am touching on the most fundamental questions of human life and of religion. I hesitate in formulating them because they seem so pretentious and presumptuous. I have no awareness of having formulated them. They arrive in my consciousness without any conscious invitation on my part, and they do not take offence at my lack of courtesy. They just stay in my mind like mental tinnitus, demanding attention.

One aspect of this process is that I become more aware of the enormity of my own ignorance. I delighted, over 60 years ago, when

I managed to read Plato's *Apologia* in Greek, in which Socrates speaks of what became his mission in life. He had visited the oracle at Delphi and the oracle declared him to be the wisest man in the world. Socrates knew he was not; his mission in life then became proving the oracle to be wrong. He visited all the wisest, most learned people he could find – the philosophers, religious teachers, politicians, eminent professionals. Then he made his discovery. Although all these people were much more learned than he, they all suffered from the illusion that their expertise in one discipline enabled them to speak with authority on every subject. Socrates then discovered that his wisdom lay in his acknowledgement of his own ignorance. I was very attracted by this picture of Socrates at the time. It is one of those memories which has lingered and keeps recurring.

At first, I was totally unaware of the importance of lingering memories. I now know how important they are. They are friendly reminders that I need to look at more closely, because they may contain a wisdom which is not yet accessible to my conscious mind. Why do I recognize it now?

Briefly, the reason is I now have time to reflect on the past with a degree of detachment which I previously lacked. Lest this digression becomes too abstract, let me illustrate what I mean by returning to that incident when I was not allowed to accept those ecumenical invitations for my last month in Germany. Part of my initial reaction was anger, disappointment, resentment against the official prohibition on my accepting these invitations, followed by uncomplimentary thoughts on authority's lack of understanding and their apparent inability to listen. The problem set off an inner turmoil. In those days I had a very simple view of obedience. Authority, in the person of the Jesuit Provincial, had spoken. I must obey unquestioningly. I did so, and soon afterwards I thought I was free of the negative feelings. But feelings do not die so easily. We can repress them, but until we face into them they will keep popping up in consciousness, sometimes only many years later, or we can suffer long periods of lassitude, losing interest in life and becoming increasingly listless without any apparent cause.

One lesson I learned from this German disappointment and from countless other setbacks through the years was the need to take note of our felt reactions to events in life and show them to God in prayer. Here let me condense into a few sentences what I mean and what it has taken me decades to begin to learn and am still learning. Faced with the problem of inner turmoil, negative felt reactions and condemnatory judgements against those in authority, how are we to respond? On that occasion I responded by obeying the Provincial's orders and quite enjoyed the enforced leisure. For many years I continued in this way.

My training had been such that I could never have found peace in questioning a Provincial's orders or even his suggestions. To have acted against them would have been an act of violence against my inner conviction. Fifty years of experience later I can view the situation differently. In that time the question, 'What is God like?' has always been with me and I have tried to stay with it, treating it as an invitation, not as a threat. Do not try to protect yourself against these questions. Let them be, listen to them and they will provide the answers, not in words, but in an inner assurance summoning you into the endlessly attractive mystery of God's life and love. In light of this experience, we can begin to see our own lives very differently. God is so frequently presented as external to us, a dominating, frightening Being whose main interest is in our sins. To be forgiven, we must perform religious practices imposed by those in authority. If we fail to comply we are doomed to misfortune in this life, to be followed by an eternity of fiery punishment after death. With this view of faith, held by millions, it is not at all surprising that millions have abandoned belief in such a God and feel liberated!

Despite the liberation I experienced 56 years ago and for which I am still grateful, I still have that old question – what is God like? I now know, without any shadow of doubt, that I cannot escape the question. It continues throughout this book. It is the most precious of questions. To lose touch with it would be to lose touch with the Heart of the matter in which we all live and move and have our being.

This is a gift open to everyone. It is not something outside of us; it belongs to the very essence of our being. It turns everything upside down. Its name is 'I am'. The only place anyone of us can find 'I am' is where I am.

'I am' is in every breath we breathe. The Latin word for breath is '*spiritus*': it is also a name of God. St Paul tells us 'The Spirit, who lived in Jesus and raised him from the dead, now lives in you'. That is the Good News, the News that prompted St Paul to write:

Nothing therefore can come between us and the love of Christ, even if we are troubled, or being persecuted, or lacking food or clothes, or being threatened or even attacked. For I am certain of this, neither death nor life, no angel, no prince, nothing that exists, nothing still to come, not any power, or height or depth, nor any created thing, can ever come between us and the love of God made visible in Christ Jesus our Lord. (Rom. 8.25-39)

Exercises

- Having read this chapter, note your predominant feelings and the word or phrase which gave rise to them.
- Are there any practical implications which you can spot in this journey into Unity in which we have engaged and which you would like to explore?

5

Wonder leading to contemplation

Tertianship is the name given to the final period of Jesuit training. In 1959 it still took place in St Beuno's, North Wales and lasted nine months. It was introduced in the early seventeenth century and was called a '*Schola Affectus*', a 'school of the affections', to develop the emotional life of Jesuits after many years of study. In this chapter I focus on my interest in Ecumenism/Unity during this time.

The parts of the tertianship which lifted my spirits were not the many hours given to prayer and the reading of spiritual books. What appealed to me most was the leisure to walk in St Beuno's spacious grounds, gazing at the hills and mountains, the vast expanse of the Clwyd Valley beneath, and the wonder of the sunsets and sunrises. I found God there and could communicate from my heart. Past teaching on prayer could still pull me back from this enjoyment, leading me to fear that I was simply allowing myself to be distracted from genuine prayer and indulging in nature mysticism. It was through giving attention to this unease that I began to see Unity as central to Christian faith, not an optional extra reserved for specialists.

We had a course of lectures from an expert on liturgy and liturgical services. I cannot remember a sentence of his that connected liturgy with ordinary everyday life. When I asked him about this connection, he dismissed my query, pointing out that his subject was liturgy, not life in general! This answer produced in me a very strongly felt reaction. On later reflection I saw a connection between his words and my strongly felt reaction. I traced it back to a longstanding problem I had with the very familiar terms 'natural' and 'supernatural'. I now thank God for the problem because it led me into a surprising and life-changing experience.

In the teaching and preaching I had received and accepted without questioning, the word 'natural' referred to all that we can experience with our senses. The natural, however, was not important: all-important was the supernatural, that which cannot be perceived by the senses and to which we give the name 'God'. Consequently, we appeared to be living in a two-tiered world. Worldly, everyday concerns are important in our everyday life, but ultimately they have no lasting value. We must always be striving to escape and find our true home in the spiritual.

The problem of the two realities, the supernatural and the natural, will occupy us throughout this book. In this chapter I am illustrating how reflection on our present 'natural' experience can lead us on a journey of discovery which enables us to discover the supernatural in the natural, the heavenly in the earthly, the transcendent in the immanent, the holy in the profane. It also helps us to see the sacredness of everything, because in God all things have their being, and in all our encounters with other beings, no matter what or who they are, we are encountering God, who manifested God's very Self in Jesus of Nazareth, and is continuously manifesting Godself in our human experience. There is no aspect of our human experience which is excluded, because God really is in all things and with us in all things, including our terrors and fears.

Christian liturgy and the nature of its celebration has been a focal point of division among Christians since the beginning, divisions which incurred the wrath of the Hebrew prophets thousands of years earlier. Liturgy itself is never the problem: the real problem goes far deeper, into depths which neither side is willing to enter. Underlying the liturgical problem there lies a whole series of religious, secularist, social, political, economic, ethnic, racial differences, which are also very divisive but seem, to many, far too complicated to deal with. It is assumed that a little tinkering here and there in liturgical practice could solve all our problems: they solve nothing. The changes may be made, but they do not alter the facts. The rancour remains and grows more intensely the more it is ignored. The cause of this rancour, and the destruction which follows, not only for the dissidents but for the whole Church, lies in the false and unexamined assumptions of the dissidents on both sides. Their real differences lie far deeper than the outward forms of liturgy. Liturgy becomes, as it were, the scapegoat for all our religious difficulties. Arguing about liturgical forms in religious worship then becomes an excuse, screening both sides from facing the much more fundamental questions of human life, of human survival – questions which can never be answered by the authoritative pronouncements from authority figures, however privileged their position may be.

This period of tertianship gave me time to reflect on the split nature of our spirituality. What I was learning was the vastness of the question; it seemed to touch on every aspect of human life. It was a question we cannot ignore. Do we choose life or death? I was becoming more aware of my own inability to face the questions it raised. Yet I was also becoming vaguely aware that the cosmic questions raised by our split spirituality were those facing every single human being. Ecumenism, the unity of all human beings, of all creation, is a joint responsibility for every individual and group. Is God really in all things, or is God a fiction of our terrified imagination? And how are we to tell the difference?

Our monastic tertianship allowed us a six-week escape during Lent, when we were allotted to various Jesuit parishes or schools or retreat houses to practise some practical ministry. Ecumenism was barely mentioned and our workplaces for this experiment in practical ministry were not only restricted to Catholic places, but to Jesuit houses. I had the good fortune to be sent to the Catholic chaplaincy at Manchester University, a house which was not part of the university, nor funded by it, but relations with the university authorities were good and we were given access to the students and staff and university facilities.

The Jesuit chaplain was then Fr Benjamin Winterborn, popularly known as 'Benjie'. I would have considered my tertianship to be worthwhile if it had only included the six weeks working with him. His chaplaincy was housed in a derelict building, previously a decadent hotel. Living conditions were primitive, meals were unpredictable, yet the chaplaincy was thriving. Benjie's favourite expression on almost all occasions, however chaotic, was 'jolly good', a habit that could have been exasperating if it had been uttered by anyone else, but he was himself 'jolly good'. Students recognized this and loved him for it. He was very open and welcoming to all, encouraged students to think and express their views, was never condemnatory, always encouraging. In our conversations he never came across as the man in charge. He invited me to do things and give lectures which were well beyond my competence and he found a church nearby, where I was invited to say Mass each day and give a five-minute homily.

Benjie's health was not good, occasionally confining him to bed for
as short a time as he could tolerate. He told me to take charge in the
meantime, then, with a 'jolly good', would retire to bed. In the midst
of all this work, he was trying to raise funds for a new chaplaincy
building, and within a few years he had a purpose-built chaplaincy.
He came across to me as a most open and compassionate man, whose
primary interest was the welfare of staff and students, welcoming, and
encouraging students to welcome all denominations and none, at a
time when priestly training put more emphasis on maintenance of the
Catholic status quo rather than on spreading the Good News. It was
the experience with Benjie that encouraged me to accept the invitation,
seven years later, to become Chaplain to the Catholics in Glasgow
University, where I had a more solid grounding in the meaning of
Ecumenism/Unity as an integral part of all Christian Faith. Benjie is
one of the many people who have attracted me by their way of life,
living examples of a spirituality which was integrated and affected
every aspect of their lives.

In the final part of the tertianship we were given some lectures on the
Spiritual Exercises of Ignatius Loyola, then asked to write out 32 retreat
talks for our future use in giving retreats to others – the others being
almost entirely Catholic Religious, predominantly women's congregations, and also to diocesan priests. I did not look forward to this study
of the Spiritual Exercises because, after 17 years' training as a Jesuit,
they had begun to raise some very fundamental questions for me.
Although I knew much about them, I experienced little enthusiasm at
the prospect of making the full 30-day retreat again in the tertianship,
having already done so as a Jesuit novice. In the following 15 years after
the noviceship, we had an annual retreat of eight days.

All these retreats, apart from the tertianship, consisted of at least
four talks each day, lasting about 45 minutes and given by the retreat-
giver. This was followed by another 45-minute period when we were
left to pray over the material given by the retreat-giver. My knowledge
of the Spiritual Exercises came from my experience of these very
instructional retreats. At the end of my training I assumed that this was
the way in which retreats should be given, and that was the thinking
shared by all my Jesuit contemporaries. Consequently, my own growing
dislike of the Spiritual Exercises did raise a major difficulty for me.
Could I remain a Jesuit, whose life was based on these Exercises,
when I was becoming increasingly bored with them? As I experienced

them over the years, I found them repetitive, uninspiring, cerebral and impersonal. On the other hand, I had found a few of these annual retreats helpful and I still found aspects of Jesuit life to be attractive. The prayer experience I had at the age of 16 was still important to me, despite all the inner confusion and feelings of frustration.

Before leaving Frankfurt/Main in August 1959, I had received a manuscript containing the 32 talks, which Karl Rahner had given when giving an eight-day retreat to young German Jesuits studying in Rome. I had briefly glanced at this, found the German style heavy and difficult to understand and put it aside for some later time. The tertianship was an ideal time, so I read it carefully. Later, I described the process as being like the pursuit of a mole underground, then returning to the surface and seeing an entirely new landscape, a metaphor borrowed from T. S. Eliot. I found the manuscript so helpful that I did a quick, rough translation for my fellow tertians, and I also had two German tertians to help me. What attracted me to Rahner and this manuscript of those talks was his ability to produce an 'earthed' spirituality, anchored in our experience of ordinary, everyday life. I was told later that his style, both in lecturing and in retreat-giving, was to speak without notes. A group of industrious Germans had written out versions of his talks, showing him the final version for his approval. It has now been retranslated and produced as a book entitled *The Spirituality of Ignatius Loyola*.

This recovery of the Rahner text was important for me and enabled me to appreciate the Spiritual Exercises in a completely new way. Slowly, I began to understand them as a constant guideline in all aspects of life, uncovering connections between events, and becoming a kind of inner compass in the chaos and confusion of life, a process which opened up the meaning of Unity in its widest sense and its very practical relevance to every aspect of life. In later chapters I shall elaborate more on these points and on my experience of giving many annual eight-day retreats with my 32 talks. When I began doing this annually over many years, although I welcomed people to visit individually if they wanted to do so, hardly anyone came. Fifteen years later, in 1975, I had a few months in Rome to do some study on how the early Jesuits gave the Spiritual Exercises, and discovered that the Spiritual Exercises book which Ignatius finally published in 1540 assumes that these Exercises are being given individually. The book is a guide for retreat-givers and warns them against speaking too much to the pilgrim. The retreat-giver's task is to enable the pilgrim to discover for themselves, which is a very different art from delivering instructions. The next time I was invited to give an eight-day retreat to a group of Religious Sisters, probably around 1975, I invited them, at our first meeting, to consider just one question: did they really want to make this retreat, or would they prefer to be left to spend the following eight days as they felt most inclined? As some might want to make a silent retreat, the rest were asked to observe silence in the house, but outside the house they were free to spend the time as they liked.

The Religious Sisters were very cooperative. They were given time to reflect on their own, then, if they wanted to do so, to consult with others, and on the first morning of the retreat they were invited to give their felt reaction to this proposal at a general meeting. The majority welcomed the proposal. They had come on retreat because that was the custom, a regulation imposed by their superiors. They were a hard-working and hard-worked group, who lived a very strenuous daily programme. Most of them just wanted a rest. They had the opportunity and, in fact, enjoyed it. The retreat house was in Northern Ireland, near the sea and with spectacular views of the coastline. I very rarely gave a preached retreat after that experience.

What has this description of a retreat given to Religious Sisters got to do with Unity, the topic of this section of the book? The experience made me more aware of my own boredom with the Spiritual Exercises after 17 years of instructional retreats, most of them reminding us of the importance of obedience and loyalty to our Jesuit tradition. These Religious Sisters to whom I gave this experimental retreat had been much influenced by Jesuit training with its emphasis on conformity. They were full of goodwill, but their regime was burdensome, full of 'oughts' and leaving little scope for initiative. Given the opportunity to use this time of retreat in whatever way they liked, they showed great initiative, had the opportunity to consider what they desired in the depths of themselves, began to get more in touch with the 'natural world' and to discover that this process helped them to appreciate the Scriptures in a new and life-giving way.

'But', many religious people will say, 'what you have written here is all about the past. We no longer suffer from this narrowness today, so why drag it all up again?' My reason for dragging it all up again is because we have not yet recognized in ourselves the continuation of those stifling attitudes of the past. Circumstances have changed dramatically in a very short period of time, but our tendency to conform to present-day attitudes is stronger than it ever was. I see this very clearly in spirituality development among Jesuits. Our understanding of Ignatius of Loyola's Spiritual Exercises has developed rapidly in the last 50 years. After around 400 years of preached retreats, we have recovered the original practice of giving these retreats individually in a great variety of forms. But underlying this remarkable change and progress in promoting and developing Ignatius of Loyola's Spiritual Exercises there lies an unexamined question, which leads us into areas which are very disturbing to the core of our being. We prefer to avoid them and keep ourselves safely within our comfort zone. In this way, we avoid entering into the path of life.

What the early members of the Society of Jesus had in common was the experience of the Spiritual Exercises, given individually. They then initiated a new missionary movement in many parts of the world, and effective methods of evangelization among native peoples. Their first ministry after their foundation in 1540 was the giving of the Spiritual Exercises. Increasing numbers of people were asking to make the Spiritual Exercises in Rome. By the beginning of the seventeenth century, as the numbers of applicants far outstripped the available retreat-givers, some suggested that individual retreat-giving should be replaced by group retreats. There is a letter written by a German Jesuit novice master in 1601AD, in which he tells the Jesuit General in Rome, Fr Rudolph Aquaviva that he has so many novices that he cannot possibly give them their 30-day retreat individually. The novice master suggests group retreats. The General replies that this suggestion is contrary to our Jesuit tradition and that the novice master may cut down the length of the retreat – not necessarily 30 days – but that he must give the retreat individually. There were more requests for group retreats, especially among Jesuits working in rural areas in France. Eventually the group retreat became the norm, so that for 400 years the individually given retreat disappeared from Jesuit life and only returned after Vatican II.

Why did this happen? The usual explanation is that the individually given retreat was too labour-intensive. I question this explanation. I believe the reason could be that Jesuits themselves were becoming uneasy about the individually given retreat. If the Exercises were given to enable people to discover for themselves what God is like, what guarantee can be given that as a result of this process they do not become a subversive influence to the authority of the Church? By the end of the sixteenth century, Jesuits had become much more aware of the damage already done, and continuing to be done, by the Reformers to the Catholic view, summed up in the phrase 'Outside the Church there is no salvation'. The objection within the Catholic Church to the Spiritual Exercises in the sixteenth century was that they were subversive of the Church's authority. It is extraordinary that Ignatius never mentions 'the Holy Spirit' in his official text of the Exercises, although the Spirit's presence pervades the book, which is about 'God in All Things'. Letting people discover for themselves is always a risk, most especially when they are convinced that they have God on their side. I hope I am totally wrong in thinking this could explain the 400 years of preached retreats which followed. When the thought first came to me, after my experience of giving that group of Sisters a retreat in which they could choose how they wanted to use the eight days assigned to it, I dismissed the thought of Jesuit connivance at the abolition of the individually given retreat. To entertain the thought seemed to me then to be a form of disloyalty to the Society of Jesus, which had given me so much, and had effected so much in society in general as well as within the Catholic Church itself. But the dismissed thought kept returning as I reflected on the present crises afflicting the Catholic Church today – crises which, in so many cases, the Catholic Church brings upon itself and is continuing to do so.

I believe the root of the crisis is our failure to recognize an attachment in our lives, the attachment to honour, reputation and power, which is contrary to the one attachment to which we bind ourselves by our vows – the attachment to God for whom we are created, so that our lives become such a total abandonment to God that our greatest and most overwhelming desire is to let the Spirit of God be the Spirit which is constantly transforming us to become the love, compassion and goodness of God. This is the path to freedom. No one can take it from us. It is a treasure beyond price. Therefore, as a human being, I can never find God's love and God's peace through my own efforts. I am constantly dependent for every moment of my existence on this loving God. 'God became a human being, so that human beings might become God', wrote Ireneus in the third century, and this God is not limited by time and space. Paul writes in 2 Corinthians 5.21: 'For our sake God made the sinless one into sin, so that in him we might become the goodness of God.' God really is in all things, not apart from things. We live in a one-tier world: the supernatural is in the natural, the transcendent is in the immanent. Bearing witness to this reality in the quality of our lives is the longing of our lives and the source of our restlessness.

Towards the end of the tertianship, the Jesuit Provincial, superior of all Jesuits of the British Province – which included Jesuits working in South Africa and in what was then called Rhodesia, the modern Zimbabwe, as well as those working in Guyana – came to visit us at St Beuno's to let us know where we were to begin our active ministry as Jesuit priests. I went to this interview and spoke to him of my own growing interest in Ecumenism, of the offer I had received a year before in Paderborn to do a doctorate there, and of my dream of being allowed to work in Scotland, land of my birth, on Unity. He listened. He then opened a large folder on his desk. The folder included the names of all Jesuits in what was then called the English Province, and where they would be working in the following. Our numbers in 1960 were in excess of 900. It was a large folder. He then told me I was needed at Stonyhurst, where I had already taught for two years as a scholastic, a time which I had thoroughly enjoyed nine years earlier. My heart sank at the news. Ecumenism was not discussed at our meeting. I was needed at Stonyhurst and I was now qualified to teach the dead languages, Latin and Greek!

In September I reported at Stonyhurst for duty. I was there from September 1960 until September 1967. In the next chapter I shall reflect on those years insofar as they deepened and developed my understanding of Ecumenism/Unity as a movement which is not only integral to Christian Faith, but also to the future of the whole human race.

Exercise

- What are your own felt reactions on the natural/supernatural distinction?

- Is this a theoretical question without any practical applications to everyday life?

6

Uniformity destroys unity

What I am relating here are my own felt reactions on the seven years I spent teaching at Stonyhurst from 1960 to 1967 with the focus on my broadening understanding of Ecumenism as a movement towards Unity which affects all humankind and all creation. I use the word 'Unity' because 'Ecumenism' is so commonly understood as limited to Christians. I am most grateful for those years and for the help of so many people who, by being themselves, enabled me to glimpse the immensity of God, whose love for all knows no boundaries.

As long as I could focus my attention on the immediate present, I was happy and content to be teaching at Stonyhurst. When, however, I raised my head above the parapets of school life, I felt uneasy at being engaged in teaching in a private, fee-paying school. I did not therefore believe that all private education should be abolished. This uneasiness about private education was later to spread to uneasiness about denominational education, but it did not lead me to think the answer was the abolition of all religious schools. These issues were for me dilemmas.

Without developing these points in detail here, they do present a very serious question for all who are engaged in unity work concerned with the public good. The whole ecumenical movement, in Christian understanding, must be concerned with all humankind, not with particular groupings or particular individuals. The sun shines for the whole planet, and creation itself is a sacrament of God – that is, a created and an effective sign of God's reality.

In any conflict situation or dilemma, should it not be possible, through open communication, to find a solution through which both parties benefit? When we talk about forgiveness, reconciliation, healing, is it not a solution for the benefit of all parties concerned that we are looking for?

Ecumenism and cream teas

Soon after my arrival at Stonyhurst I got in touch with a Catholic priest, Dean Linehan, who lived in nearby Blackburn, and asked him whether there was any ecumenical group I might join. I cannot now remember the details, but Dean Linehan did gather a group of local clergy, mostly Anglican and Catholic, inviting them to a meeting. A small group of about ten met at Dean Linehan's house, meetings which I attended regularly while living at Stonyhurst. I shall not give details of our meetings, but describe just one feature, because it illustrates another essential aspect of all unity work.

We were, theologically and in character, a very varied group, the Anglicans providing a vast spectrum from radical-evangelical to Anglo-Catholic, the latter group far outstripping the Catholics in their Roman tendencies. Among the Catholics, Dean Linehan had very clear ideas about Ecumenism. For him, the answer was simple: all non-Catholic Christians must become Roman Catholic. The Dean's theology was all contained in *The Penny Catechism*, a series of questions and answers about Catholicism to be learned by heart at Roman Catholic schools. The answers were, in very abbreviated form, the decrees of the Council of Trent, summoned in the mid-sixteenth century to defend the Catholic Faith against the Reformers, the Lutherans and the Calvinists, and to remind Catholics of their own sinfulness and how to remedy it. Our ecumenical group could have been an explosive mixture likely to divide us even more; in fact, the group lasted for years. I believe the bond that held us and nurtured us was the natural kindness and generosity of Dean Linehan, who never failed to provide lavish afternoon teas with cream buns! This hospitable gesture created a warm and friendly atmosphere, enabling us all to thaw out. Our disagreements were never doctrinal, as far as I can remember, nor were they on denominational lines. It was a gradual process, which taught all of us the value of listening. Friendships were formed and we began to learn from each other. Through our interchanges we began to see clearly that what separates us as Christians is our failure to share what we have in common, what it is that brings us to life and makes us more aware of our common bond in the Living Christ at work within us and around us. We learned how to speak openly about our differences in a non-condemnatory way, a habit which helped us to appreciate, rather than fear our differences.

All ecumenical work, in Christian understanding, is for the unity of all humankind. A necessary first step in all such work must be the opportunity for differing parties in any dispute to meet and to listen to one another. Without this kind of open communication, lasting agreements cannot be achieved. This kind of communication cannot be achieved through power struggles; it is only possible where there is a measure of trust growing among participants. Mutual hospitality, focus on matters which are of interest to all the various parties, for example food, shelter, wealth, protection from violence, freedom to grow, education, human rights, and the willingness to listen to one another are necessary foundational elements for any effective and lasting agreements.

The Second Vatican Council 1962–5

This section is not attempting to give a comprehensive account of the Second Vatican Council; rather it focuses on those themes of the Council which affected me while I was at Stonyhurst and have continued affecting my understanding of Ecumenism/Unity ever since.

The documents of the Second Vatican Council, which I shall refer to as Vat II, were unique in the history of all Catholic Church Councils. They did not state articles of belief to be held by all Catholics under pain of grave sin; they were more like invitations, explanatory documents, enabling us to recognize the reality of God's love and compassion at work in all human situations and especially in the working of our hearts.

The documents came as a surprise to a Catholic generation which had grown accustomed to increasingly centralizing tendencies in Church leadership, which insisted, for example, that there was no salvation for any human being outside the Roman Catholic Church. I was of that generation. Vat II brought great relief, joy, delight and enthusiasm not only to Catholics, but also to other Christian denominations and other religions and to the millions who still had a love/hate relationship with the Catholic Church. However, Vat II was not unanimously accepted by the Catholic bishops and archbishops or by the clergy, an opposition which still exists, is still growing and spreading. The Vatican's centralizing tendencies are now more manifest and unrestrained than at any other period in our

Christian history. I know I am touching on very difficult and sensitive questions. But in all the uncertainty, I also know with certainty that no amount of threats and authoritative orders imposed from on high can ever restore peace to the Church. We need open communication and shared responsibility.

Pope John XXIII, who called Vat II, was elected, after the death of Pius XII, as a caretaker Pope, a safe pair of hands, who could hold things together until a younger, more vigorous candidate could be found. John XXIII, to the astonishment of many in the Vatican, announced this new Ecumenical Council shortly after his appointment. When the Council began, he ensured that the assembled bishops should be free to choose the subjects to be considered and also should be encouraged to speak their minds. The bishops did so and produced very radical documents on the nature of the Church, the nature of Divine Revelation, the pastoral role of the Church in the modern world, on the nature and meaning of Ecumenism/Unity, on the training of priests and bishops in the Church. The documents also included documents about the role of Religious Orders in the Church, both the active and contemplative, women and men, and, most important of all, on the role of the laity in the Church, the nature of Christian education, Christian mission, the relationship of the Catholic Church to other religions and to people of no religion. Vat II also included a fundamentally important document on Religious Freedom, recognizing it as a human right for all people, atheists and agnostics included. It is these Vat II documents which encourage the Church to think beyond itself and its ecclesiastical boundaries. The opponents of Vat II today fail to distinguish the all-important distinction between the UNITY and the UNIFORMITY of the Church.

The UNITY of God is a unity, mirrored in creation, which delights in variety, in difference, in multiformity. Every single human being is composed of trillions of cells, yet each of the cells is unique to that individual. I have read that no two snowflakes are identical, no two grains of sand! In Christian belief, this variety lies within the very essence of God, three distinct Persons within the one God! This is a belief which goes beyond the boundaries of our usual understanding of logic, but which launches us into mystery, into beliefs which go beyond the capacity of our finite minds and hearts, beliefs which transcend reason but are not irrational!

If this last paragraph baffles you, offends you, worries you, your reaction is not wrong, nor irrational: it is natural and healthy, a promising sign. How can it be promising when such reactions evoke such negative feelings?

Our felt reactions are not, in themselves, right or wrong, true or false. The categories of right, wrong, true, false do not belong to the feelings themselves, but they come from the decisions we make in response to these feelings. This is an essential point we need to grasp if we are to learn how to live in harmony within ourselves and in our relations with others. The harmony depends not only on our human relationships, but also with the way we relate to reality as we encounter it in our own immediate surroundings. Most importantly of all, for the Christian believer this harmony is the result of our harmony with God, in whom, we believe, all created reality lives, moves and has its being. Our subject matter, like the Universe, is constantly expanding. This sense of wonder and amazement helps us to appreciate that wonderful painting of St Augustine of Hippo with the child, who is trying to empty the ocean by pouring it into a hole in the sand with the aid of a seashell!

This sense of God being in all things, at all times, in all places is, for most of us, a very slow and gradual process. I find it helpful to think of God as shy, a God who is not intrusive on our lives, a courteous God. Even saints like St Paul on the road to Damascus, who was thrown to the ground, blinded, heard voices 'Paul, Paul, why are you persecuting me?', spent the rest of his life discovering the meaning of the incident, and of the breadth and the length, the height and the depth of God's goodness in which he found himself enveloped (cf. Eph. 3.16–21).

Now to return to Vat II in light of the distinction we have been making between unity and uniformity. On reflection, it should not surprise us that Vat II should still be the occasion of unrest in the Catholic Church 50 years later. All human beings have a very strong self-preservation instinct, which is in itself a very precious gift. That instinct enables us to hold together under crises, to learn from our mistakes, to hope even when everything around us, including our very selves, seems to be disintegrating. But this felt reaction to change can also imprison us in ways of thinking and reacting which can stifle our lives. Our self-preservation instinct can be so deeply ingrained in us by our upbringing and our own habitual safety-first priority that we are no longer conscious that our way of life is leading us into a state of death before dying. Vat II encouraged Catholics to think beyond their ecclesiastical boundaries, exposing them to a God at work in all peoples, of every faith and of no faith, and also at work in all aspects of creation. This God, in St John the Evangelist's words, is 'Love'. Vat II is a liberating document, produced by a gathering of predominantly conservative bishops who, through the influence and example of Pope John XXIII, were enabled to listen to each other and to their theological advisers with their hearts and in freedom for the benefit of all peoples who were prepared to listen.

Vat II did not cause the divisions in the Church: it has uncovered them. Acknowledging our failings and the truth of things is not a sign of failure; it is a sign of life and of hope. God really is in all things and our spiritual journey through life is like a treasure hunt. The treasure is not buried deep in the earth, it is buried deep in our layers of consciousness and is indestructible. We can ignore this treasure, prefer not to look at it, because we have been so accustomed to our imprisoning conditioning that we are terrified of surrendering ourselves to anything which is not under our control. The infinite love and compassion of God cannot be limited. That is why we struggle against it. God, being love, is not deterred by our fears: God's invitation can never be withdrawn.

This surrender to God is not surrender to servitude; it is surrender to the deepest longings of our hearts, a longing to be free and to be life-giving, a longing to-be-at-one. Our frustrations, if we can acknowledge them and bring them into prayer, are invitations to discover the truth of our identity, a surrender into the very life of God, the source of all love, of all creation.

I had glimpses of the liberating power of Vat II when I first read accounts of its progress from 1962 to 1965, but what has taught me most in subsequent years are encounters with people of different Christian denominations, different faiths, and with the many who do not know whether they do have any faith. They have helped me to realize that, as the Hebrew prophets remind us, 'God's ways are not our ways and God's thoughts are not our thoughts'. Through contact with this wide range of people, I discovered that God does not seem to be as concerned about our religious denominations/faiths as we are. I am speaking of those people who show their love and compassion in action, people who are welcoming, respectful and naturally caring for others, who bring hope into situations which seem hopeless and are so devoid of egocentricity that they seem to have learned 'other-centricity', whoever the other may be! This is the kind of holiness taught by the

Hebrew prophets and expressed in Jesus of Nazareth's manifesto in the Sermon on the Mount, lessons which are in harmony with the teachings of the mystics of the major world religions!

I conclude this section on the effect on me of Vat II while at Stonyhurst with a question, which has remained with me ever since. The question arises in all situations and for all kinds of people. It lies at the heart of Unity. How are we to react creatively in life when we find ourselves in situations which militate against our own deepest longings? Although I did enjoy and am grateful for my Stonyhurst teaching years, my natural inclination would have preferred teaching poor children in an ecumenical setting. Stonyhurst was privileged and it was not ecumenical. I could see, at the time, that there was nothing wrong in my having this inclination, but I could also recognize that this longing could prevent me from giving full attention to the boys entrusted to me. My attraction to Unity could also lead to disaffection for all those aspects of religious teaching which were specifically Roman Catholic!

I have no neat answer to give to this question, but I am grateful for the question itself: it opens up more general questions, which occur in any state of life – they are not peculiar to Stonyhurst. Through asking myself the question, although I had no clear answer, I did see the attractiveness of being no respecter of persons, nor of status – whether my own or other people's – nor of race, ethnicity, wealth, reputation, religious affiliation or lack of it. These questions made me more aware of my own unconscious prejudices and failures.

Stonyhurst, in its own way, offered me endless opportunities for trying to be no respecter of persons, for it was, in its structure, very hierarchical. The attempt to live each day as though I was no respecter of persons did not feel like a duty. I enjoyed the friendships I made there with pupils, serving staff and teaching staff, becoming more aware of the narrowing effect being a respecter of persons can have on our freedom and prevent us from meeting others as unique human beings.

What is the connection I now see between my feelings of uneasiness at teaching in a private school for nine years and my present state of mind 50 years later? I now see very clearly that the purpose of Unity, as far as Roman Catholics are concerned, is not that I should be trying to convert all Christians into Roman Catholics. Ecumenism is a movement whose ultimate purpose is the unity, as distinct from the uniformity, of all humankind.

In Scripture this unity is grounded in God's Covenant with the Jewish people, who were chosen to be the nation which would reveal this Covenant to all nations, 'A Light to the Gentiles' – the title given in Vat II to the document on the nature of the Church. It is a Covenant which enlightens all peoples about the nature of God, that God is One, that God is all-inclusive, barring no one from the invitation to share in the very life of God.

This God, made manifest in our humanity in Jesus of Nazareth, identifies Godself with every single human being. In Matthew 23. 31-46, Jesus describes the Final Judgement. The passage could also be described as Jesus' answer to the question, 'What matters most in human life?' Jesus' answer is astonishing, not only in what it says, but also for what it omits. Jesus says nothing directly about prayer, religion or liturgy. This fact can be misinterpreted to mean that ultimately, religion and prayer do not matter. The truth of the matter is that the heart of all religion and prayer is not about our religious performance, but about God's very Self dwelling in and being at home in the heart of every single human being and in all creation. This is the heart of Unity, the essence and the ultimate identity of every single human being without exception. Being taken up in this awareness of our identity in God and letting it guide us in all our human encounters is an invitation ingrained in every unique atom of our being. This is not a flight from the harsh reality of life into fantasy – it is a plunging into reality, the plunge which God is constantly drawing us to take, the plunge which evokes from the depths of us our 'Cry of Wonder', as we encounter God, who has manifested Godself in all of creation and who will never leave us.

The Whalley group

During Vat II a priest from Whalley parish, near Stonyhurst, invited me to meet with a group of 12 of his parishioners, who were interested in learning something of what was happening at Vat II. Reflecting on this invitation nearly 50 years later, I can see, in spite of all the crises and divisions within today's Catholic Church, the progress we have made in some respects since Vatican II. I also see how clericalized I was in my thinking and my own reactions, an affliction of which I was not conscious at the time and with which I still have to struggle.

The group used to meet monthly for about two hours, our meeting place a local pub, where the local landlord gave us a private room, took our orders, delivered them before we began the meeting, then left us till the meeting ended. This section does not record details of the monthly meetings. I write about the group here because it broadened my understanding of the nature of Unity and because such informal groups are essential in the Church of the future. They do not have to meet in pubs!

For our first meeting of the group I brought along a few recently published books on Vat II so far and gave them a very brief summary of what had been happening. I was amazed, at our next meeting, that many of them had copies of these books borrowed from their local libraries. I was even more amazed at their comments and reflections on what they had read. It was generally assumed by the Catholic clergy in the 1960s that the laity were neither interested in nor capable of theology, unless they happened to be members of Religious Orders who, if not ordained, rank as laity, not clergy.

These meetings made me aware of the general neglect in the education of Catholic laity once they had left school. In the early twentieth century, the majority of Catholics in the UK, being poor, would leave school at the age of 14. The Whalley group were mostly professional people, but not considered by clerics as capable of theology! The Whalley group experience helped me to see the narrowness of my own vision, the crippling effect clericalism can have on the Church's call to universal mission, the neglect of the latent spiritual wealth and capabilities of the laity. This clericalism is destructive of the laity, of the clergy and of the mission of the Church.

I am conscious, in writing this, how easily it can be misinterpreted as an attack on the Church. What I am attacking is not the Church, but tendencies within the Church, and within myself, which are destructive. I point them out because I know the Church, as the people of God, is a reality, our most precious reality, the core of our being and the source of it. I shall be returning to these thoughts more explicitly in Part 3 on Holiness. It is on prayer, the meaning and practice of prayer and its relation to every aspect of human life that the clerical Church has been most neglectful of the laity. And this neglect is still evident in spite of the heroic work being done in this area by small groups of people, clerical and lay.

I continued attending these Whalley meetings until I left Stonyhurst in 1967, but the group carried on. During my time with them we focused on the document on the nature of the Catholic Church entitled *Lumen Gentium*, the first two Latin words of the document and meaning 'Light of the Nations' – a very significant title, because it emphasized the essentially ecumenical nature of the Church, which does not exist for itself and its members, but as a sign for all peoples, whoever they may be. To neglect, ignore this universality is to neglect, ignore the very essence of God who, in Christ, has become one of us and identifies God's very Self with every human individual.

Lumen Gentium appealed to the Whalley group and brought them to life as they considered what their own parish community might become if it followed through its teachings. For them the Church was no longer an isolated, well-ordered barque of Peter, raised high by God and God's angels above the stormy waves of life below them, a sea full of all the drowning people who are not Roman Catholic. The barque of Peter was for all humankind. God is not only at work across all the Christian denominations; God is also at work in all religions and in people of no religion.

After a year of our meetings, the group were discussing how they could spread this good news to other local parishes and encourage them to read and reflect on the Council documents. When I reported on this to the local bishop, he listened politely, but did not show any great interest or surprise. The group, however, did continue to work in their own area after I left Stonyhurst in 1967.

I mention this Whalley group of 50 years ago because such initiatives are still active and desperately needed today when Christianity is facing the most threatening crisis in its history in our post-Christian, postmodern world. I can only speak from my own experience, of having lived through the years of lived Ecumenism/Unity, of hope and euphoria in which so many people were enlivened and encouraged, followed by years of decline and division within the Church, the division infecting all ranks of clergy and laity in their attitudes to Vat II. Fifty years later, in the developed countries especially, there has been a massive exodus from the Catholic Church, a most dramatic drop in numbers of priests and vowed Religious throughout the world. In spite of these facts, which are there for all to see, there is a deep denial of the reality of the crisis by those clergy and laity who regret that Vatican II ever took place. Why do they not care, not listen to the grief and sadness of their people, why do they revert to blame, to accusing any who disagree with them for being disloyal, disobedient, treacherous?

Could it be that what they are resenting and regretting is the passing of a faith which gave them clear rules, clear explanations of sacraments to which they had exclusive rights, and which would free them from all their sins, and a clear understanding that they, the Roman Catholics, belonged to the one true Church outside of which there was no salvation? Vat II, with its emphasis on the universality of God's call, on God's love for all humanity, of all religions and none, was and still is a severe blow to those whose hope lay in their own certainties about their own temporal and eternal security. When that security is questioned, those questioned can be vicious in their reactions. It has ever been so, as Jesus pointed out to the Jewish religious authorities, whom he recognized as legitimate, and who eventually had him crucified as a blasphemer and a criminal.

The lesson which the Whalley group taught me so clearly, and which all of us Christians need to keep learning, is that in the Church of the future the clergy and laity must be encouraged and taught to practise a ministry, not only within their own denominations, but to practise it ecumenically, in the widest sense of that word, which includes all humankind. 'Ministry' is not restricted to 'Church' matters; it is about answering human needs, whatever they may be, and that is where we meet and minister to God. I have had the privilege of living among people who do this in areas of great need. There was much laughter among them and they were especially strong on frequent celebrations of life events, birthdays, welcoming newcomers and departures. They had the great gift of enjoying the present even when they knew tomorrow would be another difficult day for them.

Fifty years later, lay groups like the Whalley group are to be found in all kinds of places, thank God, and theology is no longer considered a subject for clergy and professed religious only. In spite of our being known as the 'Post-Christian Age', it is becoming generally recognized that religion and spirituality are not limited to specialized libraries for those interested in antiquities. These subjects are more closely connected with every aspect of human life than we realize. This should not surprise us: God, who holds all creation in being, has identified us with God's very Self. We live in mystery. Believers and unbelievers, we all have more in common than separates us – our humanity! Acknowledging this can be an excellent starting point for all of us.

The Agnostics Club

Besides teaching Latin and Greek, I also had to teach Religion to a variety of classes throughout the school. This included a class of 15 to 16-year-old boys who, having passed their O-level exams in between five and eight subjects, had begun to prepare for their A-level subjects for the next two years. O-level stands for ordinary level, A-level for advanced level. A-level, in those days, normally consisted of two main subjects, either science or humanities, and possibly one or two subsidiary subjects, which demanded a nodding acquaintance only. Religion was in a class of its own. It was not a public examination subject and was provided for mixed groups of scientists and humanities students.

Stonyhurst, in spite of its enclosed atmosphere, was not totally impervious to outside influences. The early sixties introduced the Beatles, was the decade of student unrest and the decade of questioning of all established belief systems, most of which were being rejected.

In all my teaching, I found religion classes to be by far the most difficult, both to prepare and to deliver. I think it was in September 1964 that I had prepared a term's classes on Liturgy. Boys had to attend Mass every morning, so I thought I would provide them with some information on how Eucharistic liturgy had developed through the ages, the meaning of the signs and symbols, the dress worn by those who celebrated, and how the whole liturgy related to everyday life. I spent many hours reading Jungman, an acknowledged authority on the subject. Within a few minutes of my first class, I knew I had already lost my audience, who were busy gazing out of the windows, examining the ceiling's cobwebs, or studying their fingernails. At the end of class, John approached me. I knew John well, knew he was not easy to please. Having now successfully passed his O-levels, he was more self-confident than ever. 'I suppose', he began, 'you realize you are wasting your time?' 'Why do you say that?' I asked, suspecting he was right. 'Half of us are atheists', was his answer. 'Which half?' I asked. 'I shall have to consult the others before giving you their names.' 'How long have you been atheists?' I asked. Without any hint of a smile, he replied: 'Ten days.' Finally, I asked him: 'Are you atheist or agnostic?' This was not a topic John had studied in his O-levels, so I explained the difference.

Next day John appeared, having consulted his friends, who willingly gave their names and, being open-minded lads, preferred to be known as Agnostics. They were also very willing to meet and discuss their new status. We met regularly once a week in my room in their free time, to discuss whether God was, or was not! I think they numbered about eight. One of their number was a very gifted mathematician, who had been reading a book by Bertrand Russell. The Russell argument, as the Agnostics had understood it, was very simple – an idea borrowed from the ancient Greeks four centuries before Christ. They believed that we are all composed of tiny bombarding particles. When the particles begin to separate to form new patterns, then we cease to exist. If we could discover more about the movement of these particles, we could eventually know all that we need to know about life without having to consult religious experts, or ancient texts written in dead languages.

I cannot now remember the details of our discussions, but I do remember some of the lessons I learned, and am still learning, from the experience. One lesson was that whenever I find myself making judgements about others, as for example, 'They seem to be very bored in my religion classes', I now ask myself, 'Am I also bored with my classes?' This usually gets me to the heart of the matter very quickly. In this case, I realized I was bored, but it was not something I was ready to admit. As a Jesuit priest, I should not be bored with teaching religion! After years of listening to lectures in philosophy and theology, I was bored. And the reason I was bored was because I was constantly being given answers to problems which did not interest me at that time. In fact, religion does interest me, an interest which began when I learned to approach it with the question, 'How does this theology I am being given relate to my everyday experience?' How does it enable us to become more aware that every bush is burning, if we had the eyes to see? How does theology help us to trust that God really is present in all the facts which surround us? Live theology opens our eyes to see: dead theology introduces us to word games, restricting our vision and awareness to the ever-narrowing world of its own creation and dehumanizes us in the process.

The Agnostics Group were not passive; they were willing to accept information like blotting paper, able to reproduce what had been said for examination purposes without the process leading to any inner transformation. These agnostics were entering into one of the vital stages in all human growth: the critical stage. This is the name that Baron von Hügel gave to this process of growth in his book *The Mystical Element in Religion*, in which he writes of the three essential elements to be found in all major world religions. He calls them: 1) The Institutional; 2) The Critical; and 3) The Mystical. These three elements correspond to three stages of human growth, namely: 1) Infancy and childhood; 2) Adolescence and 3) Maturity. All three elements are necessary in the growth of any human being. They are not mutually exclusive. No matter how old we may be, we shall always need the Institutional element in some measure. Although it is no longer the priority in our needs and desires, we still need it as a kind of anchor to ensure that our spirituality is 'earthed', reminding us that our spirituality must always have its base in human experience.

The Institutional element corresponds to our predominant needs in infancy and childhood. We need to be instructed because we are at our most vulnerable and impressionable stage of life with only a very embryonic self-awareness, a consciousness which grows and develops through all subsequent stages. Failure to nurture at this stage – lack of care and tenderness, of attention and affection – can affect us severely in later life.

The Critical element corresponds to adolescence, when we begin to question what previously we had accepted passively. We begin to rebel against the impositions of authority figures, beginning with those who are closest to us, who have nurtured and cared for us. The dawn of the critical faculty results in a growing interest in 'why?' questions, a stage which older people can find increasingly irritating, hurtful, and which they can easily misinterpret as being purely destructive. Consequently, they can tend to react with threats, prohibitions, punishments, which can later produce a whirlwind of resentment in their children.

The Critical element is a most valuable stage of life: it influences our future growth or diminishment. If this stage is not tolerated with patience, openness, tolerance and encouragement, it can do permanent damage to both parents and children, teachers and pupils. Development of our critical faculty is an essential element in our growth into personal integrity, in our ability to love others, to be tolerant and inclusive in our attitude to strangers, to becoming more free, in beginning to know and love God. Unless our critical attitude is practised, nurtured and encouraged, we cannot practise Unity, an essential element in our Christian faith.

Without this element, we are in danger of remaining stuck within our own narrow understanding, considering any deviation from what we were taught as infants to be a betrayal of God. Through acting in this way, we shall be convinced of our own loyalty and fidelity to God and so resist to the death any criticism from those who question our beliefs. The stronger our loyalty to our own beliefs, the more unscrupulous we can become in our opposition to those we consider to be our opponents. The murderous wars waged in the history of Christianity are the outcome of rigid attitudes, not only among Christian believers, but among adherents of any ideology which teaches them to consider any who disagree with their way of seeing the world to be inhuman objects.

We all need to have beliefs, we are all in need of instruction, but the following of Christ is not primarily about our creeds: it is about letting God be the Spirit of love and compassion to us and through us in every moment of our lives. All our creeds are means to enable us to live in this way. When they fail to do this, we must use our critical faculty, not because Christian belief is wrong, but because our understanding of it is wrong. To admit this is not to water down our belief system, but to submit ourselves to its truth in all its everyday implications.

This surrender brings with it two conflicting reactions: fear and, at the same time, attraction. The attraction is like light, gives life and hope, peace and joy, but, by its very nature, it also shows up our darkness. Caught up in this process, we become aware of our powerlessness, so inwardly devastating that we are driven to cry out, from the depths of our being, for help. It is in this process we begin to sense the truth of our being – that we are not isolated creatures, but caught up in something greater than anything our minds and imagination can grasp. This is the 'Cry of Wonder', but use of our critical faculty is a necessary step on our way.

The Agnostics Club was a life-giving and freeing event for me and, as far as I know, for those who took part. I used to meet with John occasionally after he had left Stonyhurst, but heard he had abandoned a prosperous job to go travelling. I had a letter from him from South America which was all about religion, tried to get in touch with him, but failed. About 20 years later, when I was preparing to work ecumenically for a few months in New Zealand, I had a phone call from John, then living in Wellington. He had heard I was coming, offered to meet me on arrival and was a wonderful guide and companion during my three months. He was busily engaged in ecumenical work!

The disabled childrens' holiday

This section describes events in my Stonyhurst years which gave me a glimpse of the uniting and transforming power of Unity in reconciling divisions in society and bringing life, hope and unity to all the parties concerned. Another way of describing the process is learning to cherish and value our differences.

In my years at Stonyhurst, the school was involved with an organization now called HCPT The Pilgrimage Trust. In Easter week, volunteer members from among Stonyhurst's staff and pupils would volunteer their services as helpers at Lourdes, a place of pilgrimage and healing in southern France. We were divided into groups of 20, ten being disabled children with ten helpers. We lived together in small hotels, not in a hospice or hospital. After a few years experiencing these wonderful pilgrimages, I planned a summer holiday experience at Stonyhurst in 1967 for children in the Lancashire area. I cannot now remember the details, but I shall never forget the felt experience of delight in being involved in it.

The disabled children numbered about 12. They were housed in the school infirmary, where the matron, Sister Mary Featherstone, volunteered her invaluable services during the week. To look after the disabled children I had two other groups. One group, numbering about 12, were pupils at a school for so-called 'delinquents' in nearby Blackburn. They were offered a camping holiday in the spacious grounds called 'Paradise', belonging to Hodder, the preparatory school of Stonyhurst, overlooking the river Hodder. They were also invited to spend some time meeting with the disabled children, joining them on expeditions, helping those in wheelchairs and playing with them. The third group was drawn from some of the senior boys at Stonyhurst, who should have been attending an inter-school Combined Cadet Force (CCF) camp for military training. The Colonel in charge readily gave permission when I presented him with a list of those who had volunteered to work with the disabled children. I had approached boys who I knew were not over-enthusiastic about CCF summer holiday courses and were more likely to find kindred spirits among the delinquents! The Colonel approved of the arrangement.

It was a risky venture, but the school authorities had agreed and were very helpful. The disabled children brought out the best in the other two groups. There were occasional difficulties, but no serious crises. The holiday ended on the morning of 31 July. About 6.30 p.m. that evening, I met three brothers, all from the delinquent group, aged between eight and 14, walking in the school grounds: they wanted to stay. They had walked about eight miles from their home in Blackburn. After a meal I drove them home and met their distressed father. He was a bus driver. His wife had left him and the family. He was struggling to save the children, seven of them, from having to go into homes.

Reflecting on these events, I begin to see more clearly how they illustrate some of the essential features in all ecumenical work. I know that excellent work has been done and is being done and that what I write will be so obvious to those actively involved that it appears not worth mentioning, yet 50 years later these essential features are still being ignored by the majority of Christians in the 'developed' countries. In the UK, for example, there is widespread assent that Ecumenism, after a brief flourishing between the 1960s and 1980s, is now moribund. What is most alarming for the future of the Church is that this condition does not appear to be a matter of great concern among the religious authorities. We appear to be content within the narrow parameters of our religious thought, a narrowness that the Hebrew prophets and Jesus himself declared to be idolatry and blindness.

Another essential feature of Ecumenism/Unity which the holiday manifested was the importance and breadth of the Institutional element in all ecumenical work. It is not only that we should meet together across our religious and non-religious boundaries; it is essential that these meetings should be enjoyable for all parties – including, where possible, meals together, walks, outings etc., so that we can meet as human beings, not simply as religious denominations or interfaith groups. These thoughts are implied in what von Hügel states when he elaborates on the Institutional element. Although in von Hügel this element belongs specially to infants and young children, it still remains a human need in us as we enter the adolescent and mystical stages. Hints, flashes, glimpses of both later stages can already be detected in the child.

This holiday also manifested another basic truth about Unity, a continuous truth on which we all need to focus our attention as human beings. To be effective in promoting unity among others, we have to practise unity within ourselves. We discover that we can break through the walls that our fears construct and begin to see things differently, that we are not essentially isolated: we are caught up in something greater than our minds and imagination can grasp, a vision that evokes the 'Cry of Wonder' that speaks to the deepest longings of our hearts.

The holiday week brought life to all who were involved in it. The life came to each of us from each other. We all received a concentrated dose of the joy that comes from giving. And I still enjoy recalling the event. I am no longer in touch with most of them, but in recalling the event they become present to me and I can wish them well and thank them through 'The Self' who holds all of us in being.

The Vatican II Conference in 1967

In August 1967, I organized a conference for Jesuits in what was then called the English Province, although it included a substantial number of Scots and a few Welsh members. Ecumenism in its wider sense had yet to infect the English members. Today we are called the British Province (which also includes South Africa and Guyana) and feathers can now be unruffled! The object of the meeting was to help us all to deepen our understanding of Vat II and to give us time to reflect together on its practical implications for the ministry in which we are engaged as Jesuits in Britain today. In this section, I do not attempt to give a report on that Conference, which lasted for the inside of a week, but I mention only one incident, which occurred a few months before the conference was due to begin, because it illustrates something of the challenges, the risks and the dangers that are inherent in Unity, as well as the limitless opportunities it offers for broadening and deepening our own understanding of Christian Faith. The incident also confirmed a previous lesson I had learned about Ecumenism and have to keep re-learning daily – *viz*, that in promoting Unity among others, we must constantly be working on it among ourselves, as Jesuits, and within ourselves. If we fail to do this then, despite our best endeavours, our efforts will foster not unity, but destructive uniformity.

One of the lecturers I had invited to the conference, and who had agreed to speak on the topic 'Authority in the Church', was Archbishop Thomas Roberts s.j. He had been teaching at St Francis Xavier's college in Liverpool when suddenly – I think it was when listening to BBC Radio News – he discovered that he had been appointed the Archbishop of Bombay. The Archbishop was not at ease in this role. India, by this time, had been independent of Britain for ten years. The new Archbishop, a short time after his arrival in Bombay, took off to become chaplain on a cargo boat, leaving his assistant bishop, a native Indian, in charge. The Archbishop later resigned from his post and returned to England, spending the rest of his life in Jesuit houses in England. I had first met him at Campion Hall, Oxford in the 1950s, where he had been appointed as Spiritual Father to the Jesuit community there. He was a very charming, helpful, generous, down-to-earth and unpretentious man. He later became well known for his views on nuclear defence and on Catholic teaching on contraception. He had also written a short history of some of the outstandingly immoral Popes in Christianity, pointing to the need to define the limits of papal power – a subject which had been on the agenda of the First Vatican Council, but war in Italy abruptly ended the Council before they had begun considering the limits of papal power. This failure is still damaging the Church over a century later.

A few months before the Jesuit conference was due to begin in August 1967, I was summoned to meet our Provincial in London. He told me that I must withdraw the name of Archbishop Roberts from the list of lecturers. I suggested that the demand for withdrawal should come directly from himself, as he had made and was responsible for the decision. He accepted the point and did not withdraw Archbishop Roberts' name. Archbishop Roberts came, was made most welcome by the 40-plus, mostly Jesuits, who attended, and he made a most useful contribution.

Reflecting on this event nearly 50 years later, I now see its significance in the context of Unity much more clearly than I could recognize it at the time. I also see connections between that conference and our present attitudes to religious belief and opinions which can deprive humankind of our basic needs for community, for mutual respect and trust, and for compassion.

Here is my reflection:
Any idea, decision, movement, however small and apparently insignificant, which is directed to the benefit of humankind, to our growth in freedom, love, compassion, reconciliation, will also, by its very nature, also activate our dark side, threatening our security, promoting division not only within each individual, but also within groups, religious and secular, however high-minded they may appear to be. The line, 'Lilies

that fester smell far worse than weeds', refers to religious lilies and to secular lilies alike: that is one point we both share in common!

Yes, religion can be very dangerous. Why, as a religious believer, do I assert this?

The reason for mentioning the danger of religion is not because I believe that human beings are intrinsically evil and doomed to destruction unless a saviour figure comes to save us. I do believe a saviour figure has appeared who can save us from destruction, but not because we are intrinsically evil. This belief in our intrinsic evil is the foundation stone of many religions, which can then instil such fear into their adherents that they can no longer trust themselves; their salvation lies in their willingness to submit themselves entirely to the belief system, imposed upon them by those who know, and who lead them to cling to that system under all circumstances. We can be so conditioned by our culture, upbringing and formal education that we assume the way we perceive things must be the way things are. Jesuits, or any other religious grouping or individual, are never excluded from this fact.

Before the mid-sixteenth century, it was generally believed that the sun, moon and other stars circled round our planet earth, the centre of the Universe. In the mid-sixteenth century, Galileo, a very sincere Catholic, was declared a heretic by the Catholic Inquisition because he believed the findings of Copernicus to be true. Galileo's conviction was based on his own careful observations over many years, leading him to conclude that the earth, the moon and others stars do, in fact, revolve around the sun.

Our differences in the way we perceive things are not defects caused by our sinfulness: they are gifts given to all and each of us, a source of blessing, enlightenment, of growth and of unity. If these gifts of seeing things differently are not recognized as such, the differences can quickly lead to violence, a passionate love of sameness and of uniformity, all fuelled by the devouring flames of fear. When I asked the Provincial why he wanted Archbishop Roberts to be banned from the Vat II conference, he told me that he had received complaints from other Jesuits, including one who had forbidden any member of his Jesuit community from attending. This action disturbed me at the time, but later reflection has led me to a much more fundamental point which will keep recurring throughout this book. It is an enormous question because it is something which affects not religious believers only, but every single human being. It is the question of 'God's Will'.

How are we to understand this concept of 'God's
is a word of Latin origin, '*obaudire*', to listen carefu'
human activity from 'doing what we are told', which
understanding of 'obedience'. The distinction between the two m
is of fundamental importance; it can become a matter of life or death.

For the Christian, the first step in what is called 'evangelization',
which means obeying the Risen Lord's final instructions to his followers
'to proclaim the good news', is to give priority to their own conversion.
As a Catholic, I continually hear this official call to evangelization:
what I do not hear are reminders of the endless daily opportunities
for collaboration with people of other denominations, other faiths
and with people of no faith in those areas of life which mean most to
all of us. The areas are feeding the hungry, giving drink to the thirsty,
clothing the naked, visiting the imprisoned, the sick, the disabled.
These people number many millions and they are in that state because
of institutional sin. 'Institutional sin' means those unjust rules and
regulations imposed on the majority for the sake of a minority, a
state of affairs which is more critical today than ever before in human
history with our alarming disparity of wealth. It is a murderous disease
imposed in the name of peace, right order, and even of 'God's Will'.

'Dear God, restore to life our fearful, withered hearts, so intent
on defending ourselves against others that we can no longer hear
Your Voice in our hearts, constantly calling us back to the love and
compassion for which you created us before time began. Let us hear
you speak again, "Before the world was I had you in mind", calling
us to fulfil our unique role in collaborating with You in Your care
and love for all creation.'

Exercise

- Having read this chapter, did any of its seven sections evoke
  a strongly felt response? Note down which and the nature of
  your response.

- In reflecting on your response, can you spot any connections
  with your daily experience, which you would like to pursue.
  Then keep pursuing them!

7

Our hearts are being drawn continuously into unity

In August 1967, I was asked whether I would be interested in working as Catholic chaplain to staff and students at Glasgow University and at other colleges for tertiary education in the city. With little knowledge of what this might entail, but with vivid memories of my short stay at Manchester University, I agreed. In September 1967, I was appointed assistant chaplain and in January 1968, my predecessor having moved to parish work in England, I took his place, and remained there, somewhat unsteadily, until May 1975.

It was through the events of these years and the people I encountered during them that I began to understand that Ecumenism might mean much more than persuading other denominations to become Roman Catholic! The experience, which I now call 'Unity', became attractive, life-giving, freeing and full of wonder, introducing me, as though for the first time, to a new way of seeing the reality which surrounds all of us: no one is excluded! In this chapter, I select a few events from the chaplaincy years, which led me in this way: ordinary everyday events, ordinary everyday encounters with people who shared their humanity.

Turnbull Hall – The Catholic Chaplaincy

Bishop Turnbull (1400–50) was the Roman Catholic bishop who founded Glasgow University. The 1967 chaplaincy building was at one end of Southpark Terrace, a few hundred yards from the main university buildings. It was a large building of four floors with an adjoining chapel, which could hold 200 people comfortably, or 300 uncomfortably, by using stacking chairs. It had a large hall for meetings, which could also be used as a refectory, dance hall, for social occasions, and there were plenty of smaller meeting rooms, a lounge and chaplains' rooms on the ground floor, a basement, including a small flat for caretaker and family, and residential quarters for chaplains and students on the top floor. The rest of Southpark Terrace included a few private houses, but also the Soviet Studies department, our next-door neighbours, Ecclesiastical History, and the University Theology Department. At the other end of the terrace was the Orange Lodge, a Northern Ireland organization named after William of Orange and founded in 1795 to uphold the Protestant religion and firmly establish Protestant supremacy over the Irish Nationalist Roman Catholics. I saw my new geographical position as an invitation to engage ecumenically!

My first impression as chaplain was bewilderment. I had been living for years in institutional establishments with a clear-cut programme for every day and every hour. In the chaplaincy I found myself sitting alone in a large building, which was rarely used by students. My predecessor was more interested in ministry to staff.

My appointment as chaplain was made by Archbishop Scanlan. He was very welcoming at first and solicitous about my physical welfare in Turnbull Hall.

In most developed countries, the 1960s were years of student unrest, a time when the media were beginning to describe our times as post-Christian and postmodern, when all major institutions were being questioned, including Christianity and all other religious faiths. Interest in religion/spirituality was not fashionable. Debunking both was a preferred activity.

Looking back on this period nearly 50 years later, I can now see that most of the events which brought life to the chaplaincy and beyond happened, apparently, by chance, and were beyond the bounds of what we normally term 'religion'. The observation is not an attack on religion: it is opening up the meaning of religion to show that 'religion' is not a neat little department of human life, of primary interest to those interested in antiquities. Religion can break open the categories of thought to which we have become so conditioned that we are no longer aware of them. The dawning of a new vision of the reality in which we are held not only introduces us to a new vision of our world, it helps us to see that we are not only recipients of new objects on which we can gaze: we are creative parts of it, unique agents, continuously being invited to step out of the imprisonment of our conditioning to collaborate and promote the unity of all things. If all this seems to be gibberish, the ravings of a very senior citizen, do not let that reaction prevent you from looking at your own experience of life, for that experience is your pearl of great price. You do not have to create it, you do not have to deserve it, or merit it: all you have to do is look at it, and the pearl of great price, which is within you as well as surrounding you, will do the rest!

'Solvitur ambulando' 'By walking the problem unravels' (Tacitus 55–117AD)

I enjoy hill walking. It was one of the ways I dealt with bewilderment on being appointed a chaplain. Glasgow is surrounded by most attractive scenery. One decision I did make was to take Saturdays off to walk the nearby hills and mountains. I did not reflect on this activity at the time. I always enjoyed it and felt better able to face the coming week because of the break. Fifty years later I look back on those hill walking days with great gratitude; they were teaching me far more than I realized at the time.

After a few Saturdays I was joined by Jim Gallacher, a sociology student with a persistently searching mind. I had never before encountered anyone who could start on a question at the foot of a mountain and still be pursuing the same topic on the descent with hardly a trace of a full stop or breathlessness in between. Others began to join us until Saturday walks all the year round became a permanent feature of chaplaincy life, and they became ecumenical. They were open to all.

William Blake once wrote: 'Great things happen when men and mountains meet.' I can confirm that observation, but avoiding the sexist language! Friendships were formed on those walks which have lasted through the years, and not a few became marriages. More immediately, from the core of walkers, small groups emerged throughout the years I was there, who initiated all kinds of things within the chaplaincy itself: dances, celebrations of birthdays, welcoming arrivals and departures, concerts, recitals, presentations and lecture series, travels abroad.

These core groups also worked on liturgies, attracting some very talented musicians, and developed many kinds of para-liturgy – the name given to religious services in which everyone, of whatever faith, or even of no professed faith, could feel welcome.

During my first year at the chaplaincy, I spent one summer holiday in Oban, a well-known coastal resort on Scotland's west coast, where I volunteered my services for two weeks to Mgr Ewan MacInnes, a Gaelic speaker and a native of the Isle of Barra in the Outer Hebrides. He lived next door to the bishop in a house attached to Oban Cathedral. The Monsignor was a fund of knowledge on all that was to be known about Highland and Islands' life, from its ancient history to its contemporary gossip. One evening he mentioned and spoke very highly of a Mrs Cameron-Head, the widow of the Laird, who had inherited Inverailort Castle on the edge of Lochailort, in the West Highlands. This was a massive building, which had been taken over by the military in World War II, where it had become an ideal training centre for commando units with its challenging mountains, fast-flowing rivers, providing naturally formed obstacle races on every side. After the war, the Laird died and the castle, apart from its central building where Mrs Cameron-Head lived with a tiny staff and hosts of visitors, remained as it had been under military occupation. Mrs Cameron-Head offered this freely, or at minimum cost, to any groups within the area who were looking for short-term accommodation.

With Jim Gallacher I visited Mrs Cameron-Head to discuss the possibility of using Inverailort for the inside of a week in September for a group of about 30 students. The week was to be an intro-duction for new students from Glasgow's many Catholic schools to university life. About 20 of the group were new students, the rest were already university students or staff. Mrs Cameron-Head welcomed the proposal and showed us the premises. They were very primitive. A very large room with a huge fireplace on the ground floor that had been the ballroom in its days of glory was now bare floorboards, stacking chairs and a few folding tables. This became our all-purpose room, for meals, for Mass every evening, for all plenary meetings, for dancing, indoor games. There was a very diminutive kitchen attached, where our volunteer cooks worked daily miracles in feeding the ravenous. At night, the room served as dormitory for the men: our beds were the floorboards and all had been warned to bring their own sleeping bags. The girls slept in the upstairs dormitories, bare rooms with ancient iron bunkbed accommodation with lumpy mattresses, defective springs occasionally breaking free of their covering. Jim and I were won over by the place, by the natural beauty of its surroundings, but above all by the generous welcome and natural eccentricity of Mrs Cameron-Head, who showed great interest in everyone and everything, her hospitality including innumerable cats, ducks and the occasional sheep. After a few years we also met there in Easter week, volunteering our services in tree felling, log chopping and spending our evenings in chatting, singing and setting the world aright.

In the autumn week we started meetings with a one-hour session after breakfast, beginning with a short stillness exercise, then introducing the topic for the day. The topics were always centred on the theme 'God in All Things' and what that can mean in our everyday life. In my early days, I tended to give lectures. Later, I learned to initiate conversations on a topic, encouraging people to express their own thoughts and feelings. The sessions were for listening to each other rather than discussing world problems. This method enabled all of us to benefit rather than scoring points against one another. It is a method most of us find difficult, in practice, because it upsets our previous conditioning. Breaking through our conditioning introduces us to a new and exciting world and to a Universe which is continuously sharing with us the miracle of existence.

For the rest of each day we went walking, sometimes together, sometimes in smaller groups. We had Mass together before supper and instead of a homily/sermon, everyone was invited to comment on the Scripture readings if they wanted to, and they were encouraged to speak their own prayers of intercession. Singing at Mass became increasingly important to them. Then we would meet after Mass to reflect together on the themes we had been considering during the day and how they linked in with everyday life.

What has all this to do with Unity? Unity is about enabling us to be at home in the world, wherever we may be – at home within ourselves, at home between ourselves and at home with God in whom we all live and move and have our being. These lofty ideals, if they are to be effective in transforming us, must be translated into ordinary everyday events of our own earthy human experience. If we fail to move in this direction, then we can create, both individually and corporately, an imaginary world of unachievable ideals, creating for ourselves a tormented life of permanent frustration from which there is no escape, because we have ourselves blocked the one escape route, scorning it as both debased and debasing: the route of looking at our own experience lived in the now of our world. This can bring us to glimpse something which is of concern to all human beings: it concerns our continuing survival as humankind on our planet. If we continue to exploit the resources of our planet as we are presently doing, then we can create the conditions which will make human life unsustainable within a few generations. In our present state of knowledge, in our vast and expanding Universe with its trillions of planets, we are the only planet inhabited by beings capable of self-reflection, capable of responding consciously to the reality around us. One way of expressing this truth is to state that, as far as we presently know, we are the only living species who are capable, by our own decisions, of making our planet uninhabitable for all organic life, for terminating all human life in the Universe. It is an awesome responsibility, unthinkable and unimaginable by past generations, apart from the occasional seer/mystic/prophet – people who are generally considered impractical in a post-Christian world.

As chaplain to the university, the predominant need of the students in von Hügel's terms was the Critical element, but students were still in need of human support and encouragement in expressing their own needs, their hopes and ambitions, their fears and their dreads, without being judged, assessed, threatened or frightened. Practice in listening to one another and to ourselves is vital if we are to learn how to relate openly to others and to ourselves. Students need to be encouraged in their search for knowledge, in their fascination with their own emotional states and daydreams, with their own inner longings and ambitions. Above all, they need to feel at home and confident in themselves, so that they can be free to grow in wonder at the mystery of their own being and their essential relatedness to the reality in which they find themselves. These lofty ideals do not require years of academic study, but what they do require is the gift of friendship. I slowly began to see this with increasing clarity through chaplaincy work. In brief, I saw my job as an invitation to provide opportunities for people to meet together, to enjoy themselves together, to grow in trust in others and in themselves.

Experimental liturgy

Today, 50 years after the Second Vatican Council, the phrase 'experimental liturgy' can be inflammatory, if uttered in a growing number of Catholic circles, leading to accusations of disloyalty, heresy, of having lost faith, etc. My reason for using it here is not to stir up more division. I simply want to record a past experience, because I know it has something very encouraging to say to all human beings, whatever their religious affiliations or lack of them.

In the late 1960s it was no longer fashionable, especially in student circles, to be known as a religious person. Vast numbers of former churchgoers across the Christian denominations had either abandoned the practice altogether or were seriously considering doing so. The Catholics were no exception. On the Lochailort courses I celebrated Mass daily, but there was no obligation on either the students or staff to come. The general theme of these weeks was 'Finding God in All Things'. In fact, almost all attended the daily Mass. They were encouraged to take an active part, to express their views in response to the readings, to listen to each other, to make suggestions. The Mass is a corporate act of worship, not a free-for-all. Argument was not allowed. Our experiments were limited to those parts of the liturgy which allowed for lay collaboration. They were not attempts to change the fundamental structure of the traditional Eucharist, but these changes brought life, revived interest among the students, because they were listened to, consulted, and came to see Eucharistic celebration not as an obligation, but as an invitation to search for and celebrate the longing of their heart.

We always had periods of total silence within the celebration – an unusual experience in most churches, which tended to regard silence as a sign of failure and to be filled at once with the spoken word, hymns or organ recitals. Singing could create problems, because there were many charismatic hymns/songs appearing at this time with catchy tunes but vacuous words, which ensured that God was kept at a safe distance and had little to do with anything earthy. However, we had some very gifted musicians among the students and a few who had some knowledge of liturgical structure, having spent some years studying for the priesthood.

The guiding principle for these experimental liturgies was to help us all to be still and through the stillness become more aware of the mystery binding us all together with all creation in our living and moving and experiencing life. The students were allowed to introduce readings, poems or reflective songs which they found to be helpful in raising their hearts and minds to God. These innovations were vetted beforehand for length and their ability to raise our sense of wonder.

The effect of this experimentation was to enable those participating to open and widen their minds and hearts to new ways of seeing, to catch a glimpse of this God, who delights in our being. For any Christian brought up to believe in a God whose main interest in us is in our sins, and whose main preoccupation is devising suitable punishments for our delinquency both in this world and eternally in Hell, it is very difficult to break down the deep self-defence barriers which such threatening images build up in our consciousness. Just talking about the limitless love and compassion of God cannot penetrate these barriers.

These experiments did change attitudes. I am not here advocating free-for-all liturgies, nor did I ever come across any student who did. What students appreciated was the opportunity to express their own views, their own beliefs, and to hear others express theirs and to bring this into eucharistic celebration. To forbid any such opportunity is the surest way of building up resistance and rejection of whatever those in authority are attempting to impose. I mention this now, 50 years later, because within the Catholic Church enormous damage is still being done to the people of God by the misuse of authority, by mistrust, adamant refusal to listen to any opinions which are contrary to our own, and by restricting liturgical forms and language.

In Catholic Church circles today, I hear this complaint regularly and from increasingly large numbers of people. What is most disturbing is that such complaints are being made mostly about the rigidity and inability to listen on the part of younger priests, who show no sign of awareness of the damage they are doing. Unfortunately, it is older clerics, many in high positions of authority in the Church, who have educated them in these rigid and deadening ways. These men are not challenged by the greater number of clerics who do see the damage that is being done, but they are unwilling to face the consequences of 'rocking the boat'.

This is the problem to which Church authorities should be giving their attention today, instead of encouraging and fomenting the deadly disease of fear and mistrust which is threatening the very survival of Christianity.

Who are we to blame? We are all to blame and our failure is in our silence. 'All that is required for the triumph of evil is the silence of the good.' And what must I do? Learn to speak the truth in love. To whom? To myself, to God in prayer and then speak the truth in love to those who are stifling the life out of us by their unwillingness to listen.

What lies beneath this refusal to listen? Is this silence compatible with the truth that God really is at work in all things? Could my refusal to listen to others be interpreted as an assertion that God must be confined to what I think? Does refusal to listen on the part of official Church authorities rule out the teaching of the Church that God is truth? Why not speak the truth in love and listen with love to those who speak, whoever they are? We are not being asked to agree with everyone, but to find God in whoever we encounter. We all have to put these questions to ourselves constantly, to uncover the hidden motives behind our own silences.

In general, the Catholic students in Scotland were not encouraged to question the religious teaching they were given: they had to accept it. It was this Catholic teaching, on sexual ethics in particular, which encouraged them to question and then abandon the Catholic Church and its ritual practices.

Without the Critical element, all human beings and not just religious people are more likely to renounce their human freedom in favour of being accepted by whatever power may be most prevalent at the moment. All forms of totalitarianism deplore human freedom and favour conformity to what they consider necessary for the welfare of society as they understand it. Religions and religious believers of whatever persuasion who forbid or discourage their members from exercising their critical faculty can be more effective destroyers of religion than any militant atheists.

To return to the 1960s and the sexual revolution ... Within the chaplaincy, we had conversations. They were listening exercises, not debates or arguments. I found these conversations to be very instructive. The participants did not harangue one another, blame or judge. It was a slow process, because they had first to build up trust and begin to feel safe. There were no subtle arguments, but they began to see more clearly the superficiality of the arguments swirling within and around them. They focused on what they most desired out of life. They did want to learn to love. They did long to be loved. They did not want to damage others emotionally or in any other way. They did not want to be treated as things. Such conversations can only happen in an atmosphere of mutual acceptance. Listening without judgement, without condemnation was a relief to them, but also it enabled them to enter a relatively new world to many – a world of learning how others felt and reacted to things that really mattered to them. To forbid open and honest exchange is an abuse. To do it in the name of Christian religion is a blasphemy.

It was for blasphemy that Jesus was condemned when he spoke the truth. Our present climate of fear within the Church, of condemnation of men and women who dare utter what they see to be the truth, is symptomatic of a disease which threatens the future of all humanity.

Over the years, Sunday Mass at the chaplaincy ceased to be an obligation: it became something life-giving and creative. The congregation were consulted and allowed to participate as far as possible. Our numbers, especially at the Sunday evening Mass at 7.00 p.m., increased. Our music improved and occasionally we had shared homilies. After the Scripture readings, we invited the congregation to comment by repeating some word or phrase which they had heard and which had evoked a felt reaction in them. They could then, in a sentence or two, say why the word or phrase had evoked such a reaction. Argument was forbidden, or any attempt to preach to others. I thought this was worth experimenting with but, at first, I always felt apprehensive – my desire to be in control! In fact, these sessions were always helpful and improved with practice. The prayers of intercession, which followed the Scripture readings, were open to anyone who wanted to utter them and this created a prayerful mood and not a little laughter.

One Sunday at the end of evening Mass, there was standing room only for those who came late, in spite of 100 extra stacking chairs and the 200 bench places. At the end of Mass I was approached by a young man who asked: 'What are you going to do about the crowds?' I replied: 'What would you do?' 'I would tell the Catholics not to come', was his Presbyterian reply, which delighted me. By this time the chaplaincy had become a place where people of all denominations and none could feel free to come. This was true of the other chaplaincies in the university and we tried to work together – a very encouraging atmosphere in which to live.

A leading communist becomes Rector of Glasgow University

Jimmy Reid (1932–2010) left his Catholic school in Glasgow at the age of 14 and then undertook his own education in public libraries, where he read widely in English and Scottish literature and in world affairs. He told me that he had begun training to become a stockbroker, but had a conversion. He was studying the flashing Stock Exchange's financial figures when he was suddenly struck by the question, 'Is this how you want to spend the rest of your life?'

He became a worker in the Clyde shipyards instead. He soon made his mark, had already joined the Communist Party and became a shop steward. There he led the famous shipyard 'work-in' in the early 1970s, when the workers refused to accept dismissal. The Prime Minister, Edward Heath, withdrew the state's subsidy and wanted to close the shipyards. The workers, under Jimmy Reid's leadership, about 6,000 of them, did not go on strike but staged a 'work-in' instead. This meant that the workers would continue to complete what orders the shipyard already had until the government changed its policy. Jimmy explained to the workforce what the workers' control and discipline over the shipyard would entail: 'We are not going to strike. We are not even having a "sit-in strike". Nobody and nothing will come in and nothing will go out without our permission. And there will be no hooliganism, there will be no vandalism, there will be no bevvying, because the world is watching us, and it is our responsibility to conduct ourselves responsibly, with dignity and maturity.' They received enormous support. Prime Minister Heath had to back down and the Clyde shipyards received £101 million in public support over the next three years.

I had met Jimmy at occasional meetings. I had also heard him speak on unemployment and homelessness. One evening he asked me to complete for him Jesus' saying, 'What does it profit a man if he gains the whole world ...'. I replied: 'And suffers the loss of his very self.' 'No', he replied, 'I prefer "his own soul".' I then asked him if he would give a joint lecture along with Professor Barclay of Glasgow University, if Professor Barclay agreed, on Jesus' Sermon on the Mount, Jesus' manifesto on God in our lives. They were both happy to accept this invitation.

I had met Professor Barclay on many occasions. He was a renowned biblical scholar and a prolific commentator on the New Testament, using his scholarship to enable non-academics, who form the vast majority of the human race, to grasp the significance of Scripture's message for every detail of our lives. He succeeded wonderfully and did not seem to be at all deterred by the criticisms he received from many of his colleagues, who labelled him 'a popularizer', as though his ability to communicate with all kinds of people was a proof of his failure as an academic!

The joint lecture drew a large ecumenical audience. Professor Barclay spoke first in his own homely style, opening up the Greek text of the Sermon on the Mount and its background in a clear and intelligible way for his audience and also stating the urgency of Jesus' message for our own day. Jimmy followed. His message was the text, its meaning and urgency for our day. He did not stray from his point nor did he show any trace of egocentricity in his impassioned address. He spoke with all the eloquence of Amos, the earliest of the recorded Hebrew prophets. Jimmy was inspirational, the inspiration being a combination of Amos' message and Jimmy's own years of experience in identifying with the poor and helpless under the oppression of the wealthy, manifest in the injustice of our social and political structures.

The audience, mostly students, were very impressed. Glasgow University had an ancient custom, shared with Edinburgh. In both universities the Rector was chosen by the students. The Rector did not have to be a graduate of Glasgow or of any other university. The current Rector, Revd George MacLeod, was coming to the end of his three-year tenure (1968–71). He was a man of a very different background from Jimmy Reid, born into the Scottish aristocracy, educated at Winchester and at Oriel College, Oxford. He joined the army in 1914, was awarded the Military Cross and the Croix de Guerre for bravery. His war experience affected him profoundly. After the war he trained for the ministry and became one of the most unconventional Church of Scotland ministers of the twentieth century. Postwar poverty and the depression years led him to work in one of Glasgow's poorest areas. In 1957 he was elected Moderator of the Church of Scotland, to the surprise and horror of many, including one prominent clergyman who asked whether it was appropriate that a man who had been described as being 'halfway to Rome and halfway to Moscow' should be a Moderator! George became a confirmed pacifist and founded the Iona Community in 1938, using the unemployed parishioners of his Govan church, students and Church of Scotland ministers to rebuild the ruined abbey's outbuildings. I came to know and admire George MacLeod and his work during my years in Glasgow. He was the most aggressive pacifist I had ever encountered, eccentric in his ways, but with a deep sense of compassion. He himself had suffered a breakdown and he has brought healing to many.

Glasgow University students elected Jimmy Reid to succeed George MacLeod. This was not a popular choice for the university staff.

Rectorship is an honorary post of three years' duration, but
give the holder the right to chair, if he chooses, Senate meetings o
university where the main decisions are taken. The new Rector is a
invited to give an inaugural lecture to the whole university.

I attended Jimmy Reid's inaugural lecture. The auditorium was
filled with staff and students. The address was later hailed in the USA
as the finest and most important inaugural address since Abraham
Lincoln's speech at the dedication of the national cemetery on the
Civil War's battlefield in November 1863. The Sermon on the Mount
was the underlying theme in all that Jimmy said as he described the
cruel deprivation of millions in our country, victims of the insatiable
greed which was devouring the lives of the oppressed, the poor and
the voiceless, betraying all the values for which people had given
their lives in World War II. He described our days as a 'rat race', then
adding: 'A rat race is for rats.' His speech was all-inclusive, demanding
peace, justice and freedom for every human being and respect for
the sacredness of the earth. Here was a man of deep spirituality, a
spirituality inseparable from every human activity and which could
communicate with every human heart, because it came from his
heart. His speech brought this academic audience to its feet in a
prolonged ovation. As Rector, Jimmy did chair many of the Senate
meetings where his skill, understanding, informality and humanity
were increasingly appreciated.

I have written of this encounter at length because Jimmy's life, as I
came to know it, was such a clear example of the true and fundamental
meaning of Ecumenism/Unity.

The word Ecumenism is derived from the Greek word '*oikia*', which
means 'house/home'. In Christian belief, God holds all humanity, all
creation in being and is continually drawing all and each of us into
unity, a unity which delights in diversity and elicits creativity in
every human being for the sake of the whole. There are as many
ways of responding to this invitation as there are human beings.
Whatever the nature of this response, it can never be adequately
measured in quantitative terms. In Christian understanding, if the
response comes from the heart, it is a shared response with the
Spirit of God, dwelling within us and working through us, for the
welfare of each and every one of us, whoever we are and however we
may be labelled, thought of, or measured by others. In spite of their
very different backgrounds and temperaments both these men bore

he reality of the transcendent at work within
of all.

ommunity in the Gorbals

Community is a dispersed community. They pay annual visits
to the Island of Iona but live in areas of need and have now spread
worldwide. In Glasgow I met members who lived in the Gorbals, at that
time the most deprived area of the city. I was invited to attend one of
their meetings. The Iona Community members lived in their separate
flats in the Gorbals. Once a week they met together for three hours,
which included prayer, reflection, exchange of views, ending the evening
with a celebration of the Eucharist, celebrated in the lounge of the flat
where we were meeting. They numbered, as far as I can now remember,
about eight people, Church of Scotland clergy, laity, men and women.

The evening was a revelation for me. I had read about French worker
priests and met with French Jesuits in 1949, who spoke of little else. I
knew nothing of any such movement in Britain. I knew little about the
Church of Scotland clergy, but had always imagined them to be rigid
and unadventurous. With this group I felt very at home, was impressed
on hearing the work they were engaged in, felt at home, too, with their
openness as they prayed together.

I was invited to join them in the celebration of the Eucharist at the end
of the meeting. I wanted to receive the Eucharist with them but Catholic
regulations about the Eucharist forbade me from doing so. I attended
but did not receive. My obedience to this regulation troubled me then
and it troubles me still. I shall be looking at this question more in detail
later. Here, I only want to comment that the evening with the Gorbals
group was, for me, the happiest moment so far in my experience of
Ecumenism/Unity, but it was also the most painful. This event disclosed
a pattern in all my experience with unity, peace and spirituality.

Discovering a way to Unity through von Hügel

It was about this time that I first discovered the writer Friedrich von
Hügel. I have mentioned him several times already, but shall repeat
here more fully.

Von Hügel was born of a Scots mother, Elizabeth Farquharson and an Austrian father, Charles von Hügel, Austrian ambassador to the Grand Duchy of Tuscany. Friedrich lived from 1852, born in Florence, and died in London in 1925. His early education was in Europe, but he then settled in England. He was a self-taught biblical scholar, fluent in French, German and Italian, never went to university, but is considered one of the most influential Catholic thinkers of his day and was granted honorary doctorates by Oxford University in 1922 and by St Andrews University in 1914.

Von Hügel's most famous work is in two volumes. Volume 1 entitled *The Mystical Element of Religion*, a very large volume, is an introduction to his life of St Catherine of Genoa, a fifteenth-century mystic. Volume 2, very slim and rarely quoted, gives the biography of Catherine, a historical illustration of lived mysticism.

I struggled to read through *The Mystical Element of Religion*. Slowly, I began to see that this book was also of great practical help in guiding me through the unfamiliar territory of chaplaincy work. This reading also enlightened me about the split nature of my own spirituality to which I had grown so accustomed that I did not notice the inconsistency. The Critical element has much to teach the whole Church and world about the human survival crises we are facing today. The modern Vatican authorities of recent years have shown little evidence of any awareness of the value and essential need of the Critical element today. Consequently, in their desire to preserve the authoritarian Church, as they understand it, they damage the very Church they are trying to preserve.

The 1960s were years of worldwide unrest among students, when atheism/agnosticism was much more popular than religion/spirituality. During this time, Thomas Merton produced a book that made mention of our living in 'a post-Christian, postmodern age'. The book's publication was only permitted by his monastic superiors about 40 years later; its theme was that our nuclear defence system threatened the destruction of all humankind – a very horrendous type of blasphemy!

When, in an early interview with Archbishop Scanlan, I had asked what he wanted me to do as chaplain, his reply was 'Help them to keep the Faith'. What he meant, although I did not realize this at the time, was that I should keep the students firmly in the Institutional stage. It was in this infancy stage that most adult

Christians were being educated at the time. Yes, there was great emphasis on Apologetics, that is, explaining the Catholic Faith to others with arguments produced to show the rightness of Catholic doctrine and the wrongness of those who did not accept, and the fate that would befall the wrong for their obduracy in the world to come! What was not emphasized in those years was the essential role of criticism in enabling us to appropriate the faith which had been handed on to us, enabling us to see it as answering our most basic needs and desires.

As I wrote earlier, the exercise of our critical faculty is essential for the development of true faith because it is the means by which the individual can assimilate the truth, allow it to lead us, allow God to become our rock, refuge and strength in every level of our psyche, in every atom of our being. Neglecting this gift of criticism reduces faith to an enforced assent to beliefs imposed on us by others.

Religious instruction, however well-meant, which does not nurture our critical faculty can rob us of our human sensitivity and our freedom, a very infectious and malignant disease. That is why the present tendency of Vatican authorities to show violent opposition to critical voices in the Church today is so dangerous and destructive of the Church and of its saving message.

Instead of criticizing and arguing against the failure of Catholic students to attend religious services, to pray, and 'keep the faith', I encouraged them to talk about what did concern them in everyday life. It soon became clear that it was not spirituality or religion that they were rejecting, but the manner in which it had been and was still being presented to them. Once a term we used to have all-night vigils, beginning about 10.30 p.m. on a Saturday evening and ending about 6.30 a.m. on Sunday with Mass for those who wanted to attend. There was a general theme for all vigils, usually Advent, Lent, Pentecost. The vigil began with an hour on the theme, to which all were encouraged to contribute their felt reactions, reflections, readings, poems, songs. Many of those coming had already been introduced to ways of praying, but there was a brief introduction for newcomers. Tea and coffee were available to help them keep awake. The following hour was spent in total silence in the chapel. The silence was very powerful. The only occasion when this hour in the chapel dragged and there were clear signs of restlessness among the congregation was when we invited a group of retreat-givers, all young and enthusiastic clergy, to conduct the vigil. During the sessions in the chapel, they included set prayers, lengthy explanations of the prayers and also invited individuals to pray aloud. Their motive for doing so seemed all very reasonable, but it was based in their conviction that a young congregation was not capable of coping with silence! We had to limit the numbers at these vigils because we did not want to disturb our sleeping neighbours, but there were always more applicants than places. That is why, in spite of all the crises the Catholic Church and other Christian denominations were suffering at that moment in developed countries, I know that true religion and spirituality were alive and vigorous and I believe the same is true today.

The crisis is in our Christian failure to recognize and face into our split spirituality, in our obdurate refusal to allow God to be God in *all* things, confining God to what we call the supernatural, a deeply ingrained attitude which bans God from ordinary life. We prefer God to be like that, not interfering in any way in the things that really matter, like our economy, our national defence, our foreign policy, trade agreements, access to resources, which enable us to preserve our values, our sovereignty, our freedom, while ignoring the deprivation our policies are having on the developing countries. We pray for God's blessing on our violent endeavours, perhaps adding our fervent prayers that God might enlighten these benighted peoples, make them see reason and persuade them to become Christians!

The prophet Isaiah had been warning Israel of the danger of split spirituality 2,700 years ago. He recognized then the destructiveness of a split spirituality masquerading as true orthodoxy.

When you stretch out your hands in prayer, I turn my eyes away. You may multiply your prayers, I shall not listen. Your hands are covered with blood, wash, make yourselves clean. Take your wrong doing out of my sight. Cease to do evil. Learn to do good, search for justice, help the oppressed, be just to the orphan, plead for the widow. (Isa. 1.14-17)

Two painful and practical lessons in Unity

In August 1968, Pope Paul VI published his encyclical *Humanae Vitae* ('Concerning Human Life') in which, after long deliberation with a group of experts, clerical and lay, he declared artificial contraception to be morally wrong. Volumes have been written on this topic. Here I am looking on the topic as a Catholic priest who, at the time of publication, was teaching medical ethics to medical students at the university and also giving a general course on moral theology at a teachers' training college. My reason for including this section is because I think the crisis which has followed *Humanae Vitae* has much to teach us in the much more universal crises besetting the Church of today.

An encyclical is an instructional document for the whole Catholic Church. It does not claim to be an infallible document and therefore could be changed. Also, local bishops translate the document into their own national language. I also knew that the vast majority of the experts called by Paul VI were in favour of a change in the generally held teaching of the Church that artificial contraception was always a grave sin.

Vat II had urged openness in the Church and had affirmed religious freedom. I was moved to write to the Archbishop because of the sad experience of hearing from many individuals and groups of the devastating effect this encyclical was having on their marriages. I had also come across one priest who had taken a strong line on artificial contraception with one couple, who had been warned by the medics that pregnancy could be fatal for the wife. Later, the priest learned that the wife had died in pregnancy. I did not want to be the official imposer of such teaching on anyone.

In my letter I explained that I had no intention of preaching against *Humanae Vitae* in public, but if I were asked whether I honestly believed that artificial contraception was 'intrinsically wrong' – that it is wrong under all possible imaginable circumstances – then I should have to admit that I could not, for philosophical, theological and for conscience reasons, accept such teaching.

There was a long delay in receiving a reply. The Archbishop was a kindly man, but I soon learned that theological subjects were better avoided. When he interviewed me, he expressed his disbelief that I, a Jesuit, vowed to obedience to the Pope, could possibly have any difficulty in accepting Papal teaching. He also assured me that his own clergy had no difficulty in accepting *Humanae Vitae*. I knew this was not true, because I had spoken with many of them. The Archbishop was not lying. No priests had mentioned their difficulties to him, being afraid of dismissal from the priesthood to which they had given their lives. He promised me his prayers and another silence followed until Fr Dom Doherty, my assistant, and myself were both summoned by a Jesuit, who was standing in for the Provincial. He told us that we were both to leave the chaplaincy after Christmas, that we were not to say anything about our dismissal, or make any statement on *Humanae Vitae*. At first, I felt devastated by this declaration. To cut a long story short, I met with the Provincial when he returned from Guyana. He came to see the Archbishop, and both Dom and I were given a reprieve. Dom Doherty moved a short time later to do a counselling course; eventually he left the Jesuits and married. He has spent his life in psychotherapy work.

I remained happily at Glasgow until May 1972. My work was becoming more ecumenical and my teachers were the people with whom I worked. The chaplaincies within the university worked well together to the benefit of all of us. In May 1972 I had shock number 2 – a phone call from the Jesuit Provincial, telling me that the Archbishop wanted me to leave the chaplaincy.

No reasons were given to the Provincial. I asked the Provincial if I might inform the congregations at Mass on the coming Sunday, Pentecost. Meanwhile, I phoned the Archdiocesan office asking for an interview, but no interview was granted. The evening mass on Pentecost Sunday was packed, our numbers swollen by journalists, as my dismissal became public knowledge. A group of university staff asked for an interview with the Archbishop, but were not accepted. A week later the Provincial came to Glasgow, had an interview with the Archbishop, then asked me to meet him at Glasgow airport before his departure for London. He told me I could be reinstated if I wrote a letter of apology to the Archbishop. The reason for this request was an article which had appeared in one of the Scottish Nationals. It was written by a journalist with whom I had spoken and reflected remarks which were not complimentary to the Archbishop. I regretted this hurt to the Archbishop and was very willing to write and tell him of my regret. I was greatly helped in all these negotiations by an emeritus history professor for whom Machiavelli was of special interest. I received another reprieve and remained in post for another three years, until April 1975, when I asked for a move from chaplaincy work.

Looking back now 50 years later and reflecting on these two 'dismissals', asking myself whether the incidents have anything pertinent to say about our present Church crises and Unity, two points are clear to me now, in light of further experience, which were not clear at the time.

Firstly, the hierarchical system, as it was practised at the time and still continues to be practised, does not permit direct communication between the bishop and the person being accused. The communication is between authority figures. In my second 'dismissal', it was only three months later that I discovered the reasons behind my 'dismissal'. Briefly, it was because of the way I conducted liturgy in general, that I gave Holy Communion to Protestants and that I did not believe in Catholic schools. Nothing of this was communicated to me at the time, nor was I allowed an interview to hear what the charges were, nor who had made them. Yes, I was grateful for the reprieve in both cases, but both crises could have been easily settled through openness of communication. I know my case is minuscule, but today there is a shocking crisis in the Catholic Church in the way in which women's religious orders have been treated in the USA. At the heart of it is a structural barrier to openness. These barriers engender an attitude of fear and distrust. The kingdom of tyrannical power replaces the Gospel's Kingdom of love and compassion, enforcing conformity and shattering unity. In today's Church we must practise openness, speaking the truth in love whatever it may cost. If we practise silence instead, fearful of displeasing the powerful, we can become the agents of death and disunity.

Secondly – and this is a more fundamental point that affects every aspect of Christian and human life – how are we to earth, that is, relate to our everyday human experience, such words as salvation, the Paschal Mystery, redemption, atonement, saved by the cross of Christ, etc.? I have no neat answer to this question. I do not think there can be any adequate answer in our human language. What must we do to allow this unifying process to take us over? The answer to these questions must somehow lie within ourselves. Why, then, is it not more obvious to us? Could it be that we have been so influenced through our upbringing that we cannot recognize the value of our own experience?

In life we go through stages of growth in childhood, in adolescence and middle age. In maturity we then begin to encounter decline in our physical and mental energies, failure of memory, difficulty in adapting to ever-changing circumstances, moving towards death. In this process we become more aware of our total dependence on others, of our inability to respond to our own needs. We can fight this process vigorously to the detriment of ourselves and of those around us. The psalmist knows this desperate state:

> You have plunged me to the bottom of the pit,
> To this darkest, deepest place,
> Weighted down by your anger, drowned beneath your waves.
> You have turned my friends and neighbours against me,
> Now darkness is my one companion left. (Ps. 88.6, 7, 18)

But there is another way of reading these dread experiences. They force us to cry from the depths of ourselves: 'God, be my rock, my refuge my strength. Show me Your Face.' Then, as in 'The Hound of Heaven', Francis Thompson's poem (see Preface to Part 2, page 141), we discover that what we dreaded and tried to escape from was, in fact, drawing us into this state of absolute surrender to the love that has been pursuing us and which we have been resisting. Our journey to the bottom of the pit is the most important journey of our lives for ourselves, but also for others. It is the journey into discovering that the God who brought us into being, the God of love and compassion, is inviting us and welcoming us into the life for which we are created. As St Augustine wrote 1,500 years ago: 'Lord, you created me for yourself and my heart is restless until it rests in Thee.' Briefly expressed, the truth we must keep turning to throughout our journey on earth is that God is in the facts, whatever my experience may be, so the facts must be kind. There is no end to our need of God's light, to help us read the kindness in the facts and to sense the reality of the God, who is always in the facts, sharing our burden with us and on behalf of all of us.

This abandonment of ourselves to God affects every aspect of our lives, working an inner transformation of which we may have little or no consciousness at the time. This is the process of unity within ourselves. Slowly we become more aware of the multiple forces at work within us, our longings, desires, urges, appetites, hopes and dreads, fears and reassurances. We grow in awareness of our essential relationship with all other human beings, continuously acting on and being acted upon. Simply because we are human beings, there is no depth of depravity of which we are not capable, no height of heroism, generosity, goodness, love and compassion which is beyond us. Even before birth we are being influenced by the DNA we have received through generations of ancestors, and later through the conditioning we receive, especially in our infancy, which trains us to act and respond in particular ways.

In infancy, in our adolescence and even in our maturity we may have been so trained that we are totally unaware of the conditioning being imposed on us. The training can be so thorough that we can claim to be free, balanced, righteous and religious, while living lives that are in total contradiction to the opinion we have of ourselves and expect others to acknowledge and agree with. Beginning to recognize and acknowledge this inconsistency is our first step to transformation. The next step is to fling ourselves into the welcoming hands of God and come to see that we need no longer cling to our own homemade securities. The first step, flinging ourselves into the hands of God, may take a second or two; the second step, to let the reality of what has happened sink down through our multiple levels of consciousness to the core of our being, may take decades and will never end, because it is a journey into the unfathomable mystery of God, but a journey which has a greater attraction than anything else we can think, or imagine. This is the attitude that evokes in us the 'Cry of Wonder'.

Two life-giving experiences of Ecumenism/Unity in practice

Unity is lived and experienced in very ordinary, simple ways between very ordinary people, who are unlikely to understand if you were to congratulate them on their ecumenical expertise, such is the gulf fixed between our religious language and everyday life.

I have written about both experiences in other books. This is an abbreviated version, hoping to encourage readers to recognize the value of the 'ordinary things' they are constantly doing.

The first experience is of meeting Stella Reekie. Stella trained as a nurse and in 1939, at the outbreak of World War II, she joined the Red Cross, where she served throughout the war. In 1945 she was among the first British people to witness the horrors of the German concentration camps. The experience was shattering for her and changed her life. She wanted to live the rest of her life in the relief of suffering, in healing and reconciliation work. She remained in Germany postwar, working with the countless refugees, who had lost their homes and were searching for food and shelter. Later, she became a Church of Scotland deaconess. In spite of the clerical title, a deaconess in the Church of Scotland is not a cleric, cannot conduct services etc.; she is simply a material helper in receipt of a subsistence salary. Stella then volunteered her services in Bangladesh, a new and impoverished nation split off from India. There she lived and worked for 25 years until she retired and returned to Glasgow. In her retirement she was invited by 'Churches Together in Glasgow' to serve as a Christian link for the many Muslim people living in and around Glasgow. Her job was part-time, included a small flat near the university and a very modest salary. Stella did not restrict her welcome to Muslims. The 'International Flat', as she called her tiny building, became a micro-United Nations, offering hospitality to all comers. Occasionally, arguments would start among the visitors, who would start quarrelling and threatening violence. Stella could walk through the quarrelling groups and, without saying a word, her presence would restore peace and calm. Stella died of cancer. I shall never forget her funeral service in the Wellington Church on University Avenue. There was a large international gathering of many faiths and of none.

There were many tributes paid to Stella, but the one which lingers in my memory was this one from a Sikh:

> To us, Stella was like water, she cleansed us, gave us life and assumed the shape of whoever she was with. To me she was a Sikh, to my Muslim friends a Muslim, to my Jewish friends a Jew, to Christians she was a Christian. I had never understood what Christians meant when they said, 'Jesus died for our sins', but I do know that Stella gave her life for us.

Those words linger in my memory, not only because they were a tribute to Stella, but because they go far beyond that; they sum up the essence of Christian life. Stella gave life to those she encountered. She also recognized, like the Quakers, that which is of God in every person. The Sikh expresses this truth, but in different words, when he said that Stella assumed the shape of whoever she was with. She recognized the sacredness of every human encounter. When I visited Singapore, at first I found people's way of greeting each other with a bow and joined hands to be strange. Later I came to appreciate the gesture. As far as I knew Stella, she never tried to persuade anyone to become a Christian. She just let people be. People sensed her good will and respect and felt at home with her. She was hesitant and apparently vague when asked by others to explain the nature of her work. Her actions spoke more eloquently than words. She was 'a unique manifestation of God', a life-giver, encourager, appreciative of everyone and of everything, simple, down to earth and able to laugh. These are the qualities to which all of us are called because the Holy One dwells within all of us, the ever-welcoming Heart in whom all things exist, always welcoming each one of us. And that is the Heart of the matter and the Heart of all work for unity, which must begin in each individual with heart speaking to the Heart that *is*.

The second example begins with a woman who called in at Turnbull Hall. She was a next-door neighbour from the Soviet Studies department. She wanted to have her child baptized in the chaplaincy. She was Catholic, her husband was an atheist lecturer in the department. We agreed on a date and time for the baptism. She then asked if her atheist husband might also attend and also whether her friends from the department, mostly atheist, might also attend. I told her they would all be most welcome.

After she left I began wondering about how I might conduct this baptism service in a manner which would not be offensive to the atheists. I shall always be most grateful for this 'problem' and how it enlightened me about the meaning of my own Christian faith.

The way in which baptism is commonly explained to and under-stood by Catholics and the way I had understood it for years was this: baptism is a sign that the person being baptized is now a son/daughter of God and a member of the Roman Catholic Church, outside of which there is no salvation. They are washed free of original sin, which afflicts all human beings and which derives from the sins of our first parents, Adam and Eve, when they disobeyed God by eating the fruit which God had forbidden them to eat. Also, if it is an adult who is being baptized, they are also, through baptism, cleansed and forgiven all their sins. The outward sign of this sacrament is the pouring of water on the head of the child, or the plunging into water of the person to be baptized, while whoever is administering the sacrament says the words 'I baptize you in the name of the Father and of the Son, and of the Holy Spirit'.

In the Catholic Church, apart from the sacraments of Marriage and Baptism, the other five sacraments can only be administered by a validly ordained Catholic priest. Baptism, the basic sacrament, can be administered by any human being of any faith or of no faith. The only thing they have to do is intend to do whatever it is the Catholic Church intends to do through this sacrament. The baptizer does not have to be a believer! In the early centuries of the Christian Church, only adults were baptized; the children had to wait until they could be aware of what was happening to them and what they were undertaking by receiving the sacrament.

As I struggled to prepare something for the atheist congregation, I remembered a book I had read some years before about the meaning of sacraments, with the title *Celebrating Our Awareness*, by Ivan Illich. Recalling that title gave me the answer to my problem. I could welcome the atheist visitors, explain briefly the ceremony that was to follow, telling them that all the words, signs, songs and symbols that were to follow were the Catholic way of celebrating the awareness of what God is, in fact, doing for every human being, inviting all of us to enter into the unity of God's own life, a life of love, of compassion, of truth and of justice. In Christian belief, our role in human life is to let God be that kind of God to us and through us to all those we encounter. Hence Jesus' constant appeal in the Gospels: 'Love one another as I have loved you.' We are not celebrating something which belongs exclusively to Catholics. All of us share this in common with this little child whose life and destiny we celebrate today.

In 1975, after eight years as chaplain, I wanted to move onto other work, prompted to do this by what I had experienced and learned in Glasgow. The Glasgow years had deepened my understanding of God, a God at work in everyone, drawing us into unity. This God will always be a surprising God to us, a God who breaks down the constrictions of our conditioning, a God who is always ahead of us, always greater than anything we can think or imagine. Experience was beginning to teach me that perhaps God was not nearly as fussy about religious denominations as we, the clergy. God was to be found in all kinds of people, manifesting Godself in the genuine love, compassion, truthfulness of their lives.

Exercises

- Did anything mentioned in this chapter elicit in you a strongly felt reaction?
- Can you spot any connection between your felt reaction and events in your own life?
- Can you see any connection between the content of this chapter and the crises facing us today?

8

Fascinating insights into unity

On leaving the Glasgow Chaplaincy in May 1975, I had asked the Jesuit Provincial if I might continue working on spirituality, preferably with people who were active in some form of peace/justice/integrity of creation, whatever their religious affiliation or lack of it. It was the Glasgow experience which led me to this. I wanted to be in a situation in which I could meet the people, rather than be in a Catholic establishment where they would have to come to me. The Provincial invited me to join a newly established and experimental group called the 'Way Community', named after the British Jesuit Spirituality periodical called *The Way*. The community consisted of six Jesuit priests and two Religious Sisters, all of whom were already engaged in giving the Spiritual Exercises. In this chapter, I reflect on the nine years I spent working on Spirituality from 1975 to 1984, in its ecumenical dimension, because these years further opened my eyes to the fundamental importance of Unity in every aspect of life.

The Way Community's mission was to study and reflect on the Spiritual Exercises, the sixteenth-century text of Ignatius Loyola. We were to study how these Exercises were given originally and how, historically, they came to be given. All this study was leading to the main question – namely, how can we better promote and develop the giving of the Exercises today? My time with the Way Community began to show me the vital importance of communication of our own inner experience with one another, as distinct from endless discussions about details of how to instruct others on the meaning and the value of spirituality.

I was encouraged by the Way Community to spend some time in Rome at the Centre for Jesuit Spirituality and to meet up with

Jesuits who were now, in practice, reintroducing the original form of presenting the Spiritual Exercises individually, the method which is presumed in the text itself, but which had been neglected for 400 years in favour of group retreats to large numbers with four to five lectures delivered daily. The early Jesuits had also developed methods of giving these Spiritual Exercises to people who continued their ordinary lives, but reserved one hour each day for prayer. They had also devised methods of so adapting the Exercises to the needs of the pilgrim that the majority of applicants did only one of the four weeks which the full Exercises offered. Much more detailed information on the Spiritual Exercises will be given in Part 3.

I walked every inch of the way to Rome in 1975, from my starting point in Weybridge, on the outskirts of London, until I reached St Peter's Basilica in Rome. Reflecting on the event nearly 40 years later, I now see that the pilgrimage taught me far more than I realized at the time. It taught me to make simple connections between events, and these connections revealed further questions, which I am still trying to answer. Here are some examples.

One question was about the connection between this pilgrimage and everyday life. Every decision I made on the walk was influenced by my intention to reach Rome on foot. The question that followed this banal observation was: In my journey through life, what corresponds to my intention to reach Rome? What is the overarching intention in my life which gives it meaning, holds me together, answers my deepest longings? I also noticed that these questions are not limited to those on walking pilgrimages; they concern every human being, because we are all on a journey through life.

A further question arises, a daily question on the pilgrimage: What is the purpose of the luggage I carry each day? Another banal question! The luggage is to enable me to make the journey on foot to Rome as effectively as possible. Yes, luggage is for the journey. Now transfer the statement and apply it to life's journey. Is my luggage for the journey, or is the journey for my luggage? Perhaps the question could be expressed more sharply in the phrase, 'Are my possessions for the journey, or is the journey for my possessions?' It was a question Jesus of Nazareth put so clearly: 'What does it profit you if you gain the whole world and suffer the loss of your very self?' And a further most fundamental question following on this is: 'What is this "self" that you can lose? And how is it connected with the rest of the Universe?'

A third observation which came to me on later reflection on the walk to Rome was that Ecumenism, essentially, concerns all humankind, not Christians only. It is a movement to preserve, develop and strengthen the unity of all humankind. It is in light of this fundamental truth that our Christian divisions, upheld self-righteously by the chosen, can begin to reveal themselves as blasphemies against God's self-revelation in Jesus of Nazareth.

This short period in Rome also showed me something that I had never appreciated before, but which became increasingly important for me in all future work. The very early Jesuits do not appear to have seen themselves as leaders of the Counter-Reformation. In all the thousands of preserved letters of Ignatius Loyola, who died in 1556, only three make mention of Luther! The Jesuit emphasis was on the universality of God's call to all human beings and on our need to become more aware of this call of God in and through our everyday experience.

The most valuable single incident for me during my visit to Rome was reading an account of Jerome Nadal, a contemporary and close friend of Ignatius, who had appointed him as the person responsible for introducing the Jesuit Constitutions to the increasing number of people who were becoming Jesuits. The Constitutions of Ignatius are a guide for Jesuits on their manner of life as a Religious Order within the Catholic Church. On one occasion, Nadal was asked: 'For whom are these Exercises suited?' His sixteenth-century answer was: 'For Catholics, for Protestants and for Pagans'! In those days 'Pagans' was used as a term for all people who were neither Jewish nor Christian. I have treasured those words and tried to let them guide me in all the spiritual work I have engaged in ever since. All my subsequent experience confirms the truth of Nadal's words and gives me great hope.

It was when I returned from Rome to the Way Community in London that I learned that the Jesuit Provincial had asked Fr Michael Ivens, who was also a member of the Way Community, and myself to take over responsibility for the Jesuit Tertianship in Britain, beginning in September 1976.

Michael Ivens and I were very lucky in that we were given a free hand to remodel the tertianship for the twentieth century, guided by the pastoral guidelines which Vat II had produced for the Church and the world, breaking down many of the barriers which had grown up over the centuries, separating the Church from the world. The Jesuits themselves had held two General Congregations – meetings of Jesuit representatives from all parts of the world – in 1972 and 1975, to reflect on our ministries in the Church today in light of Vat II.

To prepare for this work, I was encouraged by the Way Community to spend a few months in early 1976 visiting some Jesuit houses in the USA and Canada where Jesuits, who had made their own tertianship in England over ten years earlier, were now pioneering new types of Jesuit Spirituality centres, specializing in the giving of the Spiritual Exercises individually to laity as well as to Religious, developing training methods to enable Religious Sisters and laity to give these retreats both residentially and also in daily life. I was amazed and delighted to visit and work in some of these thriving retreat houses and the visits were a most useful preparation for work which I was invited to undertake later in the tertianship and then in developing St Beuno's as a Jesuit Spirituality Centre.

The man who had inspired these American and Canadian Jesuit pioneers was Father Paul Kennedy, who was beginning his time as Tertian Instructor in 1959, when I made my tertianship. He inherited a very monastic-style tertianship but slowly, over the years, he discovered the individually given retreat and began experimenting. His experi-mentation was more appreciated by English-speaking Jesuits from the USA, Canada, Australia and New Zealand than by the British. I benefited from Paul Kennedy's work ten years later!

I enjoyed working with Michael Ivens. He was a contemplative in action, an excellent listener, who enabled people to feel safe in his company, because he could always spot the creative and positive element in what might seem to others to be outrageous statements. 'Contemplation' and 'being contemplative' are words which, because of our ingrained split spirituality, we tend to think of as 'religious' words, not to be mentioned by any serious modern atheist or post-Christian thinker. This split is a great loss for believers and unbelievers alike.

Contemplation and being contemplative describe attitudes, not activities. Contemplation concerns the way we see the reality that surrounds us. The contemplative allows that reality to instruct us; the analyst imposes a method of perception upon what we experience, imposing our meaning on what exists. Galileo was condemned by the analysts because he failed to share their conviction that the sun moves round the immoveable earth. His contemplative attitude revealed connections that the condemning analysts had failed to notice.

The contemplative attitude is a potential in all human beings. Failure to be open to it closes us up against life in all its wonderful variety and complexity. This is the attitude condemned by the Jewish writer Martin Buber in his classic book *I and Thou*, in which he asserts: 'Nothing so masks the face of God as religion!' The contemplative attitude is vital for our human survival, a concern for every human being in every aspect of life. The contemplative attitude is different, but not opposed to the analytic; they are complementary – we need both.

In our remodelled tertianship, the first two months were spent in preparation for the 30-day retreat, to be given individually, an experience which was new to most of the tertians, who were accustomed to 'preached' retreats with four or five talks given daily by the retreat-giver, each lasting about 45 minutes. After the retreat, we had a period of reflection on the experience, considering the changes this one-to-one method might have on all our future ministries. The period after Christmas until the end of January was spent in study of the Jesuit Constitutions and history. The Jesuit Constitutions were composed as a guide, based on the Spiritual Exercises, to enable the Society of Jesus to be formed and to develop in the world as an organization within the world, bearing witness to the reality of the Risen Christ at work in all things and in all peoples. We encouraged the tertians themselves to do the research and to deliver most of the lectures on these topics.

The next major period, from the end of January until early June, was given to 'Experiments'. In previous tertianships these had taken place in Jesuit establishments, parishes, schools, retreat houses. They also lasted only for the period of Lent, after which the tertians returned to St Beuno's for another three months of monastic existence. In 1976 we extended the experiment period from the beginning of Lent until early June, when the tertians reassembled at Barmouth, in North Wales, where we had a Jesuit holiday house. There we did an eight-day individually given retreat together, then had a period of reflection on the whole tertianship experience, sharing our own felt experience of the year and how it left us as we faced our futures.

With one exception, all the experiment placements were in non-Jesuit establishments, which were founded to help the poorest and most deprived in our society. The inspiration to attempt experiments outside of Jesuit houses came from the Vat II documents and the Jesuit General Congregations 31 and 32, besides reports I had read on the development of 'Liberation Theology' in Central and South America.

It was the poor and oppressed people who had instigated this massive movement together with European-trained theologians, native to or working in those countries, who had chosen to live with the oppressed, sharing their hardships, and so rediscovering the theology, inspiration and the enthusiasm of the Hebrew prophets for Yahweh's special care for the poor and oppressed. What was so astonishing was that this movement, 'Liberation Theology', should only reappear under this title 2,700 years later! Still more astonishing was – and still is – the opposition and mistrust of Liberation Theology, which still rages today within and beyond the Catholic Church itself.

The experiments were very varied, clustered in areas of London and Liverpool. The type of work in which tertians were invited to serve included hospices for the dying, centres for refugees and asylum seekers, centres for the homeless and unemployed, centres and homes for HIV and AIDS patients, work with young offenders, teaching in schools in deprived areas, and living with people with learning disabilities in a L'Arche Community. I searched for cheap accommodation within the area of their workplaces, often unfurnished. There were hitches and last-minute crises in arranging both workplaces and accommodation. On looking back on all this, I am amazed that we did succeed in finding the basic, if not the most comfortable places. I marvel, too, at the cooperation and willingness to learn of most of the tertians, who were not accustomed to this unpredictable lifestyle; they found it a rewarding, if testing time, deepening their trust in God in all things and also in themselves. I was also amazed at the spontaneous generosity we encountered from individuals and organizations, once they knew what we were trying to do.

What were some of the insights into the nature of Unity, in general, which this period of working with Jesuits in their final year of training had to offer? Although our tertianship was for Jesuits only, the design of it was influenced by Ecumenism as I understood it at that time. The reintroduction of the individually given retreat showed me the enormous possibilities for our Jesuit ministry of giving the Spiritual Exercises to Catholics, Protestants and Pagans, as Nadal had said, and of giving it individually.

In Britain in the 1960s, this was a quantitative leap. Serious giving of the Exercises was not only restricted to Roman Catholics within the Catholic Church; it was also restricted to members of Religious Orders and Congregations and to clergy. Laity were restricted to weekend retreats, which were instructional, delivered in lecture form. To put this openness to our retreat ministry into practice would demand radical change in our own Jesuit understanding of the Spiritual Exercises ministry. Most Jesuits were themselves inexperienced in receiving individual retreats and without experience of giving them to others. How were we to learn to give the Exercises in this way to people of other denominations, of other faiths, or of no faith? How were we to introduce people to the very idea of these retreats without using 'religious' language? Might not such experimentation put at risk our faith in God, in the supernatural etc.?

So insight No. 1 was on the enormity of the task of finding the language in which to present these Exercises.

Insight No. 2, which I had already begun to discover through my own receiving and giving of spiritual direction and individually given retreats, was a much deeper and more intractable problem than that of finding a language with which to present the Spiritual Exercises in clear and intelligible language to people with little or no religious background. This was the problem for Jesuits ourselves, as well as for the pilgrims, of detecting our unconscious resistance to God, which begins with our conditioning as infants and continues to strengthen through our formative years, until we become so accustomed to our narrow vision that we no longer recognize it as narrowing: it has become our comfort zone, to be defended against all comers. It also becomes our prison, destructive to us and to those around us.

Insight No. 3 was beginning to see that these insights are not specifically 'religious questions'; they are human problems, afflicting everyone. This insight did not come in a flash; it dawned on me slowly. Could it be that the present religious crises, the mass defections in developed countries from churchgoing and religious practice, the multiplications of religious splits, not only between religious denominations, but also – and more worryingly – within the same denominations, should be seen not as threats of extinction, but as invitations to freedom, the freedom which God promises for all peoples and which the Hebrew prophets were declaring over 5,000 years ago? These promises of the prophets did not win the approval of Jewish religious authorities through the ages. The prophets were imprisoned, maligned, and many put to death because of their unorthodoxy – that is, they championed the defenceless and impoverished, 'the orphans and the widows', they shared the sufferings of their people, became the suffering servants, who healed and reverenced the victims of the powerful and ruthless. When Godself entered into our humanity in Jesus of Nazareth and identified himself with every human being, the religious authorities condemned him to death as a criminal. God's answer was not vengeance on the guilty. In Jesus, God entered into our mortal death; in St Paul's words, 'He became sin for us that we might become the goodness of God'. This God is still living, risen from the dead, 'nearer to us than we are to ourselves'. The power that raised Jesus from the dead now lives in you and me and in every human being. And if we listen to the depths of our own hearts on life as we now experience it, we shall slowly grow in awareness of those words of God, telling us always 'Don't be afraid. I am with you'. This is not a fantasy of wishful thinking. It is the truth of our being.

Insight No. 4 is a generalization, which is linked with Unity in its widest sense. It is linked with how we understand education and the effect our understanding can have in narrowing or broadening our vision of the world around us.

In the Jesuit tertianships in which I was involved, Jesuit brothers and Jesuit priests made their tertianships together and not, as previously, separately. The reason for the separate tertianships had been the assumption that the brothers, who usually entered the Society of Jesus without any academic qualifications beyond early schooling, would not be able to understand the lectures offered in the tertianship because they had no theological training. Historically, many had entered without the ability to read or write and could perform their manual tasks without further education. In the twentieth century, although candidates to become Jesuit brothers were decreasing rapidly, many who did apply were often very well academically qualified, or capable of academic qualifications, but did not feel drawn to priesthood.

What I noticed in these mixed tertianships, brothers and priests together, was that in the lengthened experimental period, working in non-Jesuit houses, caring for the sick, the dying, living in community with people with learning disabilities, with AIDS sufferers, with the deaf, with prisoners etc., it frequently was the brothers who were most at home in these environments, not the priests. All the priests had done some kind of course on Ecumenism in their theological training, instructions that were not normally given to brothers. Yet it was the brothers who adapted more easily to these environments, where people of all Christian denominations, of other faiths and of no faith collaborated in caring occupations.

The point I am trying to make here in Insight No. 4 is contained in a Rabbinic phrase, 'Do, and you will understand'. If we could apply that phrase to all our own learning and teaching, knowledge would cease to be a burden, both in its acquisition for ourselves and in passing it on to others; it would become an exciting and transformative process introducing us to a new way of seeing and of being, of benefit to others as well as to ourselves. This point will be elaborated in later sections of the book.

In September 1978, I was appointed superior of the St Beuno's community and asked to develop it as a Jesuit Spirituality Centre. Initially, I felt no great attraction to the post. However, I accepted the invitation, having discussed it with Michael Ivens and with Fr Patrick Purnell, whom I had first encountered at the age of 13 when I went to Mount St Mary's, a Jesuit school on the outskirts of Sheffield. The three of us could talk together easily. We had no clear ideas of how to proceed, but we knew the problem facing us was enormous and could not be solved by a few conversations. We could only dream of what we might possibly do.

It was a chance encounter with a seagull that helped me formulate my own dream. The encounter happened shortly after my appointment to St Beuno's. On a stormy afternoon I climbed the hill, called Maeneffa, behind the house. There were flocks of low-flying gulls circling overhead, about eight miles from the sea. Beyond the summit of Maeneffa I spotted one gull wobbling its way along the middle of the road. As I drew level it made no attempt to fly away. I picked it up, felt its wings, but could find no sign of a break. It still had plenty of biting power in its long beak, but the bite was not drawing blood; it was more like a kindly reminder of its presence. I could see no sheltered spot, so brought it back to the St Beuno's garden and placed it under a bush.

On returning to my room in the tower, which faced across the Clwyd valley with the mountains of Snowdonia to the west, I realized my own stupidity in leaving the gull prey to the many stray cats which had found refuge in our grounds and garden sheds. The room next to me in the tower was uninhabited and unfurnished. I placed the seagull on the floor with a bowl of water and scraps of bread. The gull showed no interest. For several days it remained motionless. I had even tried letting it float in the filled handbasin with bread nearby.

I phoned a vet and was answered by a cheerful, confident woman's voice assuring me that there was nothing to worry about. Exhausted gulls could remain for over a week in such a lethargic state. She suggested feeding the gull with a syringe containing milk, beaten-up white of egg, laced with a dash of sherry!

I found in the house an aged bottle of Avocat – a liqueur which, I thought, would be approved of by the vet, as well as cutting down preparation time. It took three of us to apply the mixture, one holding the gull, the second holding its beak open, while I applied the mixture through a syringe. The effect was almost instant. The gull began walking around the floor, found the water and the bread, ate and drank readily. Three times a day for the next three days, we repeated the process.

After six days of this intensive care, on a Saturday afternoon we took the gull to the garden, threw it into the air and watched, fascinated, as it spread its wings, glided gently back to earth, but showed no enthusiasm for further flight. Next day, a week after our first encounter, I left the seagull on the windowsill, the windows wide open, water and food nearby. When I entered the room about 10.00 a.m. the gull was moving from one foot to another, opened its wings and flew off into the distance, never to return!

The seagull had suggested to me what St Beuno's might become: a place of welcome and a refuge for the bruised, battered and exhausted, where they could slowly recover for themselves the reality of God, always at work with us and within us, drawing us out of death into life, from darkness into light – not because of our virtue, our efforts to be good, but simply because that is the way of God's unconditional love for each one of us.

That was the dream. The only immediately practical point I could see at the time was that this place of refuge must be as open as possible to any human being in need, whatever their religious belief or lack of it. I knew that by remembering the dream, bringing it to God in prayer, the dream itself would enlighten us about the next step to take, and each step would show us the further steps we might take.

The walk to Rome had not been a waste of time and energy, or a form of escapism: it was now proving to be very practical. Seeing the whole of life as a pilgrimage lies at the heart of all world religions, especially in Judaism, Christianity and Islam.

Another very useful memory in our bewilderment about a future St Beuno's was recalling the Gospels' portrayal of Jesus' public ministry, which lasted only from one to three years. He is presented as spending much of his time with crowds of people, listening, teaching, healing and having meals. He gives most of his time to his own close followers, men and women, having meals with them and talking with them. He also retires frequently, both from the crowds and from his inner circle, to be alone in prayer with 'Abba', a child's name for the more formal 'Father'. This inner circle is not presented in the Gospels as the brightest, most reliable, most gifted. Jesus grows irritated with them at times: 'Have you ears that cannot hear, eyes that cannot see, do you remember nothing?' His chosen disciples scatter at his death; it is the women who are the first witnesses of his resurrection. Yet it is with this chosen group that he spends most of his time.

These reflections give some very clear general guidelines for Christians in their attempts to spread and promote the Good News of the Kingdom: the need to form small core groups of individuals, whose minds and hearts are dedicated to God's service and therefore to the service of others, whatever their religious adherence or lack of it. Without this personal dedication to God's service, the inner core group will inevitably lose direction, become more entangled in their own personal or group interests, becoming causes of division in society rather than sources of unity. Most dangerous of all, they will pursue this policy of destruction in the name of God. When this happens on a large scale, it is not surprising that people should begin to think that we might all be better off without religion. The source of our difficulties is not God, but ourselves. The abolition of God will not lead us into bliss. The historical evidence for this assertion lies in the appalling slaughter of recent centuries, slaughter justified by the righteous, whether religious or atheist, who are trapped in our own certainties, convictions which blind and deafen us to the murderous effects our certainties are having on the fate of others.

A people that does not dream is doomed. Dreams are vital for humanity but, unless they are translated into some form of action, they quickly vanish. One simple example of this is in the idea of pilgrimage, an exciting dream which attracts thousands, because it appeals to something deep in our nature. The French state this clearly: '*Ce n'est que le premier pas qui coute*', 'It is only the first step that matters'.

The first problem was a purely practical one. How can we turn St Beuno's from being both a tertianship and a house for elderly Jesuits into a spirituality centre open to all comers? Our staff was Michael Ivens and myself, already running a tertianship, and Fr Patrick Purnell, who was also keen on the spirituality project but was

appointed Minister to the house, responsible for the practical running
of this large building. How were we to find and train a staff; how were
we to keep such a place running financially without making it so
expensive that only the moderately wealthy could afford to come to
it; how were we to begin to open up the house to all denominations
and none? There were five members of the community resident in five
different hospitals/hospices in the neighbourhood and very few in the
community who could drive a car. These were some of the questions
facing us. I do not want to bore the reader with detailed descriptions
of these questions, or of the other urgent questions which arose when
we tried to put our very modest plans into action, but I do want to
sketch, as briefly as possible, some of the surprising things that did
happen and which, I believe, have something useful to say about the
survival problems we are all facing today, whatever our religion or
lack of it.

As our Jesuit work had developed in the UK, it had become
centred on Catholic establishments, whether schools, retreat houses or
parishes. We ministered to the people who came to us. Consequently,
our ministry was, for most of us, limited to Roman Catholics.
Ecumenical work was not a practical occupation for the vast majority.
Also, our 'spirituality' work tended to be mostly to women and men
Catholic Religious. Eight-day retreats and the full Spiritual Exercises
were reserved to Religious; the laity would have weekend retreats only.
St Beuno's had only recently become accessible for Religious Women's
retreats. Many of these restrictions no longer exist today, but we need
to reflect on such past restrictions, because the tendency to insularity
still exists: it is something natural and congenial, a state of unfreedom,
with which we can easily become so familiar that we fail to recognize
its destructive effects.

Before setting up spirituality programmes for St Beuno's, we concentrated, at first, on giving lectures and setting up courses in other places,
where I already knew there was interest in the spirituality of Justice
and Peace from my time at Stonyhurst and in Glasgow. These were
most profitable meetings, for they allowed those present to say what
they would look for in a spirituality centre and they appreciated being
consulted and encouraged to speak their minds. At St Beuno's we also
encouraged people already working in spirituality, or interested in
doing so, to meet and speak on what they would like a future St Beuno's
to provide. We encouraged people attending to speak from their own

experience. Theorizing, discussion and argument were forbidden – not a general ban, because all these activities have their place, but the meetings we were having were listening meetings, exploratory, looking for general direction, not for reaching detailed practical conclusions. Out of these meetings we could begin to see some general characteristics which people would like to see in a future St Beuno's. Here are some of them:

- St Beuno's should be open to people of all Christian denominations and none. (This priority was not enthusiastically shared by all, but I never heard anyone speak against it.)

- Our ministry should be gratuitous. This was generally endorsed as an ideal.

- Donations to the work of the house would be welcome, but no one should be turned away because they were unable to pay.

- Those on the staff (when we had a staff!) should also engage in some form of spirituality work outside of the house (outreach work).

- The spirituality offered and encouraged should be 'earthed spirituality' – that is, based on our everyday human experience, a spirituality which finds 'God in all things', not just in what we term 'spiritual'.

- Our Jesuit spirituality, however communicated, should be connected with every other aspect of human life, therefore it should acknowledge the importance of reflecting on our images of God, our images of the Church, our understanding of faith. These are fundamental questions.

We believed the spirituality centre should provide help in exploring these vital questions, encouraging us to develop our critical faculty.

These very general pointers, which came out of listening to many groups of laity, clergy, Religious – mostly Catholic, but to which other denominations were welcome and gave their views – did make it clear that there was a great hunger for an 'earthed spirituality', which made sense, touched our hearts and restored joy and enthusiasm to the people of God, weighed down with instructions and warnings coming down on them from clerical and ecclesiastical heights.

Here are some of the suggestions from this listening to groups which we responded to through weekend courses at St Beuno's:

For divorced and separated people.
For the unemployed.
For those who have given up churchgoing.
On images of God and how they affect every aspect of our lives.
On ways of discovering our own images of God.
On the nature and meaning of Ecumenism/Unity and of Church. Does our understanding of these terms open us up to life, or do they enclose and restrict our vision?
On the Pursuit of Justice as being integral to Faith. What does it mean and what are some of its practical implications in our lives?
On Healing of memories.
On Forgiveness.
Introduction to Myers-Briggs Personality Type Indicator.

We also put on occasional mid-week courses, which were very effective in opening our minds to the wealth to be found in ecumenical collaboration. One such course was between a group of Catholics and a core group of British Communists on attitudes to politics. In the few days we had together, politics were hardly mentioned. Our meetings were about God! It was a most memorable meeting, because it helped all of us to recognize our tendencies to categorize each other and reject one another because of our thought categories, without ever having met, or seen the need to meet, in person.

Another most profitable mid-week course was between a group of people engaged in giving Ignatius Loyola's Spiritual Exercises individually and a group of Christian psychologists and psychiatrists, most of whom were not familiar with these Spiritual Exercises. The object of the meeting was that these givers of the Exercises should explain to the psychologists and psychiatrists how we conducted these retreats, the methods we used, and then invite them to comment as professional psychologists. All of us found this exchange to be very profitable: the psychologists were amazed at the psychological insights of Ignatius centuries before our modern psychological vocabulary had been developed, and they helped the givers of the Spiritual Exercises to appreciate Ignatius' text.

We learned, through these experimental courses at weekends and occasionally mid-week, many elementary lessons about the meaning and breadth of Ecumenism/Unity, expressed briefly as follows:

- Our attempts to be open to all denominations and none begin to reveal a forgotten truth of our Christian Revelation: that the God of the Hebrew prophets, the God of Abraham, Isaac and Jacob, the God of the Jewish and the Christian Covenant, is also the God who is calling every single human being into unity with Godself and with all creation. God is the God of Unity, not of Conformity, the God of compassion for all creation, God of the Covenant, which is offered to all humankind, the God in whom each of us lives, is loved and has our being.

- In our attempts to encourage people to look at their own pain and anxiety in their experience of life, we began to glimpse the healing power latent in all such groups and witnessed, in practice, the power of the laity to minister to one another in such a way that both the healer and the healed benefit from the interaction.

- We began to see clearly from our own observations that a characteristic of God's action is to produce creative results of love, compassion and service to each other which are out of all proportion to the resources invested in the work.

- This creative work for the good of all is the result of non-violent communication between peoples of different backgrounds. Without such communication, our inevitable differences can easily lapse into divisions, which are destructive to all parties.

These were glimpses of possibilities, new ways of seeing things, exciting, awesome and hope-giving, but they were also a source of pain, disappointment and frustration, because the glimpses showed up our own shortcomings, the huge gulf which existed within us between our high ideals and lamentable performance. They also introduced us to the formidable difficulties and opposition which can be encountered when we suggest courses of action which run counter to the solid convictions of others, built up over decades of conditioning.

The Way Group, to which Michael Ivens and I still belonged, were always ready to give their support, and we also had three Jesuits assigned to the St Beuno's staff. The work of the Spirituality Centre developed. The main work in which we engaged during these early years at St

Beuno's was in the training of a core group of retreat-givers, willing and able to give the Exercises to others one-to-one, individually, and also train these pilgrims to give such retreats to others. Such training was not primarily about learning new techniques: it demanded a funda-mental change in outlook, the ability to be open and free before God, the willingness to surrender ourselves in the core of our being. When we began this work, I had very little idea of what it would demand and I was not alone in this ignorance. I am still learning and know I have much more to learn, but there is an overpowering attraction in the work and I have no desire to escape from it.

We put on many six-week courses on the model of those I had been introduced to in Guelph, Canada by Fr John English. They included an individually given 30-day retreat, preceded by ten days of preparation, introducing ways of praying, of being still, of reflecting on the prayer experience, both individually and in groups, learning to communicate from our felt experience in prayer, from our guts rather than from our heads. After the 30-day retreat the participants reflected together and in groups on their experience of the process and how it related to ordinary, everyday life. To most of those who came on these six-week courses, the individually given retreat was a completely new, but welcome experience.

We also put on many briefer courses lasting a week or two, on various aspects of spirituality, on the art of spiritual direction, on the meaning of discernment, on Ignatius of Loyola's guidelines on what he called 'discerning the spirits' – which means learning to distinguish those inner movements which are drawing us to be creative, outgoing, compassionate, sensitive to the needs of others, joyful and enthusi-astic about this most attractive God, from those which can drive us to destructive responses, leading us to become downcast, negative to ourselves and others, infecting us with gloom and encasing us in self-preoccupation.

At first, our participants for these early six-week courses on spiritu-ality tended to be predominantly Roman Catholic, but Anglicans and other denominations were beginning to come, too, including some Anglican bishops, who then advertised St Beuno's in their own dioceses. The trickle of other denominations became a steady stream and so Ecumenism, understood as a movement towards Unity for all humankind, began to become a more visible reality, to the benefit of all concerned.

Besides these training courses, as the numbers of people having had some training in the giving of individually given retreats increased, so we were able to put on many eight-day retreats for laity, an innovation in the late 1970s, when laity, who were not members of a religious order were limited to weekend 'preached retreats'. Applicants for these retreats, open to all denominations and none, increased, leading to a very practical earthy problem – finances. This is a problem affecting all residential retreat houses today, leading to the closure of many.

Ideally, the dream was to enable St Beuno's to offer its services gratuitously, without any fixed charge, even for residential courses and retreats. Ignatius Loyola in the Jesuit Constitutions was very clear: all our ministries should be gratuitous. Donations to the retreat house were welcomed, but those who could not contribute were not to be excluded. In the early years at St Beuno's, we offered all services gratuitously, but invited donations for the upkeep of the house.

I know that, in general, retreat houses and spirituality centres are generous and do not turn away applicants who are in financial difficulties, but what happens, in fact, is that people who are poor do not apply for residential retreats/courses. Consequently, the residential spirituality centre becomes a place to which only the better off have access. It was Michael Ivens who pointed out the problem to me. We were in danger of building up a spirituality centre catering for the very tiny minority of people who had the time and the means to afford what we had to offer. But how is spirituality – that is, raising our own and other people's awareness to the reality of God, present and active in our lives and in all human lives – to be made available to all sections of our society? To ask such a question is not to devalue the excellent work which can be done for the more affluent, but why is it such an unpopular question and, in my experience, hardly ever raised?

The first answer I came to in considering this question of the availability and accessibility of spirituality work to all was simple, clear and obvious. Not only was it possible to do this – it had already been done in Jesus' short public ministry. The spirituality of Jesus was embraced most eagerly by the poor, the oppressed, those without prospects of escape from the harsh conditions imposed on them. The Spirit of the Risen Christ is still at work in us today, therefore there must be some answer.

Whatever the future for spirituality work today, it can never effectively be done by residential retreat houses alone, no matter how many were built and however much money might be available. We need to learn from the early Christian Church, when there was not the money to build churches, when the majority of members were slaves and people met in the open air or in private houses.

Spiritual/religious renewal cannot begin with plans imposed by hierarchical, ecclesiastical authorities to which the rest of the People of God, millions of them, must submit. Such plans may produce a brief period of enforced conformity, but they will not encourage creativity, spontaneity, wonder and joy in God's people. This is a lesson we desperately need today, not only in our churches but in all human institutions which claim to be working for the common good. They must constantly ask themselves, for whose benefit do we exist and what opportunity is given to those we claim to benefit to express their needs and influence our decisions? These questions are not being faced; they are resolutely ignored by those in authority.

These were the considerations which led me to propose a three-month course, to be held initially twice a year at St Beuno's. The thinking behind the proposal was that there can be no effective renewal in the Church unless, in some way, we can restore the pastoral ministry of lay person to lay person, a ministry declared to be a ministry for all in the Sacrament of Baptism.

This conviction about the need to develop the ministry of lay person to lay person was rooted in my experience as a Jesuit. I had been trained for many years in an instructional and controlling method of pastoral ministry. Pastoral experience, especially after ordination, as I have already explained in previous chapters, revealed to me the depth and richness of spirituality already in lay people of all denominations and none, but the majority were unable to recognize the gifts they had received, because the instructions given to them had so convinced them of their spiritual and religious inadequacy. The teaching they received tended to demoralize them. Their minds and hearts were so focused on their own failures and inadequacy that they failed to focus on the goodness and love of God for them, leaving themselves without the time or energy to gawk in wonder at God's presence in all creation – gifts freely given to them to enjoy and enable others to enjoy.

The hope for the three-month course was that it should enable St Beuno's to become a resource centre for training people in lay ministry. To qualify as a candidate, applicants must have had some experience of working in some form of justice/peace work, and to have fire in their bellies for this kind of work – in the Gospels this qualification is expressed in Jesus' words: 'Blessed' (which in the Greek text can be translated 'blissfully happy') are those 'who hunger and thirst after justice'.

We would offer a three-month course, the core of which would be an individually given, 30-day retreat, introducing participants to Ignatius Loyola's full Spiritual Exercises to enable them to grow in awareness of 'God in all Things', in all the mess and chaos of things, in our fears and terrors as well as in our delight and laughter. The first part of the course would be preparatory exercises in prayer, grounded in our own human experience, and delivered not by lectures, but by praying, reflecting on the prayer, sharing the experience in small listening groups. Hopefully, this process would enable people to trust each other and so be able to explore their experience at a deeper level, enabling them to become more aware of the miracle of our own existence and of the nature of this God of Self-giving, closer to us than we are to ourselves.

After the retreat, participants would spend another few weeks reflecting on their retreat experience both individually and in groups, spotting for themselves some of the practical implications which came to mind as a result of their beginning to see their lives as a partnership with God, who is continuously inviting us into deeper union with Godself. In the final part of the course they would each give a three-day, individually given retreat to another, under supervision, and then receive such a retreat. Care was taken to ensure that those who had given a retreat to another never received their retreat from that same person. We also ensured that those who had been working together in small groups of six did not give or receive retreats from each other. The reason for that prohibition was the preservation of strict confidentiality in their group work previous to their retreat-giving.

The hope was that this first step might produce a number of people willing to venture into this type of one-to-one retreat-giving in their own local area. Therefore it would be multiplying work. The three-month course was not designed to produce thoroughly equipped spiritual directors – its aims were far more modest. It was designed as a step in enabling lay people to minister to one another.

How to finance such a venture? My hope was that those who felt drawn to this kind of course, enabling them to learn how to accompany others without doing them damage, could be funded by their own bishops. Was that hope unrealistic? When I read some statistics for the annual cost of building programmes in regional dioceses, the cost of subsidizing a candidate for a three-month course was very minimal. Also, those attending who could afford to pay their own normal daily living expenses were encouraged to do so. Beneath the surface level of this finance problem lay a much wider question. What is the underlying understanding of the meaning of 'Church', out of which the hierarchy is making its financial decisions? Jesus speaks frequently on this subject, especially in Chapter 4 of St John's Gospel in his conversation with the Samaritan woman (Jn 4.1-42).

In case the length of the course might deter many from applying, we broke it down into sections, so that, for example, someone might come only for the full Spiritual Exercises but not for the other sections. In fact, there was such a demand for the whole three-month course after the first one that we no longer had to offer it in sections.

Here is the outline of the sections of the first three-month course, which ran from 15 September to 10 December 1982. It is based on my brief notes from nearly 29 years ago. Some details may be wrong, but the substance is accurate. It was through our attempts to provide such a course that we, the retreat-givers, learned through our pilgrims how better to accompany them.

- September 15–19 Human Growth and Holiness
- September 20–25 On Finding God in Our Own Experience *(Some methods of prayer drawing on our own experience in daily life)*
- September 26–October 27 30-day Retreat given one-to-one
- October 28–31 Evaluation of the retreat

(The most important source of knowledge required for retreat-giving lies in the giver's own experience. This evaluation period is to emphasize this truth for the pilgrims, enabling them to listen to one another's retreat experience, insofar as they are willing to share it. This listening deepens the pilgrims' awareness and understanding of the art of prayer accompaniment and the freedom it can bring to both pilgrim and guide.)

- November 2–7 Learning how to listen – encouraging practice of listening skills which are of value in all human encounters
- November 9–12 Christian Faith and the Promotion of Justice for all humankind

- November 14–20 A brief study of the history of Christian Spirituality

(In Christian tradition there are many ways offered for coming to a deepening awareness of the reality of God. Ignatius Loyola's spirituality is one of them. Different approaches are helpful for different people, but what is essential for all of them, and a mark of their genuineness, is that they converge in a more wholehearted surrender to the praise, reverence and service of God, which means that the dominating factor in all our lives becomes our free, willing and total surrender to God, who has called us, before time began, to find our true selves in God's own life.)

- November 21–December 8 Workshop in Retreat-giving and Spiritual Accompaniment
  (On how to accompany another without doing damage)
- December 9–11 Evaluation of the three-month course in groups of six and in plenary sessions

After the first three-month course, numbers of applicants began to increase until we had more applicants than places available. During all three-month courses, we reserved about six rooms for eight-day retreats. We now had enough trained staff to ensure that we could do this and also to provide supervision for the retreat-givers.

A very significant change at St Beuno's in these early years from 1977 onwards was the gradual introduction of women retreat-givers to give one-to-one retreats. When we began doing this, there was much opposition. One Religious Sister, in her first interview with her pilgrim – also a Religious Sister, but from another congregation – was met with an opening salvo: 'I paid a lot of money in travelling here for an eight-day retreat, and I paid to have a Jesuit retreat-giver.' All pilgrims had received preliminary warning of this change. It is to the great credit of the retreat-giver that she was so gentle in her reaction that the pilgrim relented and found the encounter to be very helpful. It was soon after this introduction of women retreat-givers that requests frequently came in, from men and women, asking for a woman as retreat-guide.

Ecumenism/Unity is a movement which is not exclusively concerned with Christian denominational differences: it is concerned with all the boundaries that alienate us from one another. Cultural differences are very frequently far more divisive than religious differences, including racial, ethnic, national, social, political, geographical and class distinctions.

One very important leap in the development of the work begun at St Beuno's began with an invitation I received from the Bishop of Kimberley, in South Africa, inviting me to work on spirituality with his clergy. By the time I had received a visa from the Apartheid government to accept the invitation, Bishop Graham Chadwick had already returned to the UK. He was being so restricted in his movements by the government that he could no longer visit the major part of his diocese in Lesotho. I accepted the invitation, and had a most interesting and instructive three months working with both native African and white clergy. When I returned to the UK, I had my first meeting with Graham Chadwick, who was now resident in St Asaph, North Wales, where he had been invited to live and work on spirituality with the clergy. I told him about the new three-month course at St Beuno's and he signed up to come. He enjoyed the course, his first experience of an individually given retreat, felt very at home in Ignatian spirituality and made a great contribution to the first three-month course. A year later, we were both invited to give a retreat in daily life to some L'Arche assistants in Jean Vanier's foundation, an organization in which people with learning disabilities live together in community with their assistants. On a day off during the course, we went walking in the Yorkshire dales. It was during a pub lunch that the leap happened!

Graham was telling me about his work in Wales during the past year. He had been fully engaged in spirituality work not only with clergy in North Wales but also with many lay people of different Christian denominations, giving individual retreats in daily life. Many of these pilgrims had been asking him if he could give them some training in one-to-one retreat-giving, so that they could pass on to others something of what they had received through this method. To cut a long lunch conversation short, within an hour we had hatched an idea. I had already attended Fr John English's two-week workshops, one in Canada and one at St Beuno's, so we arranged to run similar two-week workshops in North Wales in the summer vacation. Graham would find accommodation for the course and I would draw up a rough programme. Graham discovered a residential agricultural college called Llysfasi which normally closed down in the summer months, but would be willing to open for two weeks, providing meals and accommodation at very reasonable cost.

It was in 1985 that we held the first Llysfasi course, facilitated by myself, Bishop Graham Chadwick and Sister Mary Rose Fitzsimmons HHS, attended by 26 people. Our numbers increased over the years until in one year we held two courses in one summer with about 60 participants in each retreat. We had a remarkable range of people attending. Some were already engaged in spirituality work, members of religious orders and congregations, members of different Christian denominations who were in charge of novices or had been appointed to develop and promote the spirituality of their own orders and congregations. Llysfasi also attracted many lay people from the helping professions, psychologists, psychiatrists, doctors and nurses, chaplains to various organizations. We also had many teachers, social workers, artists, potters and farmers. There was a wealth of spirituality in those groups. Being with them became one of my abiding memories on which I could draw in periods of frustration.

The courses were designed to be times for self-discovery with roughly two hours each day for private prayer, another two hours for individual reflection and meeting in small listening groups of six, listening to the felt experience in prayer of members of the group, then working in groups of three for practice in accompanying one another in prayer. In these triads, as we called them, each member had the opportunity to be the guide, the pilgrim, and the observer, then time at the end of each session for assessment of each other as guide in enabling the pilgrim to discover for him/herself from their own felt daily experience. Lectures were limited to 30 minutes per day in the first week. In the second week members gave individual three-day retreats to one another under supervision. In other words, the whole experience was drawing on the personal experience of each member, and it was that method which appealed to all denominations and none.

The Llysfasi groups only began after I had left St Beuno's and I continued working with them annually for another ten years, by which time we had many well-qualified regular members to keep the project going and develop it.

When the three-month courses were established and we had sufficient trained staff to continue the work, I asked the Jesuit Provincial if I might leave St Beuno's in order to work ecumenically, especially with people active in promoting justice and peace work, who were in search of a spirituality which could support and sustain them in the difficulties they encountered. I had met many such people, who complained that the churches they attended did not support them in this way: they felt estranged and alienated from their own church communities. The Provincial agreed that I might explore the possibility of such work and I have been grateful to him ever since for his trust! He knew I was starting on this work with no clear idea of how to begin.

How to begin on this grandiose project? The obvious answer is 'Consult others who are already engaged and experienced in this kind of work'. So I consulted Mgr Bruce Kent, a priest of the Westminster archdiocese, who was then chairman of CND, the Campaign for Nuclear Disarmament. Within a short time he so rapidly increased CND's membership that the government became nervous and began to keep eyes and ears on him. I told him what I hoped to do. He invited me to meet with a group of peace activists. Their very sensible and practical advice was that I should work as an office boy for a few weeks with some of the peace organizations in the London area, and so get to know some of the personnel and the kind of work in which they were involved.

I spent about two months in this kind of work, most of it on sending mail to members. Internet, e-mailing was all in the future. In each peace organization in which I had worked I asked if I might write a brief column in their news bulletin, outlining the work I hoped to engage in. I was amazed and delighted at the responses I received. Within a few weeks of writing, I had enough invitations to keep me busy for a year or more. The invitations were mostly from small groups working within the UK and the Irish Republic, some of them ecumenical religious groups, others secular.

This kind of work engaged me for the next 25 years, both in the UK and abroad. Now I no longer have the energy or the ability to continue in active work, but I hope to have enough health of mind and body to reflect, write and encourage people who are searching, as well as those who have discovered for themselves the wonder and the mystery of the human life which we are now living, eliciting from deep within each of them a cry of wonder and thanksgiving for the gift of Unity with each other, with all creation and with God, in whom we all live and move and have our being – a gift which is freely offered to each of us for our own and everyone else's good. The attempt to write keeps reminding me of my own continuous need to see all reality in the universal context of all that is, enfolded within the embrace of a love that has no limit.

Pursuing an early interest in Unity, a subject in which I was so ignorant, had led me in most unexpected ways. It was through contact with people of other Christian denominations, of other faiths and of no faith, as well as through the guidance of the Catholic Church – especially in Vatican II – and of two recent General Congregations of the Jesuits, applying the teaching of Vatican II to our own Jesuit lives, that I slowly began seeing the world in a new and exciting way.

I belonged to something much greater, more open, exciting, mysterious and attractive than I had previously thought or imagined. This something was not a new subject: it was a new way of seeing the world and in that light I was able to see the narrowness and rigidity of my previous understanding. Through this process – it is still going on in me – I began to understand and appreciate the Christian Scriptures in a new way. They are addressed to all humankind and they speak a message which is just as pertinent to us today as it was to those who heard it thousands of years ago. Through my pursuit of Unity, through meeting with Christians across the denominations, with people of other faiths and people of no professed faith, I have come to believe that God is not as concerned about religious differences among people as we religious people tend to be. God, in the Scripture, identifies God's very self with each one of us. When Jesus, image of the unseen God, speaks on the final judgement of humankind, He makes no mention of religious differences. Judgement is made on how we relate to one another: 'Love your neighbour as yourself.' And this God is always with us, 'closer than we are to ourselves', calling us all into at-one-ness.

We are all being called into this Unity. Letting this truth penetrate through every layer of my being is what I most long for and most need. I want to be caught up in this process and to share it with others. That is what kept me going – helping others and myself to become more aware of this God of gratuitous love, holding all of the Universe in Unity.

The work I did and the people I met in these years after I left St Beuno's also began to attract me to Peace and what it means. Like Unity, Peace began to lead me in unexpected directions. Peace is the topic for Part 2 of this book. It is a subject in which we are all most intimately involved, whether we realize it or not. We are all interconnected and interdependent, held in union with all things and all people in God, in whom all of us live, move and have our being.

Exercises

- Having read this chapter, do you have any felt reaction to the proposal that we need a new language in which we can better communicate the primary importance of Unity for all humankind?

- Have you any practical steps to suggest for the promotion of unity and reconciliation in your own area?

Part Two

Peace

Preface

Peace is a vast, all-life-embracing and very complex subject, praised by all, especially arms manufacturers, reflected on by few. In support of this wild generalization is a fact: in the *Encyclopedia Britannica* (1974) there are 60 double-columned pages on War – there is no entry under Peace!

Peace is not an idea, a study topic: it is a way of life which affects every aspect and every moment. Our understanding of Peace and of the ways that lead to Peace can only develop insofar as we are trying to live at peace with ourselves, with our circumstances and with all those we encounter, however impossible we may find them.

Peace is far deeper than contentment: it is possible to live in contentment with a modest fortune of stolen goods. Peace cannot be found within well-defended towers of ivory, for it is essentially a quality of relationship with all creation under all circumstances, including conflict.

Peace, within an individual, includes a 'divine restlessness', a profound discontent with what we discover around and, above all, within ourselves. Peace, in spite of our protestations of being dedicated to it, is a state against which we defend ourselves with verbal smokescreens and subtle reasoning, so subtle that we deceive ourselves, preferring violence and calling it 'Peace'.

Peace is a transforming quality, not always appreciated by those who receive the gift, for it can feel more like a psychic earthquake, as though our inner tectonic plates, on which all our security seems to depend, were shifting, leaving us in a state of dark uncertainty. This trauma can be a first step to discovering where our real security lies.

Peace is an all-pervasive presence. She permeates all things, all circumstances, all hearts, even the most obdurate. She is inseparable from her sister, Truth. That is why we find her so elusive.

Peace is a gift offered to everyone, not because we are deserving, or
specially gifted, successful or powerful, religious or spiritual, but simply
because we are human beings.

**Peace comes to us not as a personal gift for me and those like me: it
is a gift offered to each for the sake of all.**

Peace is to be found in our own experience. It is like a thread put
in our hands: we do not create it. If we follow the thread, it leads us
in unexpected ways where we are afraid of going, through doubt,
darkness and despair. To change the metaphor, Peace is like 'The
Hound of Heaven', of which Francis Thompson wrote, the hound that
pursued him down the arches of the years, finally catching him and
revealing itself:

'All which I took from thee I did but take,
    Not for thy harms,
But just that thou might'st seek it in my arms.
    All which thy child's mistake

Fancies as lost, I have stored for thee at home;
    Rise, clasp my hand and come!'

    Halts by me that footfall:
    Is my gloom, after all,
Shade of His hand, outstretched caressingly?
    'Ah fondest, blindest, weakest
    I am He whom thou seekest!
Thou dravest love from thee, who dravest me.'

*(This last line means: 'When you drive out love from me, you also
drive it out of yourself'.)*

It was my interest in Ecumenism/Unity, in the Oneness of God, that
led me on to Peace. Both topics have worked on me like drills, which
bore down through layers of consciousness with their questions – a
painful process at times, and still continuing, yet it is also a process
which I value above everything, because it gives glimpses of the
miracle in which we are all living at this moment. We are not solitary
monads struggling to survive in a hostile world. We are all caught up
in something far greater than we are. In this something, we all live
and move and have our being. We live so interconnected with each

other, in ways we are only beginning to understand, that it is through our connectedness that we become persons. We cannot exist as little independent units. At every moment, whether we are aware of it or not, our existence depends upon others and others' existence depends on us.

This way of seeing the reality in which we live does not change the world, or the Universe, but it does begin to change the core of our being, upsets our habitual ways of seeing – a painful process at first, but becoming more attractive as we adapt to this way of seeing. Our Universe is expanding and within this expanding Universe our minds are also expanding. We are being invited into a new relationship with all creation, with all living things, with our own self. Wonder and amazement begin to take hold on us; fear and guilt grow less and lose their grip. And we catch glimpses of this strange ability to delight in being and in feeling free to be the unique persons we are created to be. We now know we can never be alone. This 'something, greater than I am', 'in whom I live and move and have my being' can never leave us. I am identified with this something greater and this something greater identifies with me. My mind and my heart cannot grasp this truth. Nor do I want to grasp it, but I do want to be grasped by it. I call this something greater 'GOD'. It is shorthand, used by billions throughout the ages to put us in touch with this mysterious reality which is nearer to each of us than we are to ourselves, beckoning us out beyond ourselves.

In this Part 2, I relate incidents from my own experience, but my object is to persuade all readers that the experience they must reflect on is not mine, but their own, because the only place any of us can find God at first hand is within our own experience. God is to be found in the ordinary, in the earthiness and messiness, the chaos and strife of everyday living. We live today in an environment where such thinking is not fashionable. Self-preservation has become our God: it masquerades as peace and imprisons us in spiralling violence. The violence has its source in our way of thinking. Every individual is being invited to contribute to peace for all. We are created for glory, not for annihilation.

1

Peace reveals a split in the core of our being

It was when I began meeting with and working with Christians of other denominations, as I have explained in Part 1, that I began to under-stand Ecumenism/Unity differently. I was thrown back to a much more fundamental question, namely, what is the meaning of this one God in whom I believe? I am reflecting on what happened to me over many years and changed my understanding of God, of the Church, of myself and of everything else.

God is the one God of all creation. All God's revelation reveals a God who is always greater than anything we can think or imagine, a beckoning God, whose creation is an act of love and still continuing, a God who creates in order to share God's very Self with all creation.

Humankind, as far as we know at present, is the only species which can think, reflect, wonder, be amazed, hunger for knowledge, act freely, dream and determine the direction we want our life to take.

This mysterious God is all-inclusive, present in all things, in all people. God is not an object, a thing, an idea. God *is*, and within that *is*, all creation has its being: there are no exceptions. As a Christian I believe that whenever I meet with another person, of whatever religious belief or none, I am meeting with God, because the God I believe in has identified God's very Self with every single person. Imagine you have met this man Jesus of Nazareth and that you ask him: 'Where am I to find this God you keep talking about?' In answer, he describes the Final Judgement. The astonishing thing in his answer is that he does not mention the words God, or religion, or prayer. It does not follow from this observation that belief in God, religion and prayer do not matter. What it does do is bring religion down to earth with a thump. At the Final Judgement, Jesus says,

... when the Son of man comes in his glory – he will separate all people one from another as a shepherd separates sheep from goats. Then he will say to those on his right hand, 'Come you, whom my Father has blessed, take for your heritage the kingdom prepared for you before the foundation of the world. For I was hungry and you gave me food; I was thirsty and you gave me drink; I was a stranger and you made me welcome; naked and you clothed me, sick and you visited me, in prison and you came to see me.' Then the virtuous will say to him in reply, 'When did we see you hungry and fed you, or thirsty and gave you drink? When did we see you a stranger and made you welcome; naked and clothed you; sick or in prison and go to see you?' And the King will answer, 'I tell you solemnly, in so far as you did this to one of these brothers or sisters of mine, you did it to me.'

Through working with Christians across the denominations, and with people of other faiths and of no faith, I slowly came to recognize the signs of God's Spirit at work in all kinds of people. I came to realize that Ecumenism is about the unity of all humankind and saw the signs of it in the generosity, the openness, the joy and the faithfulness of so many people, who were complaining that the churches to which they belonged or once belonged were no longer supporting them in the problems they were encountering. The language they were hearing from the pulpit no longer spoke to their daily experience.

Increasingly, as I worked on unity, I became aware of the split nature of our religion and how the instruction that was being given in many Church circles manifested the split. This was not a 'theological' problem, which could be handled by theological experts: it was a problem of everyday life affecting all human beings. I have written of this in Part 1 on 'Unity'. It was a growing awareness of the 'Peace' issue which gave me a deeper understanding of the massive split that exists between our human experience itself and the way we describe it in words. The split threatens the very core of our being, but it is in facing that threat that we can take our first step into transformation, into real peace and freedom.

It is when I now look back that I can see the significance of an event that occurred over 50 years ago – a significance I was unable to see at the time. I can remember the moment and the place I was standing when 'Peace' first became a preoccupation. It happened suddenly, surprisingly. The moment was not solemn, awe-inspiring. It happened about 7.00 a.m. on Easter Sunday morning 1961. I was standing in the playground of Stonyhurst College, where I taught from 1960 to 1967. I cannot now remember why I went down to the playground at 7.00 a.m., but I do remember meeting an enraged Colonel, who was in charge of the Combined Cadet Force, known as the CCF. This was a compulsory organization for membership of what were then called the 'Public Schools' – which meant, in fact, private schools. The CCF was a military branch of the school, introduced as a recruiting ground for pupils who wanted a career in the army, navy or air force on leaving school. In case of war, the Public Schools could provide a larger pool of potential officers.

The CCF occupied two afternoons every week of term. Occasionally, on solemn occasions, the massed troops, in military uniform and with bugle and drum band, would perform a solemn march-past, when some eminent visitor, usually military, would stand on a raised dais and take the salute. Easter Sunday morning, immediately after Mass, was such an occasion when the Jesuit Rector, dressed in simple Jesuit gown and wearing a clerical biretta on his head, took the salute.

The distressed Colonel dispensed with Easter greetings and got down to more immediate business. 'Have you seen what has happened?' he asked, pointing to a wall in the middle of the playground, on which was sprayed an enlarged logo of the Campaign for Nuclear Disarmament. Below this was a notice, 'MARCH BEGINS HERE', and below that, in brackets and smaller script: (No children, please).

The dais, on which the Rector was to stand and take the general salute, had disappeared. The Colonel took me to see its new location. The college had a splendid avenue approaching the main entrance, the last 200 yards running between two large ponds, on one of which the dais was now afloat, equipped with a tree-branch mast and a bedsheet for sail.

As I was then in charge of the boys at the top of the school, I was also in charge of the 'criminal' investigations which followed. I soon realized that my heart was not in hunting down the criminals. This was the first of the many connections I was to notice between events that I had previously encountered without their having any conscious effect on my life.

The Stonyhurst event reminded me of another event from 20 years earlier. When I was 13 years old, I left St Aloysius College, Glasgow, a Jesuit school where I had been educated from the age of seven, and moved to Mount St Mary's College, near Sheffield, a private Jesuit boarding school, hoping to be recognized as a 'Public School'. In the year I arrived there, the school had introduced what was known in those days as an OTC, Officers Training Corps, later to be renamed CCF, Combined Cadet Force. On two afternoons each week, dressed in the military uniforms of the First World War, we would practise marching the slow march, various drills, sometimes bearing rifles and learning how to give the military salute with rifle and fixed bayonet. In the longer of the two afternoon parades, we were introduced to military manoeuvres across the school playing fields, taught to break step when crossing railway bridges lest the vibrations of our teenage pounding feet should cause it to collapse, and firing our rifles with noisy blank cartridges.

Annually on the Feast of Corpus Christi, commemorating Jesus of Nazareth's final supper with his followers before his arrest, trial and sentence to death by crucifixion, the school celebrated the Feast with a procession of the Blessed Sacrament. The celebration began in the school chapel and then proceeded through the school grounds before returning to the chapel. En route, there were two stopping places, so that there were four 'blessings' given in all. For the blessing, the priest celebrant, who held the Blessed Sacrament in an elaborate golden container, the monstrance, throughout the ceremony, would hold it aloft and the congregation would bow in silent reverence. The reason for the silent bow of reverence was the Catholic belief that this white circle of unleavened bread was a sign, signifying a reality, namely that this action of Jesus at the Last Supper is an eternal event, declaring the reality of every moment, namely that God, the ground of our being, is a God of Self-giving, a God of love without limit, a beckoning God calling each of us to share the very life of God.

At Mount St Mary's, this procession of the Blessed Sacrament had a special feature: the canopy under which the celebrating priest walked, holding the monstrance, was accompanied by a military escort of eight boys, four on each side, dressed in military uniform and with their rifles and fixed bayonets. At the age of 16, being of suitable height and capable of doing the slow march and of giving the general military salute at all four stopping places without being crippled with cramp, I was appointed to the guard of honour. We spent many hours in drill practice.

I can remember clearly that at the time I found nothing incongruous in escorting the Blessed Sacrament with fixed bayonet; nor, apparently, did the other boys, nor the Jesuit staff. I can also remember being glad to be selected and I said some prayers as we marched.

Many readers, both Christian and non-Christian, may find these accounts of Easter 1961 and of Corpus Christi 1941 either quaint, incredible or scandalous, while some Roman Catholics will regret that I have written them. I do not write them to make fun of Catholic belief or practice: I remain a Roman Catholic. I believe in the reality of God, present in every atom of our being and in every aspect of our lives. For me, that belief is the most treasured element in my life: it gives me life and hope, not in me and in my ability, achievements or virtue, but in this reality of God, whose love is unconditional and embraces all people and all creation, whose providence is boundless and who is nearer to each of us than we are to ourselves, whoever we are.

The reason why I have mentioned these stories of Corpus Christi 1941 and Easter Sunday 1961 is to illustrate a truth from my own experience which concerns not only me, but every human being. What is this truth? It is our human tendency to divinize our own experience, identifying 'God', 'God's Will' with that which is not of God. Other ways of describing this tendency are to call it 'a failure in discernment', or 'to turn faith in God into an ideology', leading us to dedicate our lives to some created thing; it might be a golden calf, as some Israelites did, or a belief system. Examples prevalent in developed countries today are the simplistic beliefs that by getting rid of 'God', 'Religion', we shall root out evil from our lives.

'Godly' people can be the most idolatrous and dangerous people of all when God is a God of their own making. 'God' can be a projection onto this name of our own identity and characteristics, thus justifying ourselves in our contempt for any who do not agree with us, in acting violently against them, killing them in the name of God, bestowing wealth on those they consider to be the loyal faithful, oppressing all who fail to conform.

The idol can assume any number of forms: a religion, a church, a group of any kind. In other words, no individual can ever claim to be free of idolatry by claiming to be a religious believer of any kind, or by claiming to be a religious authority, even if it is in a movement for a better world!

The conclusion commonly reached by many today is that religion is the root of all evils. Any who disagree with this assertion are classed as stupid, ignorant, brainwashed victims of religious education. Idolatry is not a disease from which non-religious are immune. The most fervent, faithful and dedicated idolators of today include both religious and non-religious people, whose real idols are wealth, success, status in society, who put a price on everything but value nothing beyond their own personal ambition. The Bible's description of Israel's worship of the golden calf is not a strange account of ridiculous and destructive behaviour of primitive peoples: it is a precious insight into human tendencies in all ages, from which no person, whether believer or unbeliever, is ever exempt.

There is a sense in which the problems facing us today can no longer be usefully labelled 'religious': our problems are far more fundamental! The way we understand the word 'religious', 'God' is part of the problem. Our use of language is not the problem, but it illustrates the problem. It is as though our language has cut adrift from reality, has come to develop a virtual reality, independent of our human experience. This phenomenon indicates a deep split within our self-understanding, a split which penetrates to the core of our being.

All of us have a natural tendency to protect ourselves. This tendency, in itself, is a gift. Without it our lives would be very short. Fear is the messenger of danger. When charismatic hymns were becoming popular, there was one which included the line 'Let me climb every mountain without fear'. I always prayed to be exempted from this godly request! But fear, when used as a method of controlling others, becomes violence, and violence promotes violence, leaving irreparable damage behind. 'Primitive' peoples were well aware of this fact and that is why their societies had so many and such complicated 'taboos'. The taboos were to safeguard the people against situations that were likely to promote violence causing widespread destruction. Today, in our modern societies, we have lost that sensitivity.

We have the simplistic belief that violence can only be overcome by greater violence. Hence we live with a nuclear defence policy. The very means that we employ to ensure our national safety is the very means that imperils all human life on earth.

The point of writing this is not scaremongering; it is to enable us to become more aware of the reality in which we are living. I write it because in spite of all the crises, the falseness, the escalating violence of today, I see hope for the future. The hope is not a fantasy I have created: it is something I have discovered and am still discovering. It is open and freely given to every human being. It lies in our own experience. We live in a world where our own experience is discounted, not valued. We believe in experts, successful people with lots of impressive qualifications. They, we think, are the people to trust. Consequently, we ignore the value of our own experience, our own freedom, and become model citizens for a totalitarian state. This is happening to us at the moment. It was through an interest in Unity, and then in Peace, that I began to see everything differently. I want to share this story with others in order to pass on this news. What is important for each of us is our story. To get in touch with it we have to start with our own personal experience. This will not close us up in our own ego: it will free us from it, revealing a life which is far more interesting, attractive, alive and peaceful because it is revealing to us our real identity. We are not solitary human beings, struggling against impossible odds to live: we belong to something far greater than our solitary self. We are related creatures who are in a state of continuous becoming through, and only through, our relating. What is it I am becoming? I am becoming at-one-with-God in whom all creation exists, a God who is the answer to the restlessness of my heart.

The reader may find even a short description of this unlocking to be boring, a quaint example of outdated thinking with little or no relevance to today. It was not irrelevant to me at the time it happened. It disturbed me and was threatening my religious belief, to the 19 years I had already spent as a Jesuit, and to the rest of my life, which I had vowed to live as a Jesuit. The fundamental question, although I was not aware of this until later, was about the existence of God and, even more important, about the nature of God.

The immediate question that arose for me in the wake of the Easter Sunday event at Stoneyhurst was this: Is it not a more serious offence against God and these boys that I should encourage them to celebrate the Feast of the Resurrection with a military parade than the offence the boys committed by painting CND logos on the playground wall and setting the dais, on which the Rector was to stand while they gave him a military salute, on the pond with a tree for mast and bedsheets for sails? This question was like opening Pandora's Box: it led to a host of disturbing questions.

What troubled me at first over the Peace issue was that I was aware of the magnificent heroism and generosity of those who had, in all good conscience, fought and died in the two world wars of 1914–18 and 1939–45. Some of them were personal friends, school contemporaries. Condemning war seemed to be an insult to those generous people and to their families still grieving their loss. Briefly, I admired and was grateful for the heroic generosity on the one hand; on the other hand, I deplored all glorification of war, both by State and by Church – a glorification that still continues today and promotes the spread of violence which, of its nature, feeds on violence and becomes uncontrollable. Could this 'Just War' teaching of the Catholic Church be wrong after all these centuries since Augustine first formulated the argument 14 centuries ago? Were my doubts about this doctrine a sign of my lack of faith? With my upbringing, these were terrifying doubts. Because I was so accustomed to compartmental thinking, I could put these questions aside and carry on 'normally'.

Another of the questions was my whole attitude to war. I can remember a conversation with my eldest sister, Marie, in 1940, when I had first begun to feel drawn to priesthood. In that year, Mount St Mary's offered a scholarship to boys who were about to begin what were called Advanced level studies. This was a two-year specialized course in either science or humanities subjects. I had chosen to do science because I wanted to study medicine later. The scholarship being offered would pay for the winner his school fees for the following two years. Thinking I might have a chance of winning this scholarship, I began putting in extra time in study. To give a boost to my study I thought a little extra prayer might help. In those days that meant for me reciting well-known prayers which I knew by heart. After a month or so of this, I slowly began to experience something attractive in prayer. I could, occasionally, stop gabbling like a parrot, be silent and talk to God familiarly.

I failed to win the scholarship, but it was then I began to think of becoming a priest. The inclination came and went in waves, because I also wanted to become a fighter pilot in the RAF. I confessed this to Marie and her immediate response was: 'But you may be killed if you go into the RAF.' I can also remember my reply: 'What does that matter? If I do get killed I shall go to heaven for giving my life for King and Country!'

I look back on this conversation 73 years later and I realize how in my upbringing I had been amply supplied with unquestionable certainties, which affected the decisions I made, the actions I took, the course of life I chose, convinced that I was free in my choices. When these certainties begin to crumble, life can become very threatening.

As I have mentioned, one of the questions which unsettled me in the aftermath of the parade ground offence was the Catholic acceptance of the Just War theory. As this question will recur throughout Part 2 of this book, I shall give a brief explanation of the theory here.

The early Christian Church was opposed to war and to armed participation in war. After Christianity became the Religion of the Empire under the Emperor Constantine in 323AD, St Augustine of Hippo in North Africa introduced the notion of 'Just War' to legitimize defence of the Empire against the attacks of its enemies. Both this early doctrine and its development into modern times is an attempt to strengthen agreement in the search for international peace.

Augustine's Just War theory persisted in Christianity. It was endorsed and developed by St Thomas Aquinas (1225–74) and a version of it appears in the Catholic Catechism of 1994 as the current teaching of the Catholic Church. Here is an excerpt from that Catechism:

> The strict conditions for legitimate defence by military force require rigorous consideration. The gravity of such a decision makes it subject to rigorous conditions of moral legitimacy. At one and the same time:
>
> - The damage inflicted by the aggressor on the nation or group of nations it attacks must be lasting, grave and certain.
>
> - All the other means of putting an end to it must have been shown to be impractical or ineffective.
>
> - There must be serious prospect of success.
>
> - The use of arms must not produce evils and disorders graver than the evil to be eliminated. The power of modern means of destruction weighs very heavily in evaluating this condition.
>
> *These are the traditional elements enumerated in what is called 'Just War' doctrine.*
>
> The evaluation of these conditions for moral legitimacy belongs

to the prudential judgement of those who have responsibility
for the common good.

§2309 Catechism of the Catholic Church

I give this excerpt from the Catholic Catechism here to show how the
term 'Just War' is presented in the Catholic Catechism of 1994. I do not
give it as a personal opinion, nor as a possible justification for modern
warfare with nuclear, or even with conventional weapons. I include it
here as an example of one of the troubling questions which arose for
me soon after Easter Sunday 1961. These questions came gradually. I
was able to function 'normally', with common sense firmly in charge.

Other questions which arose for me at this time were more fundamental than the Just War theory; they concerned the very nature of
religious belief in general, and of Catholic belief in particular. These
many and varied questions all concerned the split nature of our
Christian belief.

Common to all three parts of this book is this theme of 'The Split
Nature of our Spirituality'. Briefly, the phrase means the split which
there is between the reality that we experience in daily life and the
meaning of life as it is expressed in religious language. It is as though we
have been introduced to two very different worlds. One is intangible,
invisible, inaudible, pure spirit but, we are assured, of fundamental
importance; the other is the physical world, our bodily existence in
a visible, material world, with which we are continuously interacting.
This part is considered of less importance, 'purely natural', as distinct
from the higher world of the 'supernatural'. The manner in which we
are trained to think of language illustrates the split. For example, take
this modern dictionary description of 'Spiritual', which can be found in
Collins English Dictionary of 1979:

> **Spiritual** – relating to the spirit or soul and not to physical nature
> or matter; intangible.
> – of, relating to, or characteristic of sacred things, the Church,
> religion etc.
> – having a mind or emotions of a high and delicately refined quality.

Defining spiritual in this way can make the distinction between the
spiritual and the material appear to be very clear. In fact, this description
throws new light on our modern crises. By separating God, religion
etc. from everything material, people believe that we are now relieved

of a heavy and dangerous burden in our post-Christian, post-religion, postmodern world. However, the prevalence of this false distinction between the material and the spiritual has enabled others, of all religions and of none, and people who have had little or no formal education, to give more attention to the miracle of this 'matter', leading them to appreciate that matter itself is the source of what we call the spiritual. Again, by the way we have become accustomed to distinguish 'spiritual' from 'material', what I have just written can be interpreted as a reduction of everything to materialism and denying God and the supernatural!

By breaking through this lumpish notion of inert matter in which we have been educated, we can slowly begin to understand religious language in a very different way. This breakthrough leads to a new understanding of our present condition and of God, who sustains us in it at every moment of our existence. This God is not a remote, impersonal, fearful figure. This God is manifesting Godself to us in and through our material existence – not in spite of it. In Christian understanding, God did so uniquely in Jesus Christ, 'the first-born of all creation', as St Paul writes of him in Colossians 1.15. 'He is the image of the unseen God, the first-born of all creation.' The Good News is that Incarnation is not a gift exclusively given to Jesus Christ: the gift is given to Jesus, but it is also God's sharing of God's very Self with each one of us.

This manifestation continues throughout the ages: it is happening now in every single human being without exception. We are already living the life of God. St Paul's letters now suddenly come to life – for example, his telling the Ephesians:

> May your inner selves grow strong, so that Christ may live in your hearts through faith, so that grounded in love and based on love, you may with all the saints have strength to grasp the breadth and the length, the height and the depth until, knowing the love of Christ, which is beyond all knowledge, you are filled with the utter fullness of God. Glory be to God, whose power working in us can do infinitely more than we can think or imagine. (Eph. 3.14-21)

I now relate an event from 1974 which I now recognize, 39 years later, as having influenced all my subsequent decisions and it is still doing so. I relate this to emphasize the importance of our own experience as life's most precious gift to each of us, yet we live in a world which teaches us to distrust our own experience and be guided by the 'experts'. As life becomes more complex in our advanced technological world, we are frequently reminded of our own incompetence and inability and so come to discount our own experience. If this tendency continues, then we are preparing ourselves for totalitarian rule in the future without realizing that this is what we are doing. I shall be developing this theme later with regard to our national policy of nuclear defence. In describing this event, the only point I want to make applies to every human being. We must pay attention to our own experience: it is our unique source of wisdom, our hidden treasure of life. Part 3 of this book will be focusing on this topic in much greater detail.

In 1974, I was invited to a function at Glasgow University where I found myself sitting opposite a splendid figure of a man, magnificently dressed in US naval uniform. He was a submarine commander, based at Holy Loch on the Firth of Clyde, then the base for a fleet of Polaris nuclear submarines, which patrolled from there to the open sea and to the oceans of the world. The submarine commander was very affable and spoke eloquently throughout the meal of the devastating power of his wonderful machine, how far it could travel underwater and how fast, the range and destructive capability of its weaponry. He seemed to have all the desirable qualities required of a man in his position. He had a perfectly sealed and compartmentalized consciousness, which enabled him to describe these flying ovens, each of its many warheads many times more powerful than the bomb that devastated Hiroshima. The commander could relate the power of his bombs while eating his meal with obvious relish. That is a memory I can never forget because it brings with it a very sobering insight, not just about the submarine commander, but about any of us. It is possible for all of us to be trained to ignore or disregard aspects of our consciousness with such completeness that we can successfully deceive ourselves, convincing ourselves of the virtuous nature of planning and executing the mass murder of those who threaten us, or whom we suspect of doing so.

A year after this event, I had been invited by the Way Community, to which I had now been assigned, to spend a few months in Rome to do some research in the Jesuit Centre of Spirituality on how the early Jesuits gave Ignatius' Spiritual Exercises. I was free from the Glasgow Chaplaincy from the beginning of May, but was advised against going to Rome in June, July or August because most libraries would be shut and the Jesuits I hoped to meet, who were already giving the Exercises individually in a variety of ways, were likely to be away in cooler climates for the summer. Consequently, I thought of walking to Rome in the summer months and was allowed to do so. In preparation for the walk, to test my fitness for long-distance walking, I planned a cross-country route from Glasgow to the Highlands. It was on the first afternoon of this trial walk that the event happened. I began by taking a ferry from Gourock, on the south coast of the Firth of Clyde, to Dunoon on the north coast – a short sail.

As I climbed the hills above Dunoon on a perfect day in May 1975, I could look down on the Holy Loch which, since 1961, had become the only base outside the US for American Polaris submarines. The sea was deep blue and as smooth as glass. I did not see any of the submarines, but I imagined a periscope moving slowly across the loch, leaving a sparkling, triangular trace of water in its track. On the surface it was a scene of great beauty, of calm, deep blue sea, the hills covered in the fresh colours of spring, gulls gliding and wheeling against the background of a cloudless sky. Beneath the surface of the sparkling traces of the periscope was the silent submarine, a magnificent piece of human engineering, holding in its torpedo launchers nuclear warheads, each warhead many times more powerful than the bomb dropped on Hiroshima 30 years earlier, devastating the city in seconds, killing over 100,000 people instantly, the vast majority being non-combatants, many of them vaporized by the intense heat of the blast which exceeded the heat of the sun itself, leaving only shadows on the roadway to mark their passing. Within a very short space of time, another 100,000 were to die of the radiation and the horrific wounds inflicted through the bombing. There are still people living today born with deformities inherited from their parents, who were genetically and permanently damaged by the radiation.

This image lingers because it illustrates horrendously that nothing can be judged simply on its appearances. The truth is so obvious that we can dismiss it as a banal platitude, while failing to notice how easily and consciously all of us can be caught up in virtual reality. Our present worldwide financial crisis is another example of this phenomenon in which bankers and their clients were caught up in transactions not of wealth, but the appearance of wealth – billions of pounds of paper money promising wealth, but delivering disaster, irreparable debt and inescapable poverty for the majority.

This image also raises a further question. Once it is planted in the mind, it can then explore not only questions of peace and war, but every aspect of our lives, even the apparently trivial. The question which the image poses is very simple: where is the source of the destructiveness of these nuclear warheads? The source was not in the submarine itself, nor in its weaponry, nor even in its nuclear warheads, for these are all manufactured things incapable, in themselves, of being responsible for anything. Nor was the source of the destructiveness to be found in the crew and captain of the submarine, nor in the President of the USA, although they were all instrumental in its operations.

The source of the destruction lies in the human minds of all those who have been involved in the design, manufacture, use of the submarine and in the minds of all those who support the construction, possession and use of our nuclear weaponry.

This is not an attempt to answer the question, 'Who is to blame?' It is a much more general question, namely, where is the source of the destruction caused, or which can be caused, by nuclear weaponry? The answer to such a question is also, necessarily, general, and it is: 'The answer lies in the human mind and heart.'

If this line of reasoning, as far as it goes, is ruled out as being too vague to be of any practical value, then we have to ask: 'Is it legitimate to ask an even more general question, covering all forms of human violence? Where are the roots of human violence? This question underlies all that I write in this section. I do not write because I think I have the answers: I write because though I have often found pursuit of this question troublesome and frustrating and threatening, it has given me a glimpse, a different way of seeing the reality in which I find myself, and it is a glimpse which reveals a very different God, Church, planet, Universe, a glimpse which transforms everything and brings hope and trust because, as St Paul wrote to the Ephesians, 'God's power working within us can do infinitely more than we can ask or imagine' (Eph. 3.20).

I will end this chapter by telling of another event which I experienced in 1974, a year before I left the Glasgow Chaplaincy. Again I did not realize its importance at the time, yet it has influenced me over all these years.

My eight years as chaplain to Catholics at Glasgow University were very eventful. They deepened my awareness of my own dependence and fragility – a painful process – yet in spite of all the crises and uncertainty, I was and still am deeply grateful for them. They did not change anything, but they enabled me to start seeing everything differently. This memory can sum up the nature of this process.

I had been told about a small deserted island off the west coast of Scotland, called Eileach an Naoimh ('The Rocky Island of the Saints'), not far from Iona, the well-known pilgrimage centre, which lies to the south of the Isle of Mull. I went to Eileach an Naoimh to make an eight-day retreat, equipped with a tent and food and emergency water supplies to last eight days. On the evening I arrived, heavy clouds were gathering. When I awoke next morning, the island was enclosed in thick mist. I tried to cook porridge in the rain, then sat outside the dripping tent holding a cup of coffee, wondering what madness had led me to risk eight days here. Within an hour the mist began to clear and slowly the stunning beauty of this island was revealed behind the thick veil of mist. On reflection later, this one-hour experience summed up what had been happening in the 14 years, both at Stonyhurst and in Glasgow. Beneath the fears and doubts and anxieties, I had begun to see the same reality very differently. God had, as it were, emerged from the box and was now running free everywhere.

God is not an external phenomenon, an object, not even 'The Other'. God *is*. No human categories can adequately describe God, who is always greater, God in whom all creation has its being, the ground of all being, who pervades all things, permeates all things, binds all things in unity, but is bound by nothing. There is no place, no situation where God is not, no place we can find where we can escape from God. Although we can never definitely state who God is and what God is like, 'irrepressible' is a useful word; God cannot be kept out, even by our most earnest and popular atheists. I love this quotation from the Anglican Canon Max Warren. The quotation is from a preface he wrote for a book on Islam, and it includes: 'Our first task in approaching another people, another culture, another religion, is to take off our shoes, for the place we are approaching is holy. Else we may find ourselves treading on another's dreams. More serious still, we may forget that God was there before our arrival.'

Karl Rahner, one of the foremost theologians of the twentieth century, reflecting on the present state of religion and spirituality in developed countries, reckoned that for survival in the future, all Catholics would have to become mystics! As I shall show in Part 3, the phenomenon of mysticism is not a human state of being which means no resistance under any circumstances. In fact, mysticism is a human state, essentially opposed to all forms of human oppression, rejection, classification of human beings into bad or good, worthless or worthy, free or slave. True mysticism is essentially resistant to all attempts to devalue the unique worth of any human being. The mystics do not see themselves as individual monads struggling to defend themselves against a hostile, sinful world, taking up residence in remote forests, or in caves, in monasteries or convents of strict observance, where they can live in seclusion and blissful unawareness of the bloody, raging wars and oppression afflicting the rest of humankind while they enjoy beautiful experiences of God. I have met many people from many different walks of life who show signs of mystic gifts. One sign of genuine mystic tendencies in human beings is their ability to give their full attention to their present situation, or to the individual or group they engage with. They also have an acute awareness of the suffering of others, and their compassion is practical, simple and wholehearted – an attitude to which people in deep distress are usually very sensitive. Rahner believed that every human being has the potential to be a mystic. I also believe this to be true, not because Rahner has said so, but because I have experienced this truth in my encounters with people who would never have claimed to have any spiritual gifts themselves.

Exercises

- Did anything in this chapter arouse a strongly felt reaction?
- Can you connect that reaction with anything in your past or present experience?
- Can you spot any connection between your responses and the more general crises of our own day?

2

Peace connects with every aspect of human life

Chapter 1 was by way of introduction to Part 2. The following chapters look at particular aspects of Peace. This chapter focuses on the essential connectedness of Peace with every aspect of human life.

In writing this chapter, I introduce a method called 'Listening with your Midriff'. It is a method of finding Peace in conflict, which enables us to learn about peace by observing our own felt reactions.

Why is listening with our midriff so important? It is because our felt reactions, if we can learn to notice them, are in many respects far more intelligent than our conscious minds. It was my own experience which taught me this, when I began giving Ignatius of Loyola's Spiritual Exercises individually to people instead of through lectures to large groups. I introduced this method of retreat by practising midriff listening with those about to make this kind of retreat for the first time.

In the preamble to *Cry of Wonder*, on page ix, I have given methods of becoming aware of our felt reactions, especially on page xiv, 'Review of the Day'. The exercises at the end of each chapter are also designed to make us more aware of our felt reactions. The learning comes from DOING the exercises, NOT from reading about them. Remember the Rabbinic saying: 'Do and you will understand.'

When I began to learn to listen very carefully when helping others to pray and to avoid lengthy instructions, I was constantly amazed at what I learned about the wisdom of our felt reactions. In early sessions of one-to-one work, I discovered that what people said in giving their felt reactions to what had happened in their prayer almost always indicated what was going to occupy them in the rest of their retreat.

It was as though their feelings and emotions could sense what was happening to them long before their conscious minds became aware of what was happening.

Here is just one example. A person who had given up churchgoing for many years came for an eight-day retreat. I gave her an imaginative exercise, an imaginary encounter with this character, Jesus of Nazareth. What she experienced in that encounter kept her fully occupied for the eight days! She began to find herself, and in so doing her view of everything else began to change. Feelings and emotions, occasioned by particular events, can become precious indications for our direction in life.

One way of getting in touch with our own feelings and emotions is through giving our attention to the word 'Peace'. In my own experience, the word has been, like 'Unity/Ecumenism', a door opening out onto a new, strange and fascinating world. The world I now see is not something new: it is exactly as it was, but I now see it in a new way, which is always developing, never static. All we have to do is notice these feelings when they come knocking at the door of our consciousness. In reading this book, when you feel you have read enough for one session – and it does not matter how much or how little you have read – then spend a few moments just noting any felt reaction, however slight, and make a brief note of it. In this way we are beginning to listen to ourselves and discover we are also beginning to listen with greater interest to others.

How is Peace connected to every aspect of our everyday life? Here are some examples:

Where are the roots of violence to be found?

'Peace' raises an enormous number of very complex questions – about human relations between individuals, groups, nations, religions, ideologies, race, ethnicity etc. In a way, these are very superficial questions, for the root question goes beyond all these categories. The answer is not to be found by sticking labels on people: the root of the question lies in each individual, in our intellectual, emotional and spiritual character. The point of this question is not to discover a neat and clever answer. The point is to help us to become more aware of the vast complexity which underlies this word 'Peace'. Exploring the question can lift our range of awareness beyond its customary boundaries. It can reintroduce us to something we possessed in our younger days, when every day was full of wonder and we were full of questions. Education can be presented to us in a way that stifles our sense of wonder, our ability to be surprised, our endless questioning. If we do not accept this method of education we may be categorized as stupid, slow, lazy and a dreamer! The damage is done when we assume these categories, inflicted on us by others, are true, pay no attention to our own personal experience and surrender ourselves to the 'experts'.

In the previous chapter I gave many examples of the way in which memories of events I had experienced in the past, but scarcely noticed at the time, returned years later, sending me off in search of 'Peace', and enabled me to begin to see things differently and to react differently. In reading this chapter, does any simple step occur to you that you might take? It does not need to be something dramatic or risky. It might be something very simple – perhaps keeping a record of your main felt reactions during the day.

Through a little exploration of your felt reactions, you will begin to become more aware of the interconnectedness of things – how, for example, a simple misunderstanding can quickly develop into a major row within the family which can last for days, or even months and years, or how some unexpected gift from someone can raise tired spirits and infect all with energy. The other area of interconnectedness, of which you will become aware, is the interconnectedness inside you, between your own inner conflicts and your outward behaviour. This is a most important connection to notice. If we fail to do so, we shall start to blame other people for our own failures, a major source of violence within all of us. To illustrate this point, here is a quotation from a remarkable and, in the West, a little-known character. His name is Seraphim of Sarov (1759–1833), an Orthodox monk, who lived for many years as a hermit. He lived in a remote and wild part of the country, populated by bears and wolves, whom he befriended. They defended him from human visitors! He eventually returned to his monastery and became renowned as a spiritual director. News of his extraordinary gifts travelled by word of mouth. When he died, the Tsar and Tsarina of Russia attended his funeral. He wrote little himself, but his admirers took notes of his discourses. One of his discourses is on 'Gentleness'. I give here the English translation I found on Google:

You cannot be too gentle, too kind. Shun even to appear harsh in your treatment of each other. Joy, radiant joy, streams from the face of him who gives and kindles joy in the heart of him who receives.

All condemnation is from the devil. Never condemn each other. We condemn others only because we shun knowing ourselves. When we gaze at our own failings, we see such a swamp that nothing in the other can equal it.

That is why we turn away, and make much of the faults of others. Instead of condemning others, strive to reach inner peace. Keep silent, refrain from judgement. This will raise you above the deadly arrows of slander, insult and outrage and will shield your glowing hearts against all evil.

(St Seraphim of Sarov Orthodox Church [1759–1833] http://enlarg-ingthe heart.wordpress.com)

When first I came across this quotation, I found it too extreme and exaggerated, particularly the phrase 'When we gaze at our own failings, we see such a swamp that nothing in the other can equal it'. I also disliked, and still do, the sexist language in the translation from Russian. Many years and many experiences later, I began to appreciate Seraphim, especially the advice 'Instead of condemning others, strive to reach inner peace'. Here we are getting to the heart of the matter in finding peace in conflict. It is something all of us need to practise daily. Yes, peace really does relate to every moment of every individual's life, affecting all of us for better or for worse.

The ambiguity of the word 'Peace'

This is not a quibble about words: it has most important practical impli-cations for every human being. The Roman Emperors had a saying: 'To preserve peace, prepare for war'. The Romans were expert in building empires – their empire included the whole of Europe and beyond. The legacy of their policies still influences us today, two thousand years later. This influence includes our national policies on defence. No political party in Britain today, with a serious intention of becoming the ruling party, can dare to oppose our nuclear defence policy. The British Labour party was anti-nuclear and was out of power for 17 years. It then changed its defence policy under Prime Minister Blair. The Catholic

Church, as we have seen in its recent Catechism, does not condemn nuclear defence in its 'Just War' theory. George W. Bush, in declaring war on Iraq, declared 'The war in Iraq is peace work'! Yes, the word Peace is certainly ambiguous!

The Roman dictum, 'To preserve peace, prepare for war', has become a principle faithfully followed by almost all nations and all religions ever since. We are now touching on an enormous and very complex topic. All I want to do here is to point out that for Christian believers we have a most fundamental question to ask ourselves, a question we carefully avoid. This avoidance both compromises ourselves, misrepresents Christ's teaching, and is already bringing destruction through hunger and malnutrition on roughly one billion people. The question is: what is my response to this dictum? No, this is not a quibble about words!

St John's Gospel describes the appearance of the Risen Lord to his disciples on the Sunday evening after his death on the cross on Good Friday:

> In the evening of that same day, the first day of the week, the doors were closed in the room where the disciples were for fear of the Jews. Jesus came and stood among them. He said to them 'Peace be with you', and showed them his hands and his side. The disciples were filled with joy when they saw the Lord, and he said to them again, 'Peace be with you. As the Father sent me, so I am sending you.' (Jn 20.19-21)

The word for 'peace', 'shalom', in Hebrew has a much richer meaning than in English. It is a greeting which includes both the wellbeing of the person so addressed, their relationship with all those they encounter, and finally their relationship with God. As Jesus gives this greeting he shows them his hands and his side. Jesus' peace comes through his vulnerability: the world's peace comes through trying to make ourselves invulnerable. 'In his wounds we are healed.'

Is there any truth in what has been said here? In the early Christian Church, Christians were not allowed to serve in the army. After the emperor Constantine declared Christianity to be the religion of the Empire in the fourth century, I have read, only Christians could serve in the army. It was after this, when the Roman Empire was being threatened on all sides by the Goths and Visi-Goths, that St Augustine produced his Just War theory.

To illustrate briefly the importance of this question, take a text describing Jesus' temptations in the desert after he had been fasting. Here is the text in St Matthew's Gospel:

> Then Jesus was led by the Spirit out into the wilderness to be tempted by the devil. He fasted forty days and forty nights, after which he was very hungry, and the tempter came and said to him, 'if you are the Son of God, tell these stones to turn into loaves'. But he replied, '*Scripture says: Man does not live on bread alone but on every word that comes from the mouth of God*'.
>
> The devil then took him to the holy city and made him stand on the parapet of the Temple. '*If you are the Son of God*' he said, '*throw yourself down; for Scripture says: He will put you in his angels' charge, and they will support you on their hands in case you hurt your foot against a stone*'. Jesus said to him, 'Scripture also says: *You must not put the Lord your God to the test*'.
>
> Next, taking him to a very high mountain, the devil showed him all the kingdoms of the world and their splendour. 'I will give you all these' he said, 'if you fall at my feet and worship me.' Then Jesus replied, 'Be off, Satan! For Scripture says: *You must worship the Lord Your God, and serve him alone.*' Then the devil left him, and the angels appeared and looked after him. (Mt. 4.1-11)

This passage is giving the essential difference between God's power and the power of Evil. The power of evil is a power that controls, robs people of their dignity and their uniqueness as human beings, treats them as means in the service of their rulers: the power of God is the power of love, of compassion, of truth, of peace. St Luke's Acts of the Apostles illustrates this truth in his account of those early Christians, who learned the meaning of God's Spirit in their own lives, surrendering their lives to the promotion of God's Kingdom on earth and discovering an inner peace which nothing could shatter, whatever the conflicts they encountered.

The revolutionary nature of Jesus' Sermon on the Mount. Why has it been so successfully muffled?

To present this question briefly I shall concentrate on a half-sentence from the Gospel of St Luke, ch. 5 v. 20, which reads:

How happy are you who are poor: yours is the Kingdom of God.

St Luke's Gospel, like his Acts of the Apostles, is written in Greek. Greek is a very expressive language. It has many different words, for example, for happiness, for poverty and for love, not to mention its many words for God. Consequently, the English translation 'How happy are you who are poor: yours is the Kingdom of God' can sound bland, can easily slip off the tongue. The English phrase is not likely to leave us thunderstruck, or holding our head in our hands lest it explode with the power of the words. So now we shall have a short Greek lesson!

The Greeks have a rich variety of words for our word 'happy'. The ultimate in happiness, a happiness which nothing can shatter, is called '*makaria*'. It is the happiness of those who have passed beyond this life and now inhabit the Isles of the Blest. This is the happiness which Jesus is offering to the huge crowds following him to be cured of their physical and spiritual afflictions. This is not mere contentment. The *makarioi* (men) and the *makariai* (women) are bubbling with life. We might translate the word into English as 'blissfully happy', for they are in a state of happiness which cannot be surpassed: it is indestructible.

Similarly the Greeks have many different words for 'poor'. The Greek word used here means utterly destitute, the poorest of the poor, totally dependent, without help, without hope. So the first part of the sentence could now be translated into 'Blissfully happy are the utterly destitute'.

In general, the Hebrew Scriptures avoid use of the sacred name 'Yahweh', the name God reveals to Moses and is translated 'I am who I am'. The phrase 'the Kingdom of God' could be translated 'the life of God', so the whole phrase now reads, 'Blissfully happy are the utterly destitute for they are in the life of God'.

This is a startling statement, like so many of the statements in this Jesus manifesto. The shock can disappear when commentators assure us that the Hebrew prophets used exaggeration deliberately. The prophets did use exaggeration in this way. The danger is that we can then dismiss anything in the Sermon on the Mount that causes us discomfort as an exaggeration, and we do not feel the need to give it any more attention. So we do not have to worry about turning the other cheek, loving our enemies, giving our tunic to the person who has already stolen our cloak, or about lending even when we know there is no hope of return. Being efficient, practical, sensible are the attitudes we value above all. We can now live within our walls of personal security, relegating religion and spirituality to certain religious practices which we perform as if that is all that God wants from us. In this way we can keep God at a safe distance and ensure God's non-interference in our daily living. All of us can become very expert at doing this.

What Christian revelation is telling us is that God's omnipotence does extend to everything, but it is God's love which is omnipotent, the love made manifest in Jesus Christ and through Him offered to all humankind. God is not bound by space and time. God is. Consequently phrases like 'eternal God' do not mean a God who goes on and on without end: God is always in the present, as present now to us as God was present to Abraham, Isaac, Jacob and to Jesus of Nazareth. And this God is offering us a share in God's own life now, an offer which will never be withdrawn. We can experience this fact in our lives.

The key question for all of us in this process is 'What is my basic desire in life?' and to keep asking the same question. The search is a lifelong process: the question has to percolate its way through our many layers of consciousness. It can be a very painful, threatening and fearful search, because it reveals to us truths about ourselves which we would rather not know. We become aware of our own weakness, our own fragility, our own helplessness. We are on the road to making the discovery that Seraphim of Sarov made and which led him to speak on Gentleness, an attitude which permeated every moment of his life. It was the road which St Paul travelled and which brought him to write: 'I have been crucified with Christ, and I live now not with my own life, but with the life of Christ who lives in me' (Gal. 2.20).

Our Christian life is about abandonment of our whole being to God, about losing our life in this way so that we can find life, our true life, a life in God which is a life of love, of truth, of compassion. It is in the experience of this attraction that we also, slowly, become aware of our utter inability to live out, in practice, what is so powerfully attracting us. If we can bring all this into prayer, acknowledge our complete inability to live the life we long to live, to give our lives that others may live, to find the freedom to be what we most deeply desire to be, then we shall know our only response is to fling ourselves into the arms of this living God and so find ourselves at home in God, within ourselves and also with all creation, including our enemies!

A twentieth-century example of a peace activist whose life affected all aspects of human life

'The Christian Church cannot contribute to world peace until it finds peace and reconciliation within itself.'

Quotation from Fr Max Josef Metzger, executed by the Nazi government in 1944.

Max Josef Metzger was a remarkable prophet of our times (born 3 February 1887 in Schopfheim in Baden, Germany; executed by the Nazis, 17 April 1944). He was brought up by devout Catholic parents. His father was a very severe man and it may have been his controlling manner which brought out a passion for freedom in his son. Max Josef entered a Junior seminary, was ordained in his early twenties and became a military chaplain in the First World War. He was decorated for bravery, and later allowed to leave the army because of the lung damage he had suffered. He came out of the army in 1916, a confirmed pacifist, having witnessed, at first hand, the brutality of it all. 'Future wars have lost their meaning,' he wrote later, 'since they no longer give anybody the prospect of winning more than they lose.'

After the war he worked for peace, both nationally and internationally. During the war he had already been sending peace proposals to Pope Benedict XV, proposals which were well received and their substance included in Benedict's later encyclical pleading for peace in the First World War.

Brought up in Bavaria, Max enjoyed wine and beer, but when he saw the enormous social damage it was doing, not only to the drinkers but to their families and children, he renounced drink himself and campaigned against its misuse, while recognizing the benefits of controlled drinking and not demanding temperance from anyone else This was not a popular cause among his fellow clergy, where he had many enemies. One of his own diocesan chancellors told him: 'Listen, our attitude is that if a priest prays his breviary, says Mass correctly and correctly prepares himself for preaching and catechetics, that is absolutely enough – there is no need for any further organizations when we have this pastoral care.'

I give this quotation because it sums up an attitude to and understanding of Christianity which is pernicious, destructive of the very essence of Christianity, yet still passes for orthodoxy in many parts of the Church today. It is not a view uniquely reserved to Germany: it is to be found in every country. Nor is it reserved to clergy. It can infect any human being. Metzger had to face this type of opposition throughout his life, but his faith was not superficial. It was a trust in his heart in the reality of God at work throughout creation and in every person, a God of infinite love and compassion, a God of peace and of justice. It was this faith which gave him such resilience in conflict, such breadth of understanding and the ability to forgive his many enemies from his heart without any trace of bitterness.

It was through his work on Peace that he began to see the need for Ecumenism/Unity within the Christian Church. If the Church could not become reconciled within itself, it could have no contribution to make to world peace. He saw 'service of others' as an essential of Catholic priesthood, the 'others' being all human beings, especially those in need. For this to happen, he also saw the need for a radical reform of Church structures, breaking down the barriers which separate clergy from laity, enabling the laity to exercise their ministry of priesthood to one another, conferred on them through baptism, but forgotten in our times.

Metzger set up many organizations for laity, who could choose different forms of commitment which they were ready to make for serving the needs of the poor. These were forerunners of the 'Secular Institutes' which exist today, modern forms of religious life for lay people, who bind themselves with a vow of poverty, expressed in service with the poor. He also saw that Marxists were quicker than Christians in detecting human needs and answering them – an insight which did not please the Catholic hierarchy of his day.

Fifty years before Vatican II, Metzger foresaw the need for it and lived with that vision throughout his life, undeterred by the opposition, lack of support and, at times, the hostility he met with frequently from his own clergy, for many of whom enthusiasm for Ecumenism/Unity was a sign of weak faith in any Catholic.

Here is one quotation from him showing his passion for peace. It is his own commentary on an address he had given in Graz on the last Sunday of January 1917, during the Great War:

> It is as if the dumb crosses on all of the hundreds of thousands of mass graves were opened and as if hundreds of thousands of wooden crosses marched at the head of a procession of death

of numberless flowering youthful lives which were cut down so early, as if all the millions of widows and orphans joined the tragic procession ... Thus did I speak and I asked, 'Why is there no Peace?' Is there no possibility of understanding? And again I said 'Peace!' 'How humanity longs for the blessing of Peace!' 'You heavens, rain down the just: You clouds, pour him forth.'

He wrote later: 'I then developed a programme in which all Catholics of all lands can and must unite themselves – the International Peace programme.' The programme called for an end to the useless pouring out of blood on the battlefields and, at the same time, an end to the politics which obscure the problems caused by the clash of nations locked in power struggles and, consequently, condemning humanity to a constant series of wars.

He also said: 'We demand an orientation of youth education which will avoid all chauvinism, all fostering of the spirit of war, a re-orientation which will awaken the awareness of social obligations, truthfulness, honesty, selflessness, justice, fraternal love, readiness to help others, social responsibility.'

His Peace programme also included the plea 'for the elimination of all power politics from the entire social and political life of the nations'. One Protestant pastor, commenting on these words of Metzger, wrote: 'This peace programme, which all Catholics should be proud of, unfortunately could be read only in the democratic press.'

In Metzger's ecumenical work, which grew out of his Peace work, he began with Lutherans, but other Christian denominations soon joined in a movement called 'Una Sancta' – a movement which eventually produced the annual 'Prayer for Church Unity Week' now held annually throughout the world in January.

The Christian Churches have made enormous progress in moving towards more faith-filled and human relations in the last century, but I do not believe Max Josef Metzger is overjoyed when he sees the state of Ecumenism/Unity today. Yes, we are more polite to one another than we used to be, but we have regressed from the euphoric period in the 1960s following Vatican II. We exchange polite bows across four centuries, as in my youth in the 1920s, but we still avoid following the wonderful pledge between the Christian Churches made at Lund, Sweden, in 1952 at the Faith and Order Conference of the World Council of Churches. The pledge was that we would never pursue any course of Christian action or teaching separately which we could possibly do together. If Max Josef were to rise from his grave today, he would have some difficulty in finding obvious signs of the Lund principle at work throughout today's Church in the developed countries.

In 1928, Metzger spoke at an international day on Peace at The Hague, 'Peace in the Kingdom of Christ'. 'Why', he asked, 'in spite of all our efforts to suppress discussion of it, does the spectre of Peace never disappear? [...] We have neglected establishing the Kingdom of God on earth, a Kingdom of truth, of justice and of love [...] Untruthful diplomacy has built a chasm of distrust between all peoples, so deep that statesmen always conclude non-aggression pacts and immediately sharpen their daggers which they have hidden under the folds of their cloaks [...] "If you want peace, prepare for war" – this Roman imperial advice for all emperors is the arch pagan principle which is still embedded in Christian statesmen.'

'*Justitia fundamentum regnorum*' was the inscription above the city gate of Vienna: 'Justice is the foundation stone of kingdoms'. Metzger could preach his peace message pithily. 'The kingdom of Satan means war: The kingdom of God means peace. Now choose!'

In 1934, as a result of Metzger's years of efforts, there was an Ecumenical meeting held in Germany in which the Protestant Churches stated that most of their differences with Roman Catholics were canonical – questions of Church laws and regulations – rather than questions of doctrine. They gave as examples the Catholic Church's insistence on Latin in Eucharistic services, the sacrament of the Eucharist being given only under the form of bread to the laity, the Catholic Church's unwillingness to accept Lutheran liturgy, which had developed over centuries, the question of married clergy, and Catholic unwillingness to accept a simplified liturgy which Lutherans and Catholics could celebrate together for a transitional period.

Metzger also founded the 'Christ the King' movement in Germany – a movement which is still developing in Germany and in many other countries worldwide, a lay movement which gives accommodation for the homeless, for refugees, for oppressed and persecuted minorities.

Metzger had many Jewish friends and rescued many Jews during the war, risking his own life in providing safe refuges for them. Yes, he *was* an idealist, but his idealism was rooted in the Gospels and his spirituality was not in the clouds: it was solidly earthed. He knew that Peace was not an abstract ideal, which could be found by constant requests in prayer. Metzger's God is a God who invites all of us to be collaborators with Godself. If we do not collaborate, God's will cannot be effected. Consequently, each person has a responsibility to respond to this invitation in their own situation, with their own gifts, their own limitations and fragilities. The God Metzger believed in was a God present in all creation. The earth is sacred and every individual is unique and sacred before God. The action of God on human beings is to make us more aware that we are something much greater than anything we can think or imagine. Our planet, all creation, of which our planet is an infinitesimal part, is a sacrament of God, a sign. It is an effective sign of the reality which sustains all things, serves all things, loves all things. As human beings, it is through our minds and hearts that we can begin to become aware of this personal presence at work within us, and it is this awareness which leads us discover the longing of our hearts – to let this God be the God of love, the God of compassion, of justice and of peace to us and through us.

As an example of this earthed spirituality, here is a final quotation from Metzger to Pope Pius XII, after he had been arrested by the Nazis in 1939. Through their chaplains he also sent these greetings to all the other prisoners: 'In spite of all the sufferings, I have never spent happier days in all my life. My faith is in the wise providence of my Father in heaven.' In 1942 he prepared a draft letter on Peace for Hitler himself! A friend advised him against doing so! This letter then became the letter he sent to Bishop Eidem of Uppsala. His courier, a Swede, and recent convert to Catholicism, married to a German, betrayed him, and for this 'crime' Metzger was 'eradicated'.

I hope that one day he will be canonized by the Catholic Church, a mark of repentance for our silence, in action, over the Peace issue in our own days.

During the Second World War Metzger sent peace proposals to Pope Pius XII and also suggested that he call a Second Vatican Council at Assisi, which would be open to all Christian denominations and to other faiths, on the subject of World Peace and Justice. Many decades later, Pope John Paul II did not call a third Vatican Council, but he did invite members of other faiths to meet at Assisi, to consider issues of international Justice, Peace and the Integrity of Creation – issues which are of concern to all humankind, because the survival of the human race depends upon our willingness to collaborate by recognizing the dignity and worth of every human being. This meeting met with a very good response and is a most promising sign for the future.

The place of hope

Justice, Peace and the Integrity of Creation are not dreamy aspirations without any hope of being effective. We can do it! This hope is deep in human hearts and manifests itself in innumerable ways. One recent example was in the UK, where the Olympic Games were held in 2012, followed immediately by the Paralympics, in which disabled men and women from all over the world were invited to take part. While the event was being prepared there were many warning voices that this venture would be a failure and would worsen the plight of all disabled people. In fact, the event met with a success which astonished its promoters and gave hope to millions of people who, while not physically disabled, were aware of their own more hidden disabilities, yet found hope in seeing the courage and hope of all who took part in these games.

I have had personal experience of this hope and its power in situations which seemed hopeless. My nephew, also called Gerry Hughes, was born with a restriction in his oesophagus, which caused him severe pain but was not immediately diagnosed. Eventually, my brother, Joe, heard of a specialist in such ailments in Dublin, so he and his wife Margaret took Gerry over to Dublin. Young Gerry was operated on by this specialist, was twice in danger of death and received what were called 'The Last Rites', a Sacrament for those who are dangerously ill. He survived both emergencies. Soon after this crisis, his parents became worried at Gerry's inability to speak. It was only then that they discovered he was profoundly deaf.

This was shattering news for his parents. At that time, in Scotland, there was little understanding of deafness. In Glasgow there were schools for the deaf, separate schools to keep Protestant and Catholic children from religious contamination! The accepted wisdom of that time believed that deaf children should be forbidden to use sign language because their only hope for success in life was if they could learn to lip-read and learn to speak, otherwise they would be unemployable! Gerry was sent to a Catholic school for the deaf, where he was forbidden to sign. At the age of 12, he had learned to speak set prayers, knew that Glasgow had two football teams, one Protestant, called Rangers, the other Catholic, called Celtic. He was an ardent supporter of Celtic and enemy of Rangers. When my brother Joe consulted the deaf association in Scotland about employment prospects for Gerry when he left school, he was told there were plenty of jobs available, manual jobs in stacking shelves in shops and warehouses. Eventually, at the age of 13, Joe got a place for Gerry in a Catholic school in Boston Spa, Yorkshire. It was run by a Catholic Congregation, called 'Sisters of Charity', the same Congregation which ran the Catholic school he had attended in Glasgow. In Boston Spa, one of the sisters, Sister Barbara, spotted his talent and, within a year, had him reading, writing, lip-reading and beginning to speak.

To cut a very long story short, Gerry went on to study at a deaf college in England, returned to Glasgow for further study, eventually getting an Open University BA degree in Mathematics. His desire was to qualify as a teacher of the deaf. Since 1880, deaf people had been banned from teaching because they were unable to hear pupils at a distance of 30 feet! It took him 19 years of struggle before he was allowed, through the good offices of a well-known Scottish lawyer, a relative by marriage, who threatened the Scottish Education Department with the European Courts of Human Rights. Gerry was then admitted to St Andrew's College of Education to qualify as a teacher – the first Scottish deaf teacher since before 1880!

From the age of two, Gerry had been educated in sailing. His father, my younger brother Joe, had served in the Royal Navy postwar and never lost his love of the sea. When Gerry was 22 years old he asked Joe if he could borrow Joe's boat to sail round Britain with a deaf friend! To his great credit, Joe allowed him to do so and Gerry safely completed his Quest I ambition, although not without risk. On his way home, off the north-west coast of Ireland, Gerry was caught in a fierce gale. For 17 hours, with all sails down, he and his friend huddled below deck waiting for the storm to pass. When the storm abated he found himself about 60 miles off course, near the Isle of Jura, and made it safely home to his starting point at Troon, Ayrshire. His second ambition was fulfilled two decades later when he entered the OSTAR Race, sailing solo from Plymouth to the USA. Gerry had had this race in mind for many decades. While Gerry was at Boston Spa, Sir Francis Chichester had sailed round the world solo in his sixties, when he had already been diagnosed with cancer. Gerry had just learned to read and write at the time. On a magazine which recorded Chichester's feat, Gerry, aged about 14 years, had written: 'One day I will go, like Sir Francis Chichester.'

He had many scares on Quest II, as he had also named the boat. This boat was his own, a second-hand boat which he had converted. It must have looked very odd among all the streamlined craft of his 40 fellow competitors. Gerry had trouble with his electronic steering equipment. Halfway across the Atlantic he lost all communication with the rest of the world and had to choose either to proceed with only compass and sextant to steer him, or to turn back towards home. He discussed the matter with his oil lamp, his only lighting, and chose to continue through gales, fog and calm! When nearing his destination his OSTAR race flag was spotted by another yacht, which led him to his destination within a few hours! In the USA, he tried to sell his yacht, could find no buyer, so he flew home to Scotland. One year later he had gathered a deaf crew of three, two of them inexperienced in sailing, flew with them to America and sailed the boat back to the Firth of Clyde, with his deaf crew.

Quest III began on 1 September 2012. This was also a lifelong ambition – to sail non-stop and solo round the world. He undertook the venture on behalf of all deaf people, to convince them that they are capable of achieving astonishing feats if only they can allow themselves to trust their own abilities and their own dreams, rather than submit to the limited lifestyles, to the narrow boundaries, which hearing people have convinced them to accept, and which the deaf, after generations of unwilling acceptance, have finally accepted because they have been presented with no viable alternative. To learn more about this wonderful feat, see www.gerrysmhughes.com.

I include this story because of what I see as its significance. Gerry's feat is not only a sign of hope for deaf people – it is a sign of hope for every human being and we need that sign desperately in our own critical times for all humankind. All of us are created unique and called to a greatness which is far beyond anything we can think or imagine. How we become depends on how we relate to others and ourselves, a truth expressed with shattering simplicity by Jesus Christ, who said 'Love your neighbour as yourself' – a task which can never be completed, because it is always beyond us, but which teaches us in the doing it in practice. We cannot grow through the endless repetition of phrases: we do grow when we put the words into practice in the simplest of ways.

When we move towards the other in a life-giving gesture, however small, then we are in tune with God and the reverberations, however slight, re-echo in our feelings, so that we feel safe, at peace, together, free to enjoy things, to gawk in wonder and become filled with gratitude. This is what the Scriptures mean when they tell us to praise God. We cannot praise genuinely unless we appreciate something or someone; we cannot praise God unless we have a real appreciation of God's creation and a sense – however slight it may be – that what I appreciate is a personal gift to me as well as to those around me. Appreciation draws us into the true meaning of community, a being brought together in love.

Violence in Christian teaching

This is a huge subject. All I want to do here is to draw notice to the fact that there is violence attributed to God in the Hebrew Scriptures. The whole concept of 'The Chosen People', central to Judaism, Christianity and Islam, rests on the belief that God chose certain people to have their own land in perpetuity, a belief which leads to the apparently insoluble problem of modern Palestine. Both sides in the conflict are certain of their God-given ownership. Although not all those involved in the wide-ranging terrorism of today are religious believers, the core believers still justify their acts of violence by appeal to God's will. This is not simply a historical problem, or a problem for biblical scholars; it is a human problem which concerns the survival of the human race. It is not a problem which can be simply solved by enforcing atheism on all. Atheist governments are not shining examples of the way to peace. We are all involved in the problem of violence, believers and unbelievers, democracies and dictatorships, developed and developing countries.

Peace eludes all of us; violence leading to mutual destruction is the problem for all. Peace can only come about through human movements towards unity. Yes, Unity, in its broadest sense, namely as inclusive of all peoples, is the only way forward. What practical steps can we take? At this stage of affairs, we can only take small steps, small practical steps which are always directed to the service of those around us. This is being done in many parts of the world and in the last 50 years, in spite of surrounding violence, enormous progress has been made in

situations which seemed impossible to change. In 1989 the breaking
down of the Berlin Wall, a reunification of Germany after decades of
enforced separation, the end of the Cold War with Russia, the collapse
of the Marcos regime in the Philippines, of Apartheid in South Africa –
all this happened with hardly any bloodshed and few, if any, foresaw the
suddenness and relative peacefulness of these transformations. What
is common to all these sudden transformations is the fact that they
were preceded by long periods of non-violent protest, through decades
when the situation of the oppressed people seemed to be hopeless.

Some scholars claim that religion had its origin in the human
struggle to control violence. What we term today as 'primitive peoples'
were very aware of the destructive power of violence, which they
compared to a raging fire. Although many of these people were illiterate, they devised very complicated systems for violence prevention.
Their many taboos were designed to prevent the outbreak of violence.
The Aboriginal people of Australia, who had no written language, no
buildings, no private possessions, and no wars, had the most complex
rules about kinship and marriage. They survived and flourished in
Australia for about 100,000 years in a wonderful harmony with the
earth and with all living things, a very mobile people, who walked
vast distances to find food and consulted the spirits of the animals
before killing them for food. Living in this nomadic way, they had
never become agricultural until Captain Cook (1728–79) enlightened
them, and their troubles began! They were considered subhuman
by their white colonizers and were brutally treated. Many of their
white colonizers openly proclaimed that the extinction of the native
people would be the answer to the problems they were creating! Some
modern sociologists claim that Aboriginal people are probably the
most religious people who have ever lived, marvel at the wisdom of
their ways and their wonderful art work, and lament their present state
in Australia, where the native peoples have become so demoralized that
vast numbers of young Aboriginal people commit suicide while still in
their twenties, and vast numbers die of alcoholism/drugs – the only
way of escape they see from the despair which envelops them.

There is violence in the Hebrew Scriptures. Yahweh inflicts plagues
upon the Egyptians, drowns their armies in the sea, supports the
Israelites in their bloody battles and their murder of their opponents
when they enter the Promised Land. But there is a developing sense
of God within the Bible. God had been called Yahweh Sabaoth, Lord

God of Armies. The prophet Isaiah's picture of God is very different, a God who loves all creation, a God who manifests God as the suffering servant, a God of compassion. Jesus, in the Gospels, identifies God with every human being. We are all unique manifestations of God.

But what about the reality of those terrifying Scriptural passages? Are they of God, or are they not? All who call themselves Christian have to face this question. We avoid it, ignore it, fear it, do not want to hear it, denounce those who keep asking it. We take refuge in such phrases as 'God is mystery'. Yes, God is mystery, but we can grow through our lives in the awareness of God, an awareness that impels us to accept that God is mystery, meaning that there is no end to our discovery of who God is, because God is always greater. But is God the God of violence, who encourages the chosen people to slaughter the inhabitants of the lands God has promised to the chosen race of Israel?

I believe in the reality of God holding me in being every second of my existence, God of the Universe, God of Jesus Christ, image of the Unseen God, who identified himself as 'The Son of Man', the man who lived and died in Israel over 2,000 years ago. I believe that the man, Jesus, grew in his knowledge of God throughout his life. I believe that it was through his contacts with other people that he learned that God is at work in people who were not of the 'chosen race'. A striking example is in his encounter with the Syro-Phoenician woman, whom he addresses with a very racist comment, calling her 'a dog' when she asks for help. The woman does not reject him, does not confront him, but reminds him that dogs appreciate the scraps from the tables of the wealthy. Her honesty touches him, he learns and is enabled to recognize God at work within her. All of us have to grow in our knowledge of God. There are no exceptions, not even among biblical authors. We are all likely to project onto God our own private likes and dislikes and so feel justified in acting in barbaric fashion towards those we dislike, assuring ourselves that God is on our side, that we are right and all others are wrong, declaring with certainty that error has no rights.

The Bible is a document whose authors cover millennia. In it there is a developing understanding of what God is like, from God who is called 'Yahweh Sabaoth', which is translated 'God of hosts' – the hosts being 'God's Massed Armies' – to the God of whom the prophet Isaiah writes, a God of love and of peace, who turns swords into ploughshares, a God who tells us to love our neighbour as we love ourselves. And in the Sermon on the Mount, which appears in all three Synoptic Gospels,

Jesus declares his manifesto on the implications of loving God and our neighbour as ourselves: 'Love your enemies, do good to those who hate you, bless those who persecute you.' Jesus is not advocating passivity in conflict: he advocates resistance, but resistance in a way which does not inflict deliberate injury on the attacker. Jesus advocates non-violent resistance.

Non-violence in Jesus' teaching

It is astonishing to observe the remarkable silence of most Christian Churches on the Sermon on the Mount. Yes, it will appear every now and again in Eucharistic Scripture readings. No one is likely to interrupt with cries of 'rubbish', but when the readings are over we can go placidly on our way, with, for example, our firm belief in the salvific value of our Trident nuclear defence system not affected in the slightest. It is this reaction which we are to fear more than anything else. It is a reaction which lies so deep within us that we do not consciously recognize it. The source of violence lies within each of us. No one can remove our obligation to acknowledge and react to that reality. Zealous atheists and very devout and fundamental Christians, Jews, followers of Islam, or of any other religion which puts its faith in terror as the only effective means of ensuring world peace, are already doing immeasurable harm to the whole human race.

Unless we keep non-violent communication open with those whom we fear, dislike, resent, there is no hope. If we can face these questions together and learn to listen to each other, then we shall come to know a peace which no power can take from us. What gives me hope is very tangible, visible, audible: I have seen the power of this God of the impossible at work in so many lives of so many people. Nothing can ultimately destroy it. Working for peace in whatever way possible is moving into and becoming what we have been called to be before time began, collaborators with God, expressions of God's creative, loving power, which is continuously calling all creation into unity. Our assurance of this will not come from some authority figure set over us; it will come from our hearts and the drawing our hearts begin to experience from the Heart of all things.

We need to reflect on these questions posed by images of God as portrayed in Scripture and in so doing, with open minds and hearts, we shall be drawn into the vision of our present reality, of our fragility and inadequacy as our way into our deepest reality – that we are being called, since before the world existed, into the very Heart of God.

Truth in conflict

It was the prophet Jeremiah who wrote: 'The heart is more devious than any other thing, perverse too: who can pierce its secrets?' Should we dismiss this as being unduly pessimistic? If we do so, we avoid the question, 'Is Jeremiah's assertion true?'

The Greek historian Thucydides wrote in the fifth century BC: 'The first casualty in war is truth.' Subsequent human history has proved him accurate and perceptive.

In our own time, we all need to remind ourselves of this truth, then ask ourselves whether it may also refer to any kind of human conflict. We dress up the horror and destructiveness of war in fine rhetoric and call in God as our supporter, stating that war is waged 'for God and Country'. Can it be God's will that we should slaughter one another by the millions?

This opens up a host of other questions on the subtlety of destructiveness. We praise virtues like loyalty, fidelity, obedience, dedication, perseverance, resoluteness, single-mindedness. Some of the German concentration camps of World War II had the phrase *'Arbeit macht frei'*, 'Work brings freedom' over the entrances and around the camps. To discern true virtue we need to ask, in every situation, who benefits from this 'virtue' and who is victim.

Gandhi had a question for all decision-making: 'What advantage does this decision you are making offer to the world's poorest?' The poorest today, according to UN figures, number about one billion.

We need, too, to look at the violence which can lie under the phrase 'forget one's self', enslaving the weak, the poor and deprived, assuring them that their complaints are sins against God, and deserving of punishment. Women and children have been victims of this phrase for centuries, and the bullying still continues among religious believers, but also among unbelievers.

We need to distinguish the word 'self' from 'Self'. 'self' denotes the egoist self – a stage we all have to grow through, necessary for our wellbeing as we develop. The parameters of consciousness in the infant are restricted to the infant's immediate needs and desires; the infant is, at first, totally self-centred. As we move out of the infancy stage into childhood, adolescence and maturity, healthy development broadens the range of interest to mother, immediate family, school friends. Growing from self to Self is a lifelong process. In Christian understanding, 'Self' denotes the life which is discovered through the experience of living and reflecting on the process, the process St Paul was led to discover on the road to Damascus and which led him many years later to write: 'I live now not with my own life but with the life of Christ who lives in me'. And that is the belief of Christians, not only for themselves, but for all peoples. My 'self' is not an exclusive little being, totally absorbed in its own immediate needs and desires. I am an essentially related creature, in whom, in a sense, all other human beings also exist, although at first I am totally unaware of this cosmic relationship into which I am born.

Loving God is not a privilege of the chosen people; it is God's free gift to all of us, the destiny of all of us since before time began. We must resist the spirit of destructiveness that is within us all and we must do so wholeheartedly; that is why we must constantly be surrendering our lives to the Spirit of love, of compassion and of peace, which dwells within us and around us. Our devious human hearts will constantly persuade us that our first duty is individual self-protection and the protection of our group, whatever it may be, whether religious or not. Our survival as a human race, as we now realize in our own day, depends on our choosing life rather than death, love rather than self-preservation.

Where is this source of violence in us all?

This is a core question we have to keep asking, for if we do not, peace will remain elusive and our pursuit of it will lead us into further violence. One source of violence lies in the way we have been taught to think. What we call the Age of Enlightenment has delivered us from superstitions and enabled us to spot some of the crude ways in which we dominate and oppress one another, but it has also led us to divinize reason and demonize our feelings. Because we have become so accustomed to this division, we fail to notice the connection between this distinction of reason and feeling and our violent tendencies. Let me give one example.

Leonard Cheshire was one of the heroes of World War II, an intrepid and much-decorated bomber pilot. After the war, he devoted his life to the care of the war-wounded and their families and had 'Cheshire Homes' in many countries of the world, including Soviet Russia. In 1945, he had been in an observer plane on 6 August, when the first atomic bomb was dropped on Japan. About 30 years after the event, he was interviewed by a Sunday newspaper. He was asked whether, as he witnessed the atomic blast, he had given any thought to its victims below. He answered that he had not done so and went on to explain that one cannot allow such thinking in wartime, for it can lead to neglect of duty. In support of that statement he related the story of a military friend of his in World War II who had a German soldier in his telescopic gun sight. The soldier began to relieve himself. The act was so human that the soldier found himself unable to fire. Cheshire cited this as an example of failure in a military man: he had allowed his feelings to overcome his sense of duty and that must never happen when at war.

I hesitate about including this example lest it appears to question the integrity of Cheshire. I believe he was a man of outstanding bravery and generosity. But he was also a man of his times, brought up to believe that war was waged 'for God and Country' – a belief I shared until my mid-thirties. In spite of this belief, I also believe that God was at work in me, drawing me and every other human being into a new perspective, slowly enabling me to see connections between events of which I was previously unaware. Is that why Jesus tells us 'Condemn no one'? We have returned to Seraphim of Sarov's comments on gentleness!

We must pursue the implications of this comment on Cheshire: it not only concerns the military, it concerns all of us. Is it true that all engaged in war must be trained to see the enemy not as human beings, but as dangerous objects, which they must eradicate? One retired naval officer told me that in the Royal Navy, ordinary seamen are allowed to have feelings, but not officers. In nuclear submarines, permission to fire nuclear weaponry is given by the Captain, but the Captain himself is not allowed to know the place he is about to eradicate. Yes, the human heart is devious! But the heart is also our seat of wisdom. That is why the practice of discernment is so vital.

The ambiguity of the word 'Power'

By failing to notice that there is an ambiguity in the meaning of
the word 'Power' as it appears in the Bible, we can easily be led to
inhuman behaviour towards one another, justifying ourselves by appeal
to Scripture. In Christian understanding, 'Power' has two contradictory
meanings. There is God's power and there is human power.

The account given in the Synoptic Gospels of Jesus' temptations in
the desert shows the distinction clearly and starkly. In our Christian
tradition we fudge the difference. It was this fudging which led Gandhi
to state that he loved Christ, but not Christianity.

The Romans had advice for their emperors: 'Give the people bread,
give the people circuses, make yourself divine.' This was the way to
exercise complete control over the masses. The Romans recognized
the potential value of religious belief in an afterlife. They did not try
to stamp it out like some modern militant atheists; they appropriated
to themselves the power to determine the future of their subjects after
death, thus controlling them through fear.

In the Gospel accounts of Jesus' temptations in the desert, he is
tempted to turn stones into bread, to jump off the roof of the temple,
just to give the people a hint of his power and of his divine protection.
Finally he is tempted to take over control of all the kingdoms of the
powerful on earth. Jesus rejects all three temptations because they are
contrary to God's will. God's power is the power of love, the power of
compassion, the power of forgiveness, the power of freedom. Satan's
power is the power to control others, to terrify them into submission.

In the Gospels Jesus gives no detailed instruction about rules and
regulations for the future of 'the people of God', but what he does give
with unmistakable clarity are regulations for the exercise of authority.

> You know that among the pagans the rulers lord it over them, and
> their great men make their authority felt. This is not to happen
> among you. No, any one who wants to be great among you must be
> your servant, and any one who wants to be first among you, must
> be your slave, just as the Son of man came not to be served, but to
> serve, and to give his life as a ransom for many. (Mt. 20.25-28)

In St John's Gospel, on the Sunday evening after Good Friday, Jesus
appears to his terrified disciples and greets them with 'Shalom', then
shows them his hands and his side. The power of God is manifested in

his vulnerability: the power of the world is made manifest in its attempts at invulnerability, attempts which add fuel to the fire of violence. The power of the world controls: the power of God sets free. The choice rests with us. Our hearts, if we can learn to listen, tell us the answer.

The violence of silence

To write on the violence of silence is not the best way of making friends and influencing people of good will and good intentions today. They tend to bristle with indignation when they hear the phrase uttered. Whenever we bristle with indignation about anything, it is always useful to reflect on our indignation and search for its source, because it probably has something very important to tell us.

In writing 'the violence of silence', I am not condemning silence; I am saying that silence can be used violently. I have already quoted the saying, 'For the triumph of evil, all that is required is the silence of the good'.

All of us can use silence as a most effective way of being cruel. To foment violence in any group of human beings, keep them in close proximity but forbid them to communicate with each other. To subdue a people, forbid them to use their own language, their own way of communicating. In this way you can break their morale and turn them into passive agents. To break the spirit of any child, disregard the child: treat the child as an object. The same is true for breaking the spirit of adults.

Violence abhors communication. Communication becomes very dangerous because people might become friends with each other! In the last century many of the remarkable incidents of bloodless reconciliation which occurred worldwide were preceded by years of secret meetings between the protagonists, when friendships were formed simply by meeting over years in unthreatening locations. In critical confrontations between police and armed criminals, police are trained to keep communications open for as long as possible. Similarly, within ourselves, we need to keep communications open with those aspects of ourselves which we abhor and avoid acknowledging. Our avoidance does not eliminate the problem: the aspects we abhor do not disappear. They retire into our subconscious where they exercise their destructiveness, influencing all aspects of our behaviour destructively for ourselves and for those around us. These aspects of ourselves are the enemies we must learn to love: they are our potential allies, our healers!

In today's ethos, certainly in Britain, but elsewhere too, it is considered polite to avoid confrontation, but the question we have to keep asking ourselves is: 'For whose advantage are we keeping silence?' Is our silence for the sake of those people who matter to us, or is it for the sake of those in greatest need? This is the question which brings us face to face with the truth.

A final word. Silence, in itself, is neither right nor wrong, true nor false. Those categories only apply when we look at our motives that are leading us to be silent. Silence, when it is practised as a means of teaching us how to be contemplative, how to become more aware of the miracle of the present moment, of our interconnection with everyone and with all creation, is a most valuable and peace-making occupation, not only for ourselves, but for all.

The aim of this chapter has been to enable us to glimpse something of the richness of the word 'Peace' and see how it is related to every aspect of human life, from the major global crises of our times to our minor feelings of frustration when life is not proceeding in the way we want. Hopefully, it has also helped us to see that the macro and the micro in life are all interconnected. In the following chapters we shall be looking in greater detail at some of these interconnections, opening our minds and hearts to the astonishing reality that there is nothing in reality which is foreign to me because my true identity is always greater than anything I can think or imagine. And that reality is always with us in every breath we breathe, the Spirit of love, of truth and of compassion. It is indestructible and we come to sense its reality through reflecting on our own experience.

Exercises

- After reading this long chapter, what were your predominant felt reactions?

- Do those reactions have any connection with your experience of everyday life?

- Do they draw you to any practical changes you would like to make in your own life?

3

The roots of violence are within our own hearts

We have already seen the enormity of the subject and the elusive nature of this peace for which we all long. We have been brought up to believe, and have assented to the belief, that the only answer to violence is violence. We need war to bring about peace! This thinking has been and still is accepted by the vast majority of countries. As Margaret Thatcher once put it when she was Prime Minister, 'It is unthinkable that we should abandon our nuclear defence system'. She was not lying, or being deceptive in any conscious way: she was uttering a deeply held personal conviction. It was the manner of her utterance – 'It is unthinkable' – which betrays the flaw, the kind of flaw that afflicts all of us when we utter our certainties. I may be utterly sincere in my utterance, but my assertion does not bear examination. Do I really mean that the boundaries of my mind set the bounds for every other mind, including God's? But that is what is being asserted with the phrase 'It is unthinkable'.

The image I had of the Polaris submarine's periscope gliding beneath the calm waters of the Firth of Clyde on a perfect day in the spring of 1975 has become a permanent feature of my mind. Everything looked so perfect without any visible sign of destructiveness. Where is the source of the destructiveness? The ultimate source is in the human mind and heart. Until we track down and confront this source, we can never eliminate nuclear weapons, or diminish any other form of human violence. Even if we were to eliminate the nuclear weapons, how long would it take before they reappeared? Our mind and our hearts require examination: that is where the problem lies; but it is also where the answer lies – the answer that can reveal to us the peace for which we long. Those old-fashioned phrases, 'Repent and believe in the Good News' may really have something urgent and life-giving to say to all of us.

It is useful to start noticing how our language, our gestures, our behaviour constantly mask the destructiveness of our violence – for example, our martial music, spectacular parades, statues of bemedalled heroes who devised the deaths of thousands of innocent people during the carpet-bombing raids on Germany and Japan during the war in order to break the morale of the civilian population. The very badly wounded have, in the past, been excluded from victory parades lest people should be upset at the sight of them; the large numbers of survivors who are psychologically permanently disabled, or who took their own lives, are rarely mentioned. We can boast about peace in postwar Europe, but give little attention to the wars waged and still being waged in other parts of the world in the interests of the developed world, which tries to ensure its access to the natural resources and precious minerals of developing countries. The method used is very simple: ensure that the governments of these developing countries will grant such access. Pay the chosen leaders lavishly to secure their support. This method is the reason for the notorious School of the Americas in the USA. It was built and still exists for the training of young people in South America in effective methods of overthrowing governments and securing control for themselves. The methods include blackmail, torture, bribery and murder. In its short history so far, the School of the Americas has produced a large number of notorious dictators who have displaced governments, assumed control and massacred thousands of innocent people, including women and children in Central and South America. These deaths are murder by proxy by the wealthy and powerful in the developed world for their own financial and political interests, but the deadly activity hides itself under rhetorical language about bringing prosperity and peace, democracy and freedom to these unfortunate and benighted peoples.

The greatest threat to the mighty is truth, which can unmask their pretence and therefore must be hidden at all costs. This tactic reveals a very important and encouraging truth. Their desire to masquerade as righteous champions of good causes and their fear of the truth indicates a subconscious awareness that all is not well. It is on this truth that non-violent pacifists rely in their peace efforts. Their methods of resistance are all directed to enabling the aggressor to become more aware of the destructiveness of their actions not only to their enemies, but also to themselves.

Now to return to look more closely at the assertion, 'The root of human violence lies in desire'. The Stoics were a school of Greek philosophy which was founded by Zeno in the third century BC. This is a very ancient belief, which predates Christianity. The Buddhists have a saying, 'Renounce all desire', recommending this as the way to peace and contentment. There is much wisdom in Stoic teaching, but as it is commonly understood – namely that renunciation of all desire is the path to peace – it is not surprising that in our pursuit of peace we discover that peace always eludes us.

Desire is not an aspect of our lives with which we can dispense: it belongs to our very essence. We cannot choose to live without desire unless we find life without desire to be preferable – in which case, by denying all desire we would be living out our desire! Jonathan Swift has a helpful remark on stoicism as it is commonly understood: 'If I have a desire for a new pair of shoes, then to rid myself of the desire I should chop off my feet!'

Desire, in itself, is a gift which draws us into life. Our life is, as we have seen, essentially relational. It is desire which draws us into relationship. It is also true that desire can draw us into destructive relationships. Any course of action that we pursue, and that is done without regard for other people, is a source of conflict which is damaging to me and to those I disregard. There is no way we can escape from this truth, because we are essentially related to each other and dependent on one another.

Our desire for wealth, for power, for recognition, for status, for knowledge, for health, friendship, love and support is endemic. It is not something we create; it is something we discover in life and the desire draws us into ways of acting and reacting, into patterns of behaviour which enable us to secure the object of our desire. This is where conflict arises.

Apart from killing another human being, the worst damage we can do to another is to break their desire to live, to rob them of their humanity. It is a sign of the will to live when people are fighting in the streets; when they lie dying in the streets, despair has robbed them of the will to live. It was because Mother Teresa had reached that level of awareness that she abandoned her teaching and devoted the rest of her life to ministering to the desperate. She lived out the passion of her life – to be compassionate – that was her all-consuming emotion.

How are we to distinguish the desires that are life-giving, peace-building, creative for all whoever they are, from the desires which are destructive? The first answer is a distinction. The desire in itself – for example, for success, for security, for wealth, for power – is never wrong. The categories of right and wrong cannot be applied to desire itself. Rightness and wrongness are only applicable to the ways in which we respond to the desire. All desire, in itself, is good. We can only pursue a destructive desire when we have convinced ourselves, or have allowed ourselves to be convinced, that it is in some way creative.

We are moving towards the heart of the problem! Here is a very simple exercise which can help us to see clearly our need to learn discernment. The word 'discernment' has a Latin root and literally it means 'to separate out'. As a human activity, discernment is about learning to distinguish creative from destructive decisions. As a preliminary step, take a few blank sheets of paper and without any attempt to discern, start scribbling down your answers to this question, 'What are my desires in life?' Do not analyse, approve or disapprove what you write. Scribble as freely and spontaneously as you can. Avoid all moralizing and resist any tendency to write what you *should* desire. This list is private to you. You are not writing for approval. You are simply recording the facts. As you are a human being, then potentially there is no desire, no matter how noble or how depraved it may be, which is impossible for you! In this exercise you are not assessing yourself, or claiming to be a shining example of what you have written. You can write honestly of your desires while, at the same time, being aware that, in practice, you are not living out those noble desires.

When you have finished this exercise, do you notice any trace of conflicting, incompatible desires within you? For example, I may have written 'I would love to be popular and well thought of', but I may also have written 'I would love to be transparently honest at all times'. The problem here is the fact that if you do practise transparent honesty at all times, your popularity rating is likely to drop. This spotting of the incompatibilities can keep you occupied for a long time. Do not rush the process!

From this exercise, another question inevitably arises, whether you want it or not. In your many desires, you have to decide on priorities. For example, between popularity and truthfulness, which do you prefer? If we are to live creatively for ourselves, for those around us and in harmony with creation in which we are enveloped, what steps do we need to take? This is the all-important question. In my life, what is the basic desire that I want to guide me, the fundamental desire that makes life worth living?

Discovering the answer is a lifelong task. However, to keep asking yourself that question frequently is a most valuable, useful, freeing and enjoyable practice. The question has to seep through our many solid layers of consciousness, layers we have inherited from our ancestors, layers which were laid down in our infancy when we were totally helpless and dependent on others for everything, our consciousness totally focused on me, the perfect little egocentric. Then there are the many other layers of consciousness from our upbringing, education, the people with whom we have related and how we have related to them, the environments in which we have lived, the places we have visited.

To live true to ourselves, we have to learn to relate openly with others. There is inbuilt conflict here, at the very core of our being. We are creatures at risk. If we choose to avoid risk at all costs and concentrate on self-protection, then we may succeed for a time, enclosing ourselves in a cocoon of self-preservation, convincing ourselves of the righteousness of our behaviour, banishing our doubts from our consciousness, living cosily and complacently in our very respectable ivory towers, invulnerable against the slings and arrows of outrageous fortune that afflict the less endowed of human kind.

That is why the efforts of those, whether individuals or groups, who are totally absorbed in self-protection are always destructive, both of themselves and of their enemies. Our nuclear defence policy illustrates this truth. It presents itself as the only safe method of ensuring our freedom, our values, our democratic way of life against rogue states and unreliable hordes of terrorists. In fact it increases the danger to all humankind. Nuclear defence capability has spread from the original four, USA, Russia, France and UK, to at least twice that number and many other countries are planning their own possession of nuclear weaponry. The danger to human survival can only increase, unless there is a radical change of mind and heart.

What is meant by 'a radical change of mind and heart' and how can it come about? There is a basic teaching in all major world religions. It is commonly called 'detachment' or 'indifference'. It lies at the heart of all peace work. The teaching recognizes that disordered desire lies at the heart of all violent conflict. It also recognizes that disordered desire grows through what it feeds on. If, for example, my desire is to accumulate as much wealth as possible to ensure my own financial security, my desire for wealth will increase the more I pursue it, until it becomes the overpowering force within me. All my other desires will be subordinated to my wealth-gathering – for example, my desire to love and be loved, my desire to bring life to others rather than deprive them of it, my desire to be honest and open and gentle in all my doings.

The desires we discover within ourselves are very powerful and, if we are not vigilant, they can become so overpowering that we can no longer bear to face them and can convince ourselves that they do not exist. Some signs that this is happening to us subconsciously are our growing certainty in our own conscious convictions, a disinclination to listen to anyone or anything that is not ministering to our predominant desire, a loss of interest in the world around us, a diminishing sense of wonder, a sense of uneasiness, which can become all-pervasive in our consciousness, which we struggle vainly to dispel.

To find peace in this inevitable conflict of our desires, we cannot destroy the desires without destroying the core of our being, because we are, in our essence, related beings – the extent of our relatedness going far beyond anything our conscious, reasoning minds can grasp. All the major world religions teach our human need of cultivating 'detachment' from our desires, 'indifference' towards them, 'control' over them.

'Detachment', 'indifference', 'control' are misleading and unattractive words. They suggest grim austerity, saying 'no' to everything we find attractive, becoming dull, narrow, lifeless, unresponsive. In the way it is often taught, it is not surprising that we are unable to get excited at the prospect of living in this way. 'Becoming free' sounds much more attractive and is, in fact, the whole object of detachment – to set us free from all those inner desires which want to take us over, leading to our own destruction and the destruction of those around us. And here we become aware of another fundamental truth for all human beings: attachment can only be overcome in us through a stronger attachment.

This is a conclusion which, if we can allow it to sink into our whole being, becomes transformative. The transformation takes place not in the reality which surrounds us – it remains exactly as it was – but in the way we begin to see and experience that same reality, including ourselves. We are at the heart of the matter we are investigating in this book, the answer to the question 'Who am I?' It is a very ancient question. It appears in the Bible in the story of Moses' vision of the burning bush he saw on Mount Horeb. The bush was aflame, but the flames were not consuming it. Moses stepped forward to have a closer look. 'And God said to Moses, "Take off your shoes, for the place on which you stand is holy ground. I am the God of your father", God said, "the God of Abraham, the God of Isaac and the God of Jacob". At this Moses covered his face, afraid to look at God' (Exod 3.3ff.). In this story, where is God? The story suggests that God is in the reality of things – in this case in the reality of the bush. Moses sees a bush aflame, but the flame does not destroy the bush. A few verses later (Exod. 3.13-15), after God has told Moses that he is to lead his people out of Egypt and bring them to the promised land, Moses asks God, 'If they ask me what your name is, what am I to tell them?' And God said to Moses, 'I am who I am'. There is a note in my Jerusalem Bible saying that this name becomes, in the third person, 'Yahweh', meaning 'He is'. For us human beings, God is to be found in the *isness* of things. This has cosmic implications for us. Here I want to link that statement with 'Attachment can only be overcome through a stronger attachment'. I want to link it with a very ordinary, earthy, recent experience.

A long time ago I had come across a statement – I cannot now remember the source – 'Every bush is burning for those who have the eyes to see'. It attracted me but I did not know why. Together with the *isness* of God, the two statements came together in my mind years later, recently, in a surprising manner. I had just been invited to join the Jesuit community at Campion Hall, Oxford, where I had arrived 60 years previously to spend four years studying the dead languages, Latin and Greek! As I was beginning to feel my age, declining physical and mental energy, and aware of my inability to meet deadlines, I had asked to be officially retired and hoped to be able to write this book.

Three minutes' walk away from Campion Hall, across St Aldates, is the entrance to Christchurch Meadows, a vast area of meadow bounded on one side by the river Isis, Oxford's name for the river Thames in this area, and on the other side by the river Cherwell, which flows into the Thames. It offers most beautiful walking along broad, tree-lined paths.

I enjoy walking in silence. It can be a very effective method for becoming still in mind and heart. Repetition of a word or phrase uttered in rhythm with our step has a stilling effect. To do this in a relaxed way, without trying deliberately to work anything out, is very calming. For example, I used to find on long walks/pilgrimages that repetition of the phrase 'Our Father' in rhythm with my steps, or with my breathing, was helpful. Another very helpful phrase was taken from a French woman, who was founder of the Catholic Religious communities called 'Sisters of Notre Dame'. Her saying was '*Qu'il est bon, qu'il est bon, qu'il est bon, le bon Dieu*' ('How good, how good, how good, is the good God'), a very rhythmic phrase, easily adapted to our pace.

It is difficult to describe this stillness in words without being misunderstood, nor do I feel any inclination to do so, but I can describe the after-effect in negatives.

I used this stillness method daily when walking through Christchurch Meadows. One day I became fascinated with the word 'Isis', for it put me in mind of the *isness* of God. Where is God? God is to be found, and can only be found, in the *isness* of things. Letting this play on the words '*Is–is*' play on my consciousness did not transform the scene through which I walked, but it did enable me to catch a glimpse of the scene in a new, attractive and exciting way. This scene is where I encounter God in whom all these trees, the meadows, the rivers, the bird life, the squirrels and I and all creation live and move and have our being. I cannot escape from your presence, Lord, for in your Being everyone and every thing exists. Nor do I want to escape from it. Show me your attractiveness, and plunge me into your life. Let me know and respond to your love for us and for all creation, your generosity which delights in giving, your compassion which sees into the depths of us and never rejects us. We have no means of escape, thank God!

In reading this, or in writing about it, I need to remind myself frequently of the need to remember, to re-collect my scattered self so that the truth can sink through my layers of resistance to the core of my being, thus allowing this phrase to connect with the other parts of me, enabling me to see myself in a wider context than my secure self in its shrinking cocoon of self-concern.

As Christians, if we bring this statement into contact with our religious beliefs, we can be taking a step into our journey of life which will transform us, provided we remain open to the questions the journey presents to us.

Here are some questions you can ponder and some exercises you can try to enable you to take a simple step in life which can lead you to seeing everything in a new perspective. Remember what was written earlier about change in general. We all want to change hundreds of things and the younger we are, the more vehement the urge to change things. We soon learn that changing things is not as easy as we thought. Then we realize that there is precious little in life we can change. We can change the furniture around us, we can destroy it, but we cannot change the fact that it existed in the past and still exists in our mind. We cannot change our past, we cannot change the future. The only thing we can change is the way in which we see ourselves and the world around us. We can treat people as things, enslave them, and we can treat our environment as though its only function is to serve our needs, but we cannot change the uniqueness of every person and every thing. We are essentially related and we can only live creatively if we are living in harmony with others, with our surroundings and with ourselves. This does not necessarily restrict us in any way. There is infinite variety possible in the way we relate.

One exercise you can try is a method of getting in touch with our own basic desire in life. Imagine that you have died and someone has been invited to give an address at your funeral service. Write your own obituary – the one which, in your wildest dreams, you would love to receive. Do not let the reality of your life impede you in the slightest! The more freely you can write in this fashion, the more likely you are to touch into your own deep-down basic desire. The point of doing this is because those deep-down subconscious desires have not disappeared; they are still at work and influencing your present decisions, even though they are not accessible to your conscious mind at the moment. If this sounds nonsense to you, just pause for a moment and ask yourself, 'Have I ever surprised myself by something I have said, or some action I have taken?', exclaiming 'I must be going out of my mind to have said that, to have taken that decision!'. You are uttering a truth that is more important and true than you realize. You have, momentarily, stepped out of your rational conscious mind and caught a glimpse of what is really going on within you under the surface.

Writing out your own obituary is one way of getting in touch with your deeper self.

It requires a leap of the imagination, a leap of which we are all capable, if we dare give ourselves the chance. The process is not unlike learning to dive into deep water. You have to leave the springboard otherwise you will never experience the delights of diving, even though you may spend the rest of your life giving others instructions in the art of diving!

Take your time over this exercise, read it over from time to time, revising it in light of the discoveries that you make. Would your heart leap, for example, if you find yourself writing 'S/he never lost an argument in her/his life'. Would that statement answer your deepest longing, even though you dearly love winning arguments?

So, keep scribbling to get in touch with the glory of your being. Before time was, God had you in mind. You are unique and have a special role in human history, a role which only you can fulfil. If that sounds fanciful, a wild fantasy of imagination, then pause. In fact – and this is what science tells us, not religious instruction – every molecule of your being, and there are trillions of them, is so unique to you, that if you were to leave one of them at the scene of your crime, you can be traced! And our Christian religion reveals that every human being – not just Christians – is a unique manifestation of God and that we encounter God in all our human relationships and in the way we relate to all creation.

How attractive is your image of God? Is God an authority figure or a lover? Is God a remote figure, out of reach, unapproachable, judgemental, a God whose primary interest is your sinfulness and your failures, your mistakes and your destructiveness, a God who spends eternity deciding appropriate punishment for you after death? This is not a theoretical question, it is a most practical one; it affects every aspect of your life and all the decisions you make. All that I write in this book is an attempt to glimpse, develop and become at home with the wonderful mystery and reality in which we are all now living – the truth of things!

Here is another simple exercise you can do to raise your level of awareness of your own basic desire. Take a sheet of A4 paper and divide it into four quarters. In the top left quarter, write the heading: 'God, as God was presented to me as a child'. Now focus your attention on that heading, then write or draw whatever comes up in your consciousness: it may be a drawing, or a symbol, or a single word rather than a written description. The more spontaneously you can do this, the more helpful your response will be.

In quarter No. 2, top right on your sheet, write the heading: 'God, as I now understand God to be', again using whatever comes to mind: a drawing, an image, a symbol, whatever you find most helpful in expressing your honest response. The response is for your sake alone, so there is no point in trying to deceive yourself. We can repeatedly try to manipulate the truth to our own personal advantage and succeed in deceiving ourselves in the process, but truth cannot be manipulated. Like God, truth is invincible. Perhaps that is why Gandhi once wrote 'Truth is God'.

In quarter No. 3, bottom left on your sheet, write the heading: 'God, as I would like God to be'. Give yourself plenty of time to consider this question. How much is 'plenty'? It could be your whole lifetime: it would be time well spent! Express your response in whatever way best suits you.

In quarter No. 4, the bottom right quarter, write the heading: 'Felt reaction(s) after doing this exercise'.

Of these four quarters, the most important is No. 3, 'God, as I would like God to be', because it is exploring the nature of desire as you experience it. If you have difficulty in expressing your answer, that is a very good sign. The importance of this exercise is not in finding the right answers, but the experience of discovering that although you have many desires, and they are real, you cannot find a neat and clear answer to the question, 'What is my basic desire?' Could it be that you are on the threshold of mystery, the mystery of your being? You are beginning to look into new and exciting depths of yourself. You are not alone, you are essentially a related being. 'In God you live and move and have your being.' A mystery is not something we cannot understand; mystery is something which takes hold of us, discloses itself, leaves us with a longing to know more, while at the same time we know we are on a journey, caught up in a process which has no end. We are being drawn out of our selves into a new Self, always greater than anything we can think or imagine, but also most desirable. We shall be returning frequently to this theme.

Meanwhile there are two final points to make before concluding this chapter.

Religious people keep saying that we must praise God. In this note I want to make the connection between praising God and appreciating life. Briefly, praise can only be genuine if it is based on something/someone we have experienced. The only way any of us can encounter God is through our ordinary everyday experience. That is why reflecting on our own experience is so important. A way of doing this is to call to mind each day the events, encounters, experiences for which we are grateful, no matter how trivial they may seem. Through this regular exercise, we can begin to become aware of these experiences in a new way, a way that can transform every aspect of our lives. We begin to recognize these events as personal gifts from God to us. They are freely given and they are signs indicating a reality, namely that God's will is that we should become at one with the mystery of our being, the source of all being. At every moment of our existence this is the reality which is drawing us out of our self into the Self in which all creation has its being. This is the prayer of Jesus at the Last Supper as recorded in St John's Gospel, 'that they all may be one, as Thou Father in me and I in Thee, that they also may be one in us' (Jn 17.21). This is more than our conscious minds can ever grasp directly or adequately, but we can touch into the reality of it when we become aware of our restlessness for something we cannot put into words. And although we cannot express the object of our longing, the longing itself is influencing us, for God's drawing is continuous. In three words, this note is saying 'Appreciate your experience', for in doing so, you are moving into closer harmony with your own heart, with all creation, and with God!

In doing these two exercises I have suggested, about writing your own obituary and in reflecting on your own image of God, do practise having conversations with God. In these conversations there is no need to break into 'religious' language; just be yourself, as simple, as honest, as open as you can be before a God who delights in you, otherwise God would not have had you in mind before time began. And I pray that you may also find laughter in the heart of God.

Exercises

- Write your own obituary – the one which, in your wildest dreams, you would love to have, not letting your own inadequacies limit you in the slightest!

- Do the four quarters exercise with the headings I have given. Keep going back to the exercise, revising, adding to it as your felt reactions prompt you. Let the exercise become a conversation with God, who is more concerned with your welfare than you can ever be!

4

Divinization of reason – demonization of feelings

This chapter is a further elaboration on Chapter 3 on desire as the source of life and root of anger. The roots of violence are invisible and intangible, but they produce very visible devastation. Fear of devastation focuses our attention on our own self-preservation, in itself a very healthy reaction, but the concentration on our wellbeing can blind us to other aspects of human well-being, leading us to use methods of self-preservation which are, in fact, increasingly destructive to ourselves and to those we want to protect. 'Violence breeds violence' is a well-known, but equally well-disregarded slogan. It is because the slogan is so widely disregarded that we find peace so elusive. In this chapter we are going to explore this phenomenon. It is not an abstract problem: it is very down-to-earth, it is immediate and it concerns everyone without exception.

There is a split in our spirituality. It means, briefly, that there exists a split between the language we use and the reality in which we live. We are so accustomed to this split that we rarely, if at all, notice it. If we can focus our attention on this split, we can begin to catch a glimpse of its importance. There are very deep, subconscious forces within us resisting any attempts we may deliberately make to get on track of these. In this chapter I try to explore this truth. It is a safe and simple procedure: it is based on human observation.

This split in our spirituality is not, fundamentally, a split in our use of language: it is a more fundamental split in the core of our being. It is this split which enables us to act ruthlessly against those whom we perceive as enemies, yet, at the same time, we can pride ourselves on the rectitude of our actions, perhaps even thanking God for eradicating our enemies! One outstanding example of this was during the post-World War II Nuremberg trials, when the concentration camp Nazis were on trial for the 'eradication' of six million Jewish people, as well as for the killing of thousands of others, men, women and children, who were considered a threat to German survival. The defence of all the accused was 'We were obeying orders'. Britain and her victorious allies did not have the equivalent of Nuremberg trials, but, as the war progressed, there were mass killings by the British Royal Air Force of hundreds of thousands of innocent people in dense housing areas of Germany, German-occupied Europe and Japan. The purpose of this 'carpet-bombing', as it was called, was to break German morale; in fact, it strengthened German and Japanese resistance and prolonged the war.

There can be no effective path to peace until we acknowledge this fact and then take practical steps to live the peace we profess in all our attitudes and actions towards others. 'Our good is their good: their loss is our loss.' There is no escape from this truth for any of us, because we are all essentially related creatures. This essential human bonded-ness is like gravity – something invisible in itself, but essential for the survival of all living beings.

Our question now is how are we to move together towards the reali-zation of a Peace which is for the advantage of all? How can we replace competition with collaboration? Does the impossibility of finding peace lie in some fundamental flaw in creation, or does it lie in the way in which we choose to interpret creation?

Split spirituality is not a recent affliction. What is relatively modern is the 'renaissance'. The fourteenth to sixteenth centuries in Europe were centuries of recovery of classical Greek and Roman learning bringing a great flourishing of art and architecture, the beginning of the sciences and the belief that everything could be explained through reason. This was not a new belief, but the recovery of a very ancient one. The Latin poet Lucretius (c. 96–55BC) had written six books of verse on '*The Nature of Things*'. Lucretius believed that religion was a source of violence because it made people afraid of an afterlife of painful punishment for offences committed in this life. This fear was so overpowering that if the religious authorities ordered people to go to war and they refused, they would face eternal punishment. Through their religious belief they would act inhumanely towards one another.

Lucretius himself had inherited this theory from Greek philosophers who were writing centuries before him, and his thinking is now continuing and spreading in our own post-Christian, postmodern age.

The recovery of reason rid us of much superstition, but when reason takes over and feelings and emotions are disregarded, then we can lock ourselves into a closed circuit of violence breeding violence – a circuit which is now threatening the future of humankind. It was only in the early twentieth century that the IQ (Intelligence Quotient) was intro-duced as a method of quantifying human intelligence. This remained the sole method of assessing intelligence until Daniel Goleman, in the 1990s, popularized the work of many neuroscientists and psychologists and introduced EQ (Emotional Quotient), which is equally important to rational intelligence. EQ gives a measure of our awareness of our own emotions and of how to respond to other people's emotions: it enables us to empathize, to be compassionate, to motivate ourselves and others to respond appropriately to pain and pleasure, to love and be loved. A moment's reflection can enable us to understand the funda-mental importance of emotional intelligence, but another moment's reflection will also show us the damage which has been done to us, and which we have done, and are still doing, by neglecting our emotions.

When we reflect on this distinction between rational and emotional intelligence, it is astonishing that IQ, our rational intelligence, was assumed to be the only intelligence available to human beings. IQ is the intelligence of the computer: rational, logical, quantifiable. The computer now outstrips in its speed, range and efficiency any achievements of our rational intelligence, but my computer does not shed tears or show any emotion when I am faced with disaster! The computer cannot think for itself, reflect, show love, enthusiasm, hate or boredom, although I may become enthusiastic about it, may become very attached to it, or be irritated by it. In my irritation with its failure to act as I want it to act, I may even throw it out of the window and experience momentary relief!

This journey into the IQ question is necessary if we are to begin to understand the elusiveness of peace and the devastation which follows from our divinization of reason and demonization of our emotions. If we pay no attention to this root cause of our human violence against ourselves, against others, against the earth which sustains us, then we are in danger of surrendering to our feelings of hopelessness and to the destruction of human life on earth. Whatever the answer may be in face of this crisis, it cannot come from government, from politics, or from religious beliefs that turn God into a Santa Claus, a computerized gift-giver, who has no time for anything other than showering gifts on me and is not at all concerned at my own utter disregard of anyone or anything which does not answer my immediate needs.

Peace can only come through the hearts and minds of human beings who are united in their total dedication to the love and service of one another. They may fail in their efforts, but they can never abandon the deepest longing of their hearts to love and to serve. This longing was summed up in a Latin phrase '*tremendum et fascinans*', meaning 'terrifying and attractive', by Rudolf Otto.

I read Otto's book *Idea of the Holy* many decades ago, but it did not speak to me then. It interested me, but it seemed to be referring to mental states which I could read about but could not share. I had also read books by mystical writers, again with some interest, but always with the conclusion that the wonderful inner states and inner experiences they enjoyed were reserved for a few select people living in monasteries and convents, but not for the likes of me. Now I believe that these experiences are open to every human being. We do not have to have thrilling/terrifying inner experiences to qualify: all we need to do is give attention to our own experience, for it is in that experience, and in that experience alone, that we can catch a whiff of God, brief moments of enlightenment, which can help us to begin to see things differently, myself differently and God differently. These are not necessarily 'beautiful experiences'. They can be traumatic, life-threatening, because the word '*tremendum*' is inclusive of all kinds of horrors, but what is unique to God's revelation is that there is always, along with the '*tremendum*', a '*fascinans*' element, meaning that the '*tremendum*' is always accompanied by something attractive, which keeps drawing us back into asking fundamental questions which, normally, we resist resolutely and consider our attitude to be virtuous or, if we are of a religious disposition, we call it 'doing the will of God'!

From our brief look so far at the meaning of human intelligence and the very restricted meaning which the IQ testing imposed on us for a century, we can see something of the wide range of very down-to-earth topics which confront us. The fundamental question is about the roots of human violence and the relationship between desire and violence. In noticing this relationship, innumerable questions arise concerning our wellbeing which we may never have noticed before.

In all our social activity, in our need for shelter, for medical care, for education, wealth and food distribution, the protection and welfare of all citizens, especially the poor, helpless, members of minority groups, the protection of children, in our economic legislation, our national and international policies, in facing the problem of climate change, out of what fundamental ideas are we operating? Do we consider one another as a collection of economic units, to be classified according to our earning capacity, or are we to look on one another as unique human beings with inviolable human rights and obligations, each individual with a unique contribution to make to the life of all humanity? Or are we to declare all these questions insoluble and just keep ourselves occupied with our own survival? If we can admit, in view of all this, that we need to acknowledge the need for a radical change in our thinking and our attitudes, then there is hope. If we fail to acknowledge this need, then we become in fact instrumental in our own annihilation.

These questions do not arise from some abstract philosophy or theology, or from a highly specialized think-tank: they arise out of human, earthy experience. It is in facing these facts that we discover the '*tremendum et fascinans*': in ignoring these facts, we create for ourselves imaginary escape routes, which do not relate to the facts of our experience. We are handing ourselves over to our own destructive tendencies.

Modern neurology is still in its infancy, but already it has provided us with information about the working of the human brain that was inaccessible to previous generations. 'It has been estimated that there are more connections within the human brain than there are particles in the known universe.' This quotation is from Iain McGilchrist's classic book *The Master and his Emissary*, a book about the divided brain and the making of the Western world, which took him 20 years to write!

The fundamental point he makes – a point which is relevant to every aspect of human experience – is that our complex human brain is divided into two parts and 'it contains mutually opposed elements whose contrary influence makes possible finely calibrated responses'. His book concentrates on the right/left pairing of the brain. The right-hand section of the brain sees reality differently from the left-hand section – an inherent opposition – yet both parts need each other. Their complementarity is their strength: their isolation from each other leads to destruction.

The left-hand side of the brain concerns itself with the 'how' of things, how the parts work: it is analytic, quantitative, like the brain of the computer. It enables us to make great progress in technology, mass-producing machines which are faster, more efficient, reliable and available, like computers themselves. The right-hand side is concerned with 'why' questions. Whereas the left-hand brain would say 'computers are available, so make use of them', the right-hand brain would ask 'why should we use them?', a question which the left-hand brain would have no interest in asking, although it might resent the question and try to suppress it because its pursuit is bad for the computer market.

What has all this to do with our subject, 'Peace'? It has everything to do with our subject: it lies at the heart of it. The origin of human violence among humankind and of our human destruction of the planet which sustains us, lies in the way we see the reality in which we find ourselves. The left-hand brain tends to see the world in a machine-like way: it is made up of independent parts. This leads us to conclude that we can control this world if we can understand the relationship of the parts to each other. The world, for the left-hand brain, is the sum of its parts. If we can learn how to control these parts, we can produce the perfect world. The right-hand brain is more interested in the 'why' questions of life, life's purpose, in the nature of our being and the why of it – questions which can never be answered with quantitative answers. These questions arise in and through our own human experience: they do not fall upon us, like manna in the desert, in the form of neatly formulated questions adapted to the needs of our computers. Yet it is our responses to these 'why' questions which determine the way in which we create our world of violence, of mass genocides, of destruction of one another in millions, a world threatened by climate change, a world which fails to rescue 20 per cent of the human population from avoidable starvation because we are too preoccupied with our own immediate affairs to reflect on the effect our neglect is having on the future of all humankind and on all living beings.

We have looked at the discovery in the early twentieth century of Emotional Intelligence and how its neglect is already dehumanizing us, leading us to regard one another as objects and robbing us of all that we hold most dear in life, our ability to love and be loved, our inner longings for joy, delight, tenderness, compassion. This leads us to another early twentieth-century discovery, the Spirituality Quotient

(SQ), which measures Spirituality Intelligence. Like the Emotional Quotient (EQ), SQ is not a recent invention; both have been around in human consciousness since human beings began to think. SQ has begun to reappear again in human consciousness.

SQ offers us a means of understanding our human experience in a much wider context than our immediate tasks. Consequently, we are enabled to choose our priorities more freely than our IQ or even our EQ could have enabled us to do. SQ enables us to get in touch with our deepest desires, an area inaccessible to our IQ, because those desires are not quantifiable. Our SQ also takes us beyond our EQ, because it exposes us to a world that is deeper than our conscious emotions. SQ enables us to recognize our own limitations, our own failure to appreciate the miracle of our existence and the wonder of it, because our attention is so narrowly focused on our own desires and needs that we have no energy for anything else.

SQ lights up creation from within, helps us to begin to recognize God in the earthiness of things, a God who is always greater than anything I can think or imagine, a beckoning God – yet, at the same time, a God who is at home in us and invites us to be at home with God whose centre is wherever we are and whose circumference has no bounds. The God that SQ reveals is a God of lavishness, of folly, 'for God's foolishness is wiser than human wisdom, and God's weakness is stronger than human strength' (1 Cor. 1.25). SQ takes us beyond ourselves and the present moment. It is the intelligence of Jesus, who asked 'Who is my mother, who are my brothers?' and who identified himself with everyone who is in need.

Today the brain's activity can be located. The SQ operates out of the brain's centre.

The three different Intelligences operate separately, but SQ facilitates dialogue between reason and emotion. It is the integrating, co-ordinating, unifying intelligence.

Being 'religious' does not necessarily require a high SQ. Jesus describes this fact very clearly in his parable about the Pharisee and the publican who go up to the Temple to pray. The Pharisee, a very conscientious Jew, thanks God that he is not like the publican who has broken every rule in the book. The publican has only one prayer to make: 'God, have mercy on me a sinner'. At the end of the parable Jesus declares that it was the publican, not the Pharisee, who left the Temple in a right relationship with God. The publican shows signs of having an

SQ: the Pharisee is so enclosed in his own world of conformity to the law that he can only see the publican as a despicable failure!

Spiritual Intelligence enables us to get to the heart of religion, a religion which is opposed to all forms of idolatry, all forms of self-dedication to anything that is not the God in whom all that exists has its being, the God who is always greater than anything we can think or imagine. SQ signifies an innate ability of the human mind, in all its range and complexity, to go beyond itself, beyond the ego, beyond the human psyche. It is an intuitive faculty, inaccessible to analysis, which is aware of its relatedness to and reliance upon the whole of creation and of sensing the drawing power of all creation, drawing it out beyond itself; it knows the power of compassion, a power that is not of its own creation. The SQ can enable us to face into the fear of death and in so doing discover the miracle of this life. The SQ makes religion possible, but is not dependent on religion. As Rumi, the thirteenth-century Persian poet, expressed it:

'I see and know all times and worlds as one, always one.'

Using SQ can enable us to be creative, flexible, visionary, creatively spontaneous, because it releases us from our customary 'within the box' conventional thinking which has strayed so far from 'earthed thinking' that we no longer notice the difference and therefore find ourselves endlessly trapped in a virtual world of our own construction. We are not only trapped, but all our attempts to escape from the trap lead us into courses of action which enclose us more hopelessly in it.

Our SQ has been called 'our compass at the edge'. I find that to be a very helpful comment when looking at our present-day threats to human existence. Nuclear defence is only one of many crises facing us with annihilation today. All our attempts to solve these imminent threats to our human survival by violent means of any kind are doomed not only to failure, but to massive and possibly irreparable destruction. As I write this, I can hear the complaints arising within me: 'Stop being so idealistic. We live in a violent world. What you are writing sounds like an appeal to all humanity – "why can't you just be nice and forgiving and kind to one another?".' It is like an appeal to all to become as passive as doormats, as meek as lambs, ready for slaughter at the hands of anyone. I can hear those complaints. They come from within me, not just from my imagined critics. And I think the complaints are justified and need to be listened to.

What I hope to show is that true pacifism is not meek passivity in the face of violence. True non-violence has its roots in resistance, a resistance which is invincible because it is rooted in love. It is fearless, indestructible in face of all threats. For Christians, this fearless resistance was shown in the person of Jesus, 'image of the unseen God', but it has also been seen and it is still seen today in thousands of people of all religions and of none whose lives are lived on behalf of others out of love. These people make no great claims for themselves, do not ask for acclaim, reward or recognition; they act in the way they do because they find, deep within themselves, that they are drawn to this way of life and any other way would be intolerable for them. I shall be developing this point of Peace as Resistance in later chapters, and in Part 3 on Holiness.

Rabbi Heschel, a twentieth-century Jewish mystic, wrote: 'We are closer to God when we are asking questions than when we think we have the answers.' And Blaise Pascal (1623–62) wrote: 'You would not be seeking me (God), if you had not already found me.' The SQ helps us to focus our attention on our basic desire for unity, a desire which can both torment and delight us, leading us through the darkness into a new and transforming way of seeing the reality in which we find ourselves, not as individual little units struggling for survival in a hostile world, but as participants in a dance of creation, in which each of us is inextricably linked with every other and each has a unique role to play in such a way that the other is me and I am the other. This is the vision to which we are all called.

From these considerations, the close connection between Peace and Unity can begin to become apparent: they are like identical twin sisters, or perhaps triplets, if we add in Truth!

In their book *SQ Spiritual Intelligence – The Ultimate Intelligence* (Bloomsbury 2000), Danah Zohar and Ian Marshall give the following summary of the characteristics which are likely to be prominent in people with a high SQ. As an exercise at the end of this chapter you could try reading this list very slowly, then asking yourself your own felt reactions to each phrase and writing them down. There are no marks given for your answers, no rewards, just the assurance that what you write is of unique value for you!

- The capacity to be flexible (*not living according to set instructions, as though you were a washing machine*).

- A high degree of self-awareness (*in relation to the reality in which*

*you find yourself. As an example of self-awareness, the comment of
the Latin Poet Terence, who wrote of himself over 2000 years ago:
'I am a human being. Nothing human is foreign to me').*

- A capacity to face and use suffering creatively *as distinct from
  running away from it by dulling our awareness.*

- A capacity to face and transcend pain.

- An ability to be inspired by vision and values.

- A reluctance to cause unnecessary pain.

- An ability to see connections.

- A tendency to ask 'what if' and 'why' questions, *to look for
  fundamental questions.*

- A tendency to work against convention.

This list will tend to irritate the logical, rational brain, which will want
to dismiss the statements as too vague. In reading the list, it is important
to notice that it is describing tendencies, not essential characteristics of
SQ. To get in touch with your own SQ, be content to look at the list
and notice whether the tendencies touch into your own experience of
people you have encountered in fact or fiction, and whether you might
have spotted any of these tendencies in your own experience.

Some consequences of our emphasis on IQ and neglect of EQ and SQ

US Secretary of State Madeleine Albright, on being questioned about
the death toll of 500,000 children in Iraq because of sanctions imposed
on the country in the attempt to overthrow the dictatorship of Saddam
Hussein, is reported to have said, 'It was worth it'. Underlying such a
statement are hidden assumptions.

The hidden assumption is that the unnecessary death of any child
can ever be justified. Human beings are reduced to the category of
'thing', and, like any other thing, become a commodity to be used at
the discretion of those in power. 'It was worth it', uttered in the context
of 500,000 children having died because of sanctions imposed on the
country in its efforts to depose Saddam Hussain, is spine-chilling. What
are the values which lie hidden under the assurance, 'It was worth it'?

Another sign of IQ's predominance in a society is the way in which we disguise the horrors of our actions under cosy titles. The bomb dropped on Hiroshima was codenamed 'Little Boy'. The Nagasaki bomb, three days later, was code named 'Fat Man'. In battles which we have won, our casualties are called 'acceptable losses'. George W. Bush declared the presence of the US forces in Iraq to be 'peace work'. Military who are killed by their own side in battle are said to be casualties of 'friendly fire'. All the propaganda with which the military are allowed to win recruits for a career in the army are full of promise of the excitement of life in far-flung places and the great benefits their action can bring to native peoples. The essential factor in military training is never mentioned, namely that they should be trained to see the enemy as 'things', not as human beings of infinite worth – once the military start thinking in this way, they are no longer reliable in warfare.

When Adolf Eichmann, the Nazi key figure in the Holocaust, who was captured decades later in South America, was asked at his trial what he had found most burdensome in his responsibilities in Auschwitz concentration camp, where millions had been put to death, he replied that his greatest burden was the difficulties he had experienced with the German railway timetables because of the mass transportations of Jews to the concentration camps. He appeared to be a man unaffected by any emotional or spiritual considerations, securely defended against any qualms of conscience.

Hermann Goering, one of the most forceful and influential of the Nazi leaders, announced, while Nazism was still in its infancy: 'The people can always be brought to the bidding of its leaders. That is easy. All you have to do is tell them that they are being attacked and denounce the pacifists for lack of patriotism and for exposing the country to danger.' A very perceptive comment, which was to prove so true in the devastation which followed in World War II, and is still continuing and increasing in our worldwide violence, the great and the good, people of religion and people of no religion, all united in the conviction that the only answer to human violence lies in violence.

We are inevitably influenced by the attitudes implanted in us by others from our earliest years, not to mention the tendencies we have inherited from birth from our ancestors. As we ourselves come to consciousness we can appropriate these attitudes and either confirm or reject them so that they continue to bind us, or we become free of them. Another reflection which has become much clearer to me in later life is our need for constant vigilance in ourselves for the source of our own emotional and heartfelt experiences. This, I know, may sound very unattractive, leading to intensive preoccupation with our own ego. In fact, it is very simple: notice the emotional/heartfelt experiences and simply ask yourself in what direction are they leading me? Are they leading me to the wellbeing and service of others, or to my own self-assurance, independently of other people? We shall be looking at all these questions repeatedly in what follows, for it is through these questions that we can begin to see our human experience differently and consequently act and respond differently and so contribute to the welfare of all humankind.

Exercises

- What has been your felt reaction to this chapter's exploration of our split spirituality?

- Have you found the distinctions between IQ, EQ and SQ have any connection for you with your experience of life?

- If so, then write down for yourself what those connections are, as far as you can see at present.

5

To the Heart of the Gospel

This chapter takes us to the Heart of the Christian Gospel, the Good News revealed for all peoples. The message is radical, but easily domesticated and entirely missed if it is not communicated as a message for all peoples. If narrowly interpreted, the awesome message can become a source of division, of violence and destruction between peoples, an infectious, devouring and intensifying violence which is threatening all of us today.

In this chapter, there will be repetition. When a young pupil, studying St John's Gospel, complained to her teacher that St John was always repeating himself, her teacher explained that St John was an old man when he wrote his Gospel and old men tend to keep telling the same stories! St John does repeat himself, but with every repetition there is something new added. It is a very good method of communicating, building gradually through constant reminders of what went before, repeatedly returning to the foundational statements from which the new message arises. Because Christ's Peace is such a wide-ranging topic relating to every aspect of human life, and because it is so commonly considered to be worth attention only in relation to war, in writing on the nature of Peace I find myself having to remind myself constantly of the spiritual nature of Peace. Peace permeates every aspect of human life, is indestructible, life-giving, the source of human freedom, wellspring of joy, a reality which, if we are going to relate to it, demands a response from our hearts. Peace remains an abstraction for us unless we engage with it: the same is true of love, compassion, justice, truth, forgiveness and all those other invisible realities for which our hearts crave.

In this chapter we shall be exploring in greater detail the stark contrast between Christ's peace, as the Scriptures present it, and the

world's peace. This is not an academic discussion: it is a most fundamental and personal question for each of us. How do I want to respond
to the life experience I am continuously being offered? The question is
not one imposed on us by some external authority, it is imposed on
us by our own experience and there is no way any of us can avoid it.
On the other hand, it is in acknowledging our need to respond to this
question that we can make the breakthrough to a new vision, a new
hope, a new joy. We begin to see ourselves, other people, our circumstances in a new way and it is the new vision which sets us on our way
into joy and freedom.

To begin with, we shall return to the Temptations of Jesus in the
desert as they are given to us in St Matthew's Gospel ch. 4, vv. 1-11:

> Then Jesus was led by the Spirit out into the wilderness to be
> tempted by the devil. He fasted for forty days and forty nights, after
> which he was very hungry, and the tempter came to him and said to
> him, 'If you are the Son of God, tell these stones to turn into loaves',
> but he replied, 'Scripture says:
> *'Man does not live by bread alone but on every word that comes
> from the mouth of God.'*
> The devil then took him to the holy city and made him stand on
> the parapet of the temple. 'If you are the Son of God', he said, 'throw
> yourself down, for Scripture says, He will put you in his angels'
> charge, and they will support you on their hands in case you hurt
> your foot upon a stone.' Jesus said to him, 'Scripture also says:
> *'You must not put the Lord your God to the test.'*
> Next, taking him to a very high mountain, the devil showed him
> all the kingdoms of the world and their splendour. 'I will give you
> all these', he said, 'if you fall at my feet and worship me.' Then Jesus
> said,
> *'You must worship the Lord your God and serve him alone.'*
> Then the devil left him, and angels appeared and looked after
> him.

This passage lies at the heart of the Gospels. This is a key text helping
us to glimpse Jesus' understanding of God and showing us the basic
attitude which we must have in relating to the world. This attitude is
not the world's attitude. It is counter-cultural and revolutionary. It lies
at the heart of the Peace issue, how peace can be realized, sustained
and promoted, until it becomes a way for all human beings, for God

is Peace, God is 'Emmanuel', meaning God is with us and each one of us is being invited to become the unique image of God that we were created to become. St Augustine of Hippo, North Africa, in his Confessions, written about 1,500 years ago, stated: 'Lord, you have created me for yourself, and my heart is restless until it rests in you.' By becoming aware of this deep restlessness within us we are responding to the drawing of God, who had us in mind before creation began!

Because of our upbringing, this description of the temptations is more likely to be a puzzle rather than an answer to our own restlessness of heart. When we read a passage like this, our first reaction is likely to be 'Did the temptations really happen in this way?' This can lead us into an endless series of difficult questions, a process which is like a journey through a swamp, an exhausting and dangerous journey because we cannot find any support to lift us out of the morass of our own thinking. The Hebrew way of thinking is different from our own. Their first question, on reading about Jesus' temptations, or any event in Jesus' life, is not to ask 'Did it really happen that way?', but 'What does the account mean?', 'What is it saying to us today in our situation?' This is a very different approach that engages us in the present in a totally new way.

Take, for example, the creation accounts given in the book of Genesis, the beginning of the Hebrew Scriptures. Did creation take place exactly as the authors describe it, remembering that the two creation accounts are very different? When we ask instead, 'What do these accounts mean for us in our present circumstances, in our present crises?', we discover very different and more practical questions. The first reaction – 'Did it really happen this way?' – leads us into a fundamentalist, literal explanation, which ignores the facts that science reveals to us and turns God into an all-powerful magician, who can ignore the harmony of creation at any moment to answer the wishes of the devout fundamentalists, who cannot see beyond the horizons of their own self-interest, which blinds them to the welfare of any who dare disagree with them.

To answer any of these 'what does it mean?' questions we need to give attention to the context in which the statements are made. This is a very relevant question, because this passage in Matthew's Gospel can change what at first sight seems a most unlikely story into a most apt and relevant comment on the nature of God and the meaning of our own lives now.

In Jesus' lifetime, the Mediterranean world was considered to be the largest and most significant part of the known world, and the Roman Empire to be the most powerful and well-organized empire that had ever existed. Palestine was one of Rome's smallest colonies, but also its most troublesome. The poet Virgil had described Rome's destiny and world function in these words: 'Rome, be this thy care – these thy arts – to bear dominion over the nations and to impose the law of peace to spare the humbled and to vanquish the proud' – a task which Rome fulfilled for centuries without serious challenge, leaving a heritage which still today characterizes the rule of law in many of its former colonies, now independent countries, including the UK.

How did Rome rule and control such a vast and varied empire in days when animal-driven vehicles and human feet were the only means of travel? The emperors had a pithy saying, the clue to their successful domination. In different forms, it is still the method being used worldwide today. The pithy phrase was: 'Give the people bread, give the people circuses, and make yourself divine'. The phrase did not fall from heaven; it grew out of centuries of experience – the last part of the phrase, 'make yourself divine', only becoming official policy when Jesus, son of Mary and of Joseph, was still a youth living in obscurity in Nazareth.

All the temptations of Jesus in the desert are temptations to power, to exercise control over others, and the methods seemed admirable: 'to feed the hungry, vanquish the proud' and so bring peace to the world, later called '*Pax Romana*'. It is important to recognize the attractiveness of this policy. It still attracts those in power – a superficial attraction, which masks from our minds and hearts the underlying violence.

The Roman rulers were very aware of the importance of religion in their way of governing. People embraced religion as a way of ensuring their protection in this life against the avarice of the gods, who were forever squabbling among themselves. These gods were considered to have control over human beings, but they were susceptible to bribes and so could be deterred from damaging humankind through money, sacrificial gifts of fruit, animals, human beings, especially children. By making themselves divine, the emperors could control their subjects by fear of the punishments they could inflict after death on those who disobeyed their orders while on earth. In this way the rulers could control their subjects' minds and hearts through fear.

Matthew's Gospel indicates the essential meaning of the temptations of Jesus in his lifetime. It is the temptation to control the lives of other people. The temptations also illustrate the subtlety of the evil spirit, masquerading under the appearance of good and hiding the utter disregard for the good of those who are controlled. Their goodness consists in their conformity to their rulers: their subjects have nothing else to commend them. When we have been well trained in this kind of thinking, we become capable of treating other people as things, as commodities, to be got rid of when they are no longer of use to serve the needs of those in charge. And we can be trained to comply without noticing our barbarity, perhaps congratulating ourselves on the wisdom of our subservience and on being honoured by the State for our conformity.

The subtlety of the temptation is also hidden under the apparent good of what is proposed, namely to feed the hungry – a funda-mental human response, which Jesus himself is to preach as being the will of God. The subtlety of the temptation was well expressed in the twentieth-century comment of Helder Camara, Bishop of Recife in Brazil: 'When I feed the hungry they call me a saint, when I ask why they are hungry they call me a Communist.' In itself, feeding the hungry is a basic human obligation. But the motive for such a policy, the manner in which it is performed can be as a means of holding people in subjection. For example, in many developed countries today, close on a billion people are dying of starvation, not because there is no food, but because people are being driven off their land because the local government can raise more money by using the land for the growth of luxury crops for export to wealthier countries. Meanwhile their own people perish from hunger.

Yes, feed the people, but also keep asking the question 'why are they hungry?' This questioning leads us to the heart of the matter: 'We do not live on bread alone'. Jesus' refusal points to a more basic need for humankind, the need to become more aware of our human dignity. We are all called to be unique manifestations of God, to let the Spirit of God, whose centre is everywhere and whose bounds are nowhere, be our Lord and God. This awareness introduces us to an awesome responsibility – to resist with all our being those forces which would deprive us of this gift. Jesus manifested this power against the religious and secular authorities of his time, a tradition which still continues today in people who protest non-violently, but with their whole being, against all authorities, both religious and secular, who treat human beings as commodities, as things, easily disposable when they oppose the vested interests of the powerful.

Leaping off the temple still seems to be an unlikely temptation, especially if we are liable to vertigo and carefully avoid high places. Again we catch ourselves in our own literal-mindedness. The important question does not concern questions about temple parapets, but what does the scene mean and in what ways does it suggest questions which concern us today about our own lives, our relationships with others, with ourselves and with God? The temptation is to act in a way that will impress people, make them take notice of us, envy or admire us. The temptation concerns our self-regard: looking at it in this way can enable us to see its power. Look, for example, at the times we say to ourselves, 'I ought to do this, say that, wear this, study that, choose this path of action', then ask ourselves the simple question 'why?', in order to discover the source of this 'ought'. There was a British psycho-analyst, Dr Frank Lake, who became an Anglican priest and wrote a fascinating book called *Clinical Theology*, in which he diagnosed a spiritual ailment which he named 'hardening of the oughteries'. He distinguishes the oughteries which arise from our own desires from those which arise from other people's desires. For example, if I want to become a violinist, then I may decide to practise daily for at least two hours. The 'ought' here springs from my own desire and I practise happily. But my 'ought' about violin practice may arise because my parents/violin teacher expect me to do it; consequently I practise with an inner reluctance, which will show itself in the quality of my playing. My playing may be faultless due to the enforced practice, but it will also be soulless.

On a broader scale than violin playing, look at the phrase 'It is your duty to serve others'– an admirable exhortation in itself, but, in the post-World War II example of the Nuremberg trials, when those accused of the murder of millions in concentration camps pleaded innocence on the grounds of duty, we can see the importance of distinguishing between duty which arises from our inner desires and free choice, from those duties which are imposed on us by external authorities and with which we comply through fear of opposing such authority. The external authority can threaten us with disgrace, dismissal from our job, or even with death if we fail to comply. They threaten us with the cross, the cross which Jesus tells us we are to bear!

Notice the subtlety in the temple parapet temptation. Jesus has a message to communicate, a revelation for all humankind. In his lifetime on earth, he expressed this truth in the words, 'I have come to cast fire upon the earth and I long for its accomplishment'. As a means of communicating this message, why not do something which will break through the narrow thinking of your audiences and help them to glimpse what their own hearts long for? A safe and elegant leap off the temple, ending with a deep bow to the astonished audience, will be far more effective than your many harangues in the temple itself. Jesus is aware of this subtlety; that is why he later tells his disciples: 'Be as wise as serpents and as gentle as doves'.

The final temptation is to take control of all the world's power centres, all the kingdoms of the world and their splendour. If Jesus were to take control of all the world's power centres, he could rid the world of corruption, deceit and oppression, oppose and overcome all human avarice for power. Would that not be a most praiseworthy thing to do? The only thing that is preventing him from doing so is his attachment to what he calls 'the will of my Father in heaven'. Why not renounce this attachment for the sake of peace and freedom for all humankind? Yes, it is a very subtle temptation, but Jesus answers it without a trace of hesitation: 'Be off, Satan, for Scripture says, "*You must worship the Lord, your God, and serve him alone*".'

What follows from this answer and what sense can we make of it? One conclusion we can make is that Jesus does not consider the possession of power and control to be the supreme good for human beings. The God to whom he is attached with his whole being is not a God of power and might, but a God of love and compassion, a God who so identifies with humankind that God's self enters into all the oppression that afflicts us, even into the oppression of death itself, and so liberates us. Death is not the end of our story, but the entry into a new way of being. It was when his followers began to understand his death in this way that their lives were changed from fear and guilt to peace and joy, even when they were being accused, rejected, imprisoned and beaten by both secular and religious authorities. The reason for this transformation was not because they now recited creeds at the bidding of Church authorities, but because their own inner experience was now continuously assuring them that they were not alone, that the Spirit of the Risen Christ really was at work within them and around them. They were no longer dominated by fear of death. As

St Paul expressed his own transformation: 'I can now live for God. I have been crucified with Christ, and I live now not with my own life, but with the life of Christ who lives in me. I cannot bring myself to give up God's gift' (Gal. 2.20-21).

Jesus does not promise to deliver us from pain and distress, but he does promise always to be with us, however painful and threatening our situation may be. He is constantly warning his followers of this. If we are drawn to follow his way of love and compassion, of justice and truth, then we shall meet with opposition, oppression, cruelty and disregard not only from strangers, but from our own families and friends. Later, we may come to realize that our fiercest enemy is within us. There are deep splits in the core of our being. Acknowledging these personal failures is the starting point for our journey into life, the way to salvation not only for ourselves, but also for those around us. Seen in this way, our faults become blessings. It is interesting that the word '*blessure*' in French, meaning a wound, is the word from which we have 'blessing' in English.

It was through reading Dostoevsky's novel *The Brothers Karamazov* many decades ago that I first began to see the fundamental importance of the Gospel accounts of Jesus' temptations. In the novel, Dostoevsky has a chapter entitled 'The Grand Inquisitor', in which one of the characters, Ivan, describes to Alyosha, his brother, an imaginary interview in sixteenth-century Seville between the Grand Inquisitor and Jesus, who has appeared in Seville, a quiet and gentle character with healing powers. On one day he raises a child to life from her funeral coffin, a scene spotted by the Grand Inquisitor, who has just attended the deaths by fire of over a hundred people accused of heresy. The Inquisitor has an interview with the reappeared Jesus, accuses him of destroying the Church because he gave all the wrong answers to the offers put to him by Satan in the temptations of the desert. Consequently, he has imposed an intolerable burden on humankind, a burden that will torment them throughout their lives, because they are unable to bear the responsibility of the gift of freedom. The Inquisitor claims: 'There are but three forces which can conquer and hold captive forever the conscience of these impotent rebels for their happiness. These forces are miracle, mystery and authority.' By refusing to turn the stones into bread, Jesus has rejected miracle; by refusing to leap off the temple parapet he has rejected mystery; and by refusing to take charge of all the kingdoms of the world he has rejected the use of authority to coerce others into conformity with his will.

The Inquisitor accuses Jesus of trusting humankind too much. 'Respecting man less, you would have asked less of him. That would have been more like love, for his burden would have been lighter.' The Inquisitor constantly claims that the role of the Church is to bring happiness, but the only practical way of doing this is to remove the burden of conscience and freedom from humankind. At one point in the conversation he tells Jesus: 'We have taken the sword of Caesar, and in taking it, we have rejected you and followed him.'

Near the end of the interview the Inquisitor declares: 'What I say to you will come to pass and our dominion will be built up. I repeat, tomorrow you shall see the obedient flock who, at a sign from me, will hasten to heap up the hot cinders about the pile on which I shall burn you for coming to hinder us. For if anyone has ever deserved our fires, it is you. Tomorrow, I shall burn you. I have spoken.'

The chapter ends with a final scene:

When the Inquisitor ceased speaking, he waited some time for his prisoner to speak to him [...] The prisoner listened intently all the time, looking gently into his face and evidently not wishing to reply [...] He suddenly approached the old man in silence and silently kissed him on his bloodless lips. That was all his answer. The old man shuddered, his lips moved. He went to the door, opened it and said to the prisoner, 'Go, and come no more ... come not at all, never, never!' And he let him out into the dark night of the town. The prisoner went away. 'And the old man?' asked Alyosha. 'The kiss glows in his heart, but the old man adheres to his idea', answers his brother.

This imaginative story raises a most profound question which concerns not only all who profess a Christian faith: it is a question for people of all faiths and also for people who profess no religious faith. What is the value you would most like to live for and die for? It is a question we are continuously answering in the practical choices we make in life: they speak more clearly and eloquently and truthfully than our words. It is a question we must all face if we long for peace for our world, the condition of our human survival. May our certainties never destroy our ability to sense the kiss that glows in our hearts.

The themes of the temptations permeate the New Testament: they also permeate our daily lives. Our salvation lies in allowing ourselves to become aware of these truths.

When Tony Blair became Prime Minister in the UK, the first Labour government after 17 years in opposition, he announced a priority for his government, 'Education, education, education', a subject of fundamental importance for any government and for any human being. In light of the first temptation, the fundamental importance of education becomes very clear when we ask 'why?' Do we educate in order to produce conformists, who will accept without question whatever their teachers tell them to accept, or do we educate them so that they can become free and live their own unique lives, in harmony with the core of their own being, with their essential relatedness to all that exists and to the unity into which all creation is being drawn? Do our own current educational methods encourage this notion of education, or do they militate against it? Do we educate people to collaborate, or is our emphasis on competing? Competition nurtures individualism, collaboration nurtures community. Through competition the majority are losers, begin to consider themselves failures, abandon hope, may find some passing relief in creating disruption, but easily fall into despair.

Because life becomes increasingly complicated in our technological age, and as people are increasingly separated from their own locality in their search for jobs and housing, so they begin to feel more isolated and less confident in themselves. In this way we enter the age of the expert and experience the tyranny of knowledge, which can undermine confidence and prepare us to be exemplary citizens of future totalitarian states. Modern communication methods, excellent in themselves, can easily become instruments of this tyranny of technology. Before the recent war in Iraq there were massive protests, the largest ever seen in London, against going to war. Within a few days, when war was declared, the mass protests dwindled into insignificance. Who dares oppose public opinion, especially when war is being waged? Lacking confidence in our personal worth, we can become enthusiastic supporters of officialdom. Jesus, in face of Pilate's statement, 'Surely, you know I have the power to release you and I have the power to crucify you?', answers 'You would have no power over me if it had not been given to you from above'. Jesus obeys the law of his heart, which transcends all human authority. Human legislation is necessary in human society, but it is a service to humanity, not an instrument declaring authority's omnipotence. Human legislation can never control the power of human freedom, of truth, of love, of justice.

Throughout the Gospels, Jesus says very little about the future Church, gives no detailed instructions about the organization of it; in fact, the word translated as 'Church' appears only three times in all the Gospels, and all three mentions are to be found only in Matthew. The topic on which Jesus is unmistakably clear is in his warnings to his disciples against the temptations of power and he does give very clear instructions about the way authority is to be exercised among his followers. Jesus' assurance is rooted in his experience that God is Love, a power which no earthly power can overcome, a meaning of power which transcends our human understanding of power as control, power which can enforce people to conform to a particular way of thinking and acting. Here are some examples.

In Mark, Ch. 10, James and John had approached Jesus asking if they could have the top places in the kingdom. The other ten apostles were indignant on hearing this, so Jesus addressed all of them: 'You know that among the pagans their so-called rulers lord it over them and their great men make their authority felt. This is not to happen among you. No; anyone who wants to become great among you must be your servant, and anyone who wants to be first among you must be slave to all. For the Son of Man himself did not come to be served, but to serve, and to give his life as a ransom for many' (Mk 10.41-45). The same event is described in Matthew 20.24-28, and in Luke 22.24-37.

In the Gospels it is remarkable to note the contrast between the New Testament's presentation of the apostles' lives and today's celebrity fever! Apart from listing their names when they are called to become apostles, most of them remain nameless thereafter without even a potted biography. They are not from famous families, show no signs of being powerful or influential. In Luke's account, the Sermon on the Mount, which I shall later refer to as the Sermon on the Plain, is given in a level place, to which everyone has access. The apostles' message is to be peace, not conquest, and their ministry is to give priority to the sick, the poor, the estranged and the abandoned. They are to leave the 99 sheep which are safe and go off in search of the one that has strayed. It is not, as the Grand Inquisitor kept telling Jesus, an attractive programme at first sight and it can easily be presented as though the essence of Jesus' teaching is that we should become passive, silent, uncomplaining sufferers in a very hostile world. In fact, the following of Jesus is calling us to resist with every fibre of our being those who oppress, devalue, despise and depersonalize any human being. Yet this resistance is to be exercised non-violently and with love! This can seem like a contradiction. Is that why, although it is read out in liturgical services, little attempt is made to emphasize and explain this essentially resistant element in all Christian life?

The question is how can non-violent resistance become effective in our modern era of intensifying and increasing violence? Worldwide common sense/opinion is clear. The answer is that violence can only be answered by greater violence, an assured certainty which will remain a certainty as long as we refuse to question it. Given our present record in opposing violence with greater violence, it is possible that we shall have effected an answer irrevocably with defence measures which make continuing human life impossible. This may read like scaremongering, but it is the facts of our situation which are scary, not our words about them.

How can non-violent resistance be effective? In answer, I shall comment on a passage in Luke from his Sermon on the Plain. The substance of this passage is also given in Matthew and Mark. It is part of Jesus' manifesto.

> But I say this to you who are listening: Love your enemies, do good to those who hate you, bless those who curse you, pray for those who treat you badly. To the person who slaps you on one cheek turn the other cheek too; to the man who takes your cloak from you, do not refuse your tunic. Give to everyone who asks you, and do not ask for your property back from the person who robs you. Treat others as you would like them to treat you [...] Instead, love your enemies and do good, and lend without any hope of return [...] Be compassionate as your Father is compassionate. Do not judge and you will not be judged yourselves; grant pardon and you will be pardoned. Give, and there will be gifts for you: a full measure, pressed down, shaken together, and running over, will be poured into your lap; because the amount you measure out is the amount you will be given back. (Lk. 6.27-38)

In non-violent resistance, the response of the victim of violence is not the response the attacker expects, so the attacker is taken off guard, is given a pause to come to a deeper level of themselves than their immediate fear. They expect retaliation, but the pause they are afforded allows them the chance to respond less instinctively. The victim's reaction has momentarily halted the aggressor's violent reaction. To be able to react to assault in this way requires practice and regular training. Nelson Mandela, in his 25 years of imprisonment, much of it in solitary confinement, never allowed fear to govern his reactions in face of violent treatment. This behaviour eventually began to influence his captors: he was releasing them, too, from their fears, so both parties gained from the non-resistance.

Among Jesus' contemporaries, the most dramatic way of showing contempt for another was to slap their face with the back of your hand; not with an open hand, for through such an action the Jew could incur a ritual impurity. Presenting the other cheek would create a problem for the assailant. To hit the other side of the victim's face with the back of your hand would demand humiliating contortions. The victim has resisted, but without inflicting any physical or verbal violence on the aggressor. To undergo such training and to act so fearlessly requires great courage and strong motivation.

A people trained in non-violence can defy violent and aggressive governments. In the overthrow of the Marcos regime in the Philippines in 1986, the Catholic population had practised non-violent resistance for a year and Marcos was deposed without bloodshed. In the Second World War, the Germans invaded Denmark. The Danes practised non-violent resistance. When the German authorities demanded that all Jews in Denmark should wear a yellow star, the King and Queen and the whole population wore the Star of David. The Danes also practised a non-violence policy against the occupying power. While in so many other invaded countries there was an underground resistance killing the invaders, in Denmark the people invited their invaders to meals. Post-World War II, I read an account which stated that after service in Denmark, no German divisions which had been stationed in Denmark were ever put in the front line of battle elsewhere because they could no longer be trusted! There is a vast amount to be written on the success of non-violent resistance against tyrannical forms of government, especially in the second half of the twentieth century, when so many countries collapsed from positions of apparently impregnable power. Examples are the break-up of the Soviet Union, the collapse of the South African Apartheid government, the release of Nelson Mandela and his installation as President.

'To the man who takes your cloak from you, do not refuse your tunic.' Behind this terse suggestion there is a message of non-violent resistance. In Jewish law in Jesus' time, a debtor who had no money could be compelled to hand over his cloak to his creditor during the daytime, but the creditor had to return it at night lest the debtor die of exposure. Jesus' suggestion is for the courthouse resistant. When ordered to hand over his cloak, Jesus' suggestion is that the accused should hand over his tunic as well – in other words, to expose his nakedness to all in court, manifesting his utter helplessness, a non-violent piece of resistance designed to reach out to the compassion of the creditor. St Matthew adds another suggestion: 'If anyone orders you to go one mile, go two miles with him.' Roman soldiers could order civilians in Israel to carry a load for one mile only. The suggestion is that Christian generosity should mirror the utter generosity of God, not measured or calculated.

To be Christian is to let the Spirit of the Risen Christ continue his work on earth in and through us. We need to pray constantly that we may recognize the drawing of God's love now in the details of our lives, drawing us out beyond our immediate preoccupations into the unity we are all being offered, a unity with all creation for which our hearts will always be restless. In this unity we shall be set free from our tyrannical self and able to know the inner peace and joy for which we are created as we find ourselves living for one another and for all creation.

In this chapter we have looked more closely at the nature of Peace as it is portrayed in the Christian New Testament against the historical context of those times. In the next chapter we shall look at Peace through the eyes of a twentieth-century writer, René Girard, who stumbled into Peace unexpectedly in his early twenties. He was lecturing in French literature at Indiana University, where he became interested in the relationship between Religion and Violence. This became his life interest. He had abandoned Christianity in his youth. He recovered it through his writing.

Exercises

- Did you have any felt reaction to the Scripture passages quoted in this chapter?
- Can you spot any connection between your felt reaction and your present experience?
- Does this reaction enable you to see your own life differently in any way?

6

René Girard, *Violence and the Sacred*

René Girard was born in France in 1923. He attended the Ecole des Chartres in Paris from 1943 to 1947, where he graduated as a specialist in medieval studies. In 1947 he left for the USA for a year and still lives there. It was in the USA that his extraordinary career began. He was employed by Indiana University to teach French and this included courses in literature, which was outside his subject, but it was teaching French literature that drew him into his lifetime's work on the nature of peace and violence. *Violence and the Sacred*, first published in 1972 in French, brought him international recognition.

His most famous book followed in 1978, *Des choses cachées depuis la fondation du monde* (*Things Hidden since the Foundation of the World*). Its theme includes Fundamental Anthropology, the Judeo-Christian Scriptures and Intervidual [*sic*] Psychology – massive topics. The book made an immediate impact both on Christian believers and on atheist humanists. In the book he declares himself a Christian, while advocating a non-sacrificial reading of the Gospels and of the divinity of Christ. His bibliography in his book *The Girard Reader* includes six pages of the titles of his published books and articles.

In this chapter I write on Girard because he throws new light on the Peace/Violence issue and raises basic questions that are still being widely ignored by the media and academics of today. I focus attention on his questions. I do not understand or agree with some of his answers, but I am impressed by his honesty in admitting his inability to express strongly and clearly his insights and also in noting his willingness to admit his past mistakes. Writers who can do this always inspire confidence, because their persistence in searching seems to be based on something more solid than their own self-belief. It was his study of the relationship between violence and the sacred that eventually brought Girard back to his Christian belief.

Looking back on his life, he spoke of three great moments of discovery. The first was the nature of mimetic desire. He claims that this mimetic characteristic is innate in all human beings. It is not something we learn to do: it is our mimetic desire which enables us to learn. This mimesis is also at the root of violence. If I become the model for another in my ability to build up my own kingdom of possessions, then I shall feel threatened when the one who has found their model in me then attempts to curb my own self-appropriating behaviour. In itself, mimetic desire is a good thing in that it enables us to grow, but the violence it can engender can destroy the antagonists if it is not controlled in some way. One way it can be controlled is through the imposition of 'taboos', about which I wrote in Chapter 2 of this part of the book.

Girard's second moment of discovery was the scapegoat mechanism, a means of escaping from violence when the taboos failed to halt its spread. Scapegoating is a method of reconciling enemies, individuals or groups, but it is a peace based on deception and violence. To be effective short-term, the scapegoat mechanism must convince those taking part in the reconciliation that the scapegoat really is the cause of all their ills and that if they can rid themselves of the scapegoat, then those taking part will be freed from all guilt incurred by the violence in which they have cooperated. The scapegoaters can then feel that they have been acting righteously in their violent destruction of the scapegoat. The scapegoat may be an animal, a human being, or a whole group of human beings. We have an abundance of terrifying examples of scapegoating in our own history. The Jewish Holocaust of the twentieth century, the witch-hunting in Europe in previous centuries are two instances of mass scapegoating.

As I said above, to work effectively in reconciling enemies, both warring parties must be convinced that the chosen scapegoat really is the cause of their misfortunes. The scapegoat, whether animal or human, whether an individual or a group is no longer considered to be a living organism/human being: it has been changed into a deadly infection from which the warring parties must be protected, lest they both become victims of the uncontrollable devastation in which they are trapped. The root of the violence in all scapegoating lies in the human mind.

The former enemies are thus reconciled, become friends and can collaborate creatively, both parties gaining from the bloody transaction. Once this mindset takes control in an individual, or in a group, then there is no depth of depravity of which we are not capable when our anger is fuelled with fear for our own, or our group's, safety. Scapegoating can also be seen in politics. During the years of the Cold War against Soviet Russia, Senator McCarthy ruined the lives of many individuals and groups in the USA by labelling them as 'Marxist' or 'Communist' sympathizers. All our misfortune and suffering was caused by Marxism; therefore, for our own peace and security, we must eradicate all Marxists from our midst. The doctrine is clear and simple, easy to grasp, which makes it so attractive: it is also deceitful and utterly destructive because it breeds the crisis of terrorism which threatens our survival today.

The scapegoating tendency can be seen at work in controversies about social reform in general and penal reform in particular. It manifests itself in a more general way in our apparent need to have an enemy in order that we may feel safe. At the end of the Cold War, when the Soviet Union ceased to be Enemy No. 1, it did not take us long before we discovered another: the threat of Islam.

In drawing our attention to mimetic desire and to the phenomenon of scapegoating – both universal tendencies among human beings – Girard has made a most valuable contribution to peace-making. He has exposed the breadth of the practical questions arising from our desire for peace, has shown the shallowness of the generally accepted answer to all violence issues – namely more violence. He does not claim to have simple answers, but he does uncover our pretences to be working for peace when, in fact, our peace-making methods are founded on violence.

Girard's third great moment of discovery was in discovering the uniqueness of the Bible, among all literature, in its attitude to the scapegoat.

In the myths of ancient literature, the scapegoat has always been believed to be the cause of all the difficulties besetting the warring parties. It is this unity in belief which enables former enemies to unite in friendship and collaborate creatively together. According to the myth of Rome's foundation, Romulus and Remus were twins, abandoned in childhood and suckled by a she-wolf. Later Romulus, in a quarrel over the new city, killed Remus, and the city was enabled to survive, grow and flourish. The killing was considered to be a very good thing and for the greater good.

In the Bible there are many tales of brothers/twins caught up in mimetic rivalry: the stories of Cain and Abel, of Jacob and his brother Esau, of Joseph and his brothers. In ancient literature there are also many similar tales of mimetic rivalry, but in these ancient stories peace is always restored through the death of one individual or party. The Scriptural accounts have a totally different way of dealing with the scapegoat.

When Cain, child of Adam and Eve, kills his twin, Abel, God condemns the murder, but when Cain says 'Whoever comes across me will kill me', God answers 'If anyone kills Cain, vengeance shall be taken on him sevenfold'. 'And the Lord put a mark on Cain to prevent anyone from striking him down.'

Cain's murder of Abel precipitates the first cultural revolution, from being nomads to becoming farmers, but this does not excuse the murder.

Biblical writers are unique in their treatment of the ancient myths. They defend the scapegoat victim. The prophet Isaiah's picture of the Suffering Servant makes the servant appear to be a scapegoat. In Isaiah ch. 53, vv. 2-6, for example, the Suffering Servant is described:

> Like a sapling he grew up in front of us,
> Like a root in arid ground.
> Without beauty, without majesty (we saw him),
> no looks to attract our eyes;
> a thing despised and rejected by men,
> a man of sorrows and familiar with suffering,
> a man to make people screen their faces;
> he was despised and we took no account of him
> yet ours were the sufferings he bore,
> ours the sorrows he carried.
>
> But we thought of him as someone punished,
> struck by God and brought low.
> yet he was pierced through for our faults,
> crushed for our sins.
> On him lies a punishment that brings us peace,
> and through his wounds we are healed.

We had all gone astray like sheep,
each taking his own way
and Yahweh burdened him
with the sins of all of us.

The only point I am trying to make here is Girard's emphasis on the unique way in which the scapegoat theme is treated by Isaiah. The scapegoat is not guilty. But in the mythical way of describing the scapegoat in ancient literature, the mechanism can only work because both warring parties firmly believe in the guilt of the scapegoated person/group/animal.

The violence of God, as God is portrayed in the Bible, is a vast topic, which is beyond my competence. There are many very disturbing passages in which large-scale violence is attributed to God – against the Egyptians, for example and the unfortunate native inhabitants of the Promised Land, which God made available to the chosen people. This fact has to be faced, and in facing it we can come to see that there is a developing understanding of God and the ways of God throughout the Bible. God becomes less violent as God is portrayed in the prophets, the psalms, the Wisdom books. In the Gospels, Jesus' God is not violent.

Jesus exposes the lie of our human culture that peace can be produced through violence.

Girard claims that Jesus, through his life, teaching, passion and death exposed the lie of our human culture that peace can only be brought about through violence and deceit. The violence is in the murder: the deceit is in convincing ourselves that through this action, and through this action alone, we can rid ourselves of our guilt. The human conviction that violence is the only effective means of bringing peace is a very ancient belief, so deeply ingrained in human consciousness that it appears to be impervious to any rational methods of persuasion, or to the appalling facts of the growing violence of our own age, leaving us in the developed Western countries with sufficient nuclear defence weaponry to threaten all organic life on earth, should war break out.

We seem to be incapable of freeing ourselves from our ingrained way of thinking. We are afraid to look at it; we hide from it, distract ourselves from our dread of it. We keep ourselves fully occupied with our own self-preservation, keeping the consumer society going and using the competitive measures against one another which intensify our fears, the fuel of our violence.

The Gospels can come alive for us in a totally new way if we dare to read them in our modern context of fear and dread. Jesus' teaching is not threatening us with an angry, vengeful God. He turns our attention to our own behaviour, to enable us to see beyond the narrow boundaries of our inherited vision, which persuades us that the only practical answer to spreading violence is greater violence. As I write these lines, the United Nations is facing the Syrian crisis, a civil war which has already cost thousands of innocent lives of women and children in addition to the casualties of the warring parties. The latest turn in events is the death of about 1,400 people through a poison gas attack. The Assad regime is the suspect. Investigations are still not completed, but the question now is, if the Assad regime is proved to be the guilty party, what measures are to be taken against a regime which wages war against its own citizens? One promising sign in this tragedy is the growing opposition from so many national groups against military intervention, but the fear is that our ingrained ways of thinking will prevail and action will be taken that will spread the violence even further, far beyond Syria.

God is not the problem: we are the problem. Until we acknowledge this, we can never escape from the prisons we create for ourselves. That is another way of saying, 'Repent and believe the Good News'. The Gospel message speaks clearly to our day if we have the ears to hear and the eyes to see. It is on our minds and hearts we need to work, not on devastating the earth which sustains us.

When Jesus uncovers for the people the hidden violence of the scribes and the Pharisees, he begins by saying: 'The scribes and Pharisees occupy the chair of Moses. You must therefore do what they tell you and listen to what they say, but do not be guided by what they do; since they do not practise what they preach.' He does not deny their authority, but that does not prevent him from telling them where he stands. He tells it clearly and he must have known the risk he was taking of losing his own life by speaking out in this way. Here, for example, is his seventh indictment against the chief priests, the Scribes and the Pharisees:

Alas for you, scribes and Pharisees, you hypocrites! You who build the sepulchres of the prophets and decorate the tombs of holy men, saying, 'We would never have joined in shedding the blood of the prophets, had we lived in our fathers' day'. So! Your own evidence tells against you! You are the sons of those who murdered the prophets! Very well then, finish off the work that your fathers began. (Mt. 23.29-32)

For speaking like this, the religious authorities have to get rid of him. They have to do violence to expel the truth about violence!

To allow these words to take hold of us, we must beg God to give us an awareness of our own hidden violence, of our own fragility, of our unacknowledged fears, which lead us to act in ways that are so centred on our own security that we become unaware of the destructive effects they are having both on ourselves and on those around us. It is through failure to acknowledge these fears that, as nations in the developed world, we proceed to build up nuclear defensive methods, which are already doing immense damage by diverting wealth, which could relieve world poverty, into the manufacture, preservation and multiplication of weapons of death. These present disasters are products of human minds and hearts. We are to blame. There is nothing inevitable in the crises that face us. Things can change.

Jesus the unique scapegoat

In Luke's account of Jesus' trial and Passion he describes how Jesus, after his betrayal by Judas and arrest by the temple guards, was brought next morning to appear before Pilate, who alone had the power to condemn Jesus to death. They told Pilate that 'we found this man inciting the people to revolt, opposing the payment of tribute to Caesar and claiming to be Christ, a king'. Pilate questions Jesus, then tells the chief priests and the crowd: 'I find no case against this man.' The chief priests then claim that 'he is inflaming the people with his teaching all over Judaea; it has come all the way from Galilee where he started, down to here'. When Pilate heard this, he handed the case over to Herod, the client king of Galilee, who happened to be in Jerusalem at the time. Herod was curious about Jesus, but could get no reply from him. 'Then Herod, together with his guards, treated him with contempt, and made fun of him; he put a rich cloak on him and sent him back to Pilate. And though Herod and Pilate had been enemies before, they were reconciled that same day' (Lk. 23.8-12).

Jesus is now the scapegoat deserted by the religious and civil authorities, deserted by his friends, denied by Peter. But he is not guilty. Consequently the guilt is not taken away, but it remains with those who have perpetrated his death. This is an intolerable situation. The truth of this murderous situation must be covered up. Luke describes this reaction in his description of Stephen's death by stoning in Acts Ch. 7.

Stephen has been accused of blasphemy. He was brought before the Sanhedrin and asked by the high priest whether the accusations were true. In his defence Stephen gives a long speech accusing not only his own accusers, but the Jewish leaders in general, of having murdered the prophets throughout Israel's history. He ends his speech with these words:

> 'You stubborn people, with your pagan hearts and pagan ears. You are always resisting the Holy Spirit, just as your ancestors used to do. Can you name a single prophet your ancestors never persecuted? In the past they killed those who foretold the coming of the Just One, and now you have become his betrayers, his murderers. You who had the Law brought to you by the angels are the very ones who have not kept it.' They were infuriated when they heard this, and ground their teeth at him. But Stephen, filled with the Holy Spirit, gazed into heaven and saw the glory of God, and Jesus standing at God's right hand. 'I can see heaven thrown open', he said, 'and the Son of Man standing at the right hand of God.' At this all the members of the Council shouted out and stopped their ears with their hands; then they all rushed at him, sent him out of the city and stoned him. The witnesses (those who had accused him) put their clothes at the feet of a young man called Saul. As they were stoning him, Stephen said in invocation, 'Lord Jesus, receive my spirit.' Then he knelt down and said aloud, 'Lord, do not hold this sin against them'; and with these words he fell asleep. (Acts 7.51–8.1).

They stop their ears and rush at Stephen to shut out this intolerable knowledge, the knowledge of the murder itself of which they are guilty; yet at the same time, at another layer of their consciousness, they are convinced – as was Saul, later to become St Paul – of the godliness of their actions.

Here we are at the heart of the mystery. Before his death, Jesus, teaching in the Temple in Jerusalem, had told the chief priests and scribes, who were questioning him about his authority to teach, the parable about the wicked tenant farmers who refused to hand over the share of the produce that was owing to the owner and they killed the servants who had been sent to collect it. They did this several times. In the end, the owner sent his own son to collect the revenue. The farmers killed the son, too. And Jesus ends the parable with the words 'It was the stone rejected by the builders that became the keystone', a quotation from Psalm 118 v. 22.

This rejected stone, Jesus himself, has become a new foundation stone for the building of the temple of humanity, a foundation no longer built on the scapegoating of individuals, of groups and classes of people who are sacrificed, allowing the murderers to escape their own guilt and violence.

Jesus presents a non-violent God

The death of Jesus, as it is presented in the New Testament, is an act that brings salvation to all humanity: it is never presented as a saving act produced by the murder of a victim. Yet many subsequent theologies have produced explanations of Jesus' death which makes it identical with the mythical accounts of a sacrifice in which the scapegoat is killed, and through that death, enemies are reconciled and peace is restored, but it is a peace founded on murder. Such theological explanations are then understood by many ordinary people to mean that God is a God of vengeance, who cannot be appeased by any number of human sacrifices, but can only be appeased if God's own Son is offered to God's self in this way on behalf of the rest of us. It is this way of thinking that Girard is condemning. The God whom Jesus reveals is a God of compassion, a God, as the book of Wisdom declares, 'who overlooks our sins, so that we can repent', a God who is scandalously profligate in generosity.

Writing in this way, am I denying that God is sacrificed for our sins? I believe God is love. That God's love is continuous, always in the present and present in all that exists. God is not a thought, an idea, a formula for living: God is, always greater that anything we can think or imagine, always beyond us, yet also within us both mysterious, yet most intimate, more intimate to each of us than we are to ourselves. In Jesus, we believe that God has entered into every aspect of our humanity, our fears and our frailties, our tears and our sorrows. There are no depths of loss, grief, darkness or despair that we can experience where God is absent. Why is God like this? I don't know, nor do I believe there is any explanation in words which could adequately express this mystery.

What I do know is an inner longing of heart which is real, but in the knowing I come to know this reality is not a personal manufacture. The Unity and Peace I long for goes far beyond anything I could achieve: it is about a way of living, a way of relating to all creation. To put this in another way, it is as though I want my life to be a song, in tune, in harmony with God, with all humanity, with all creation and with my whole inner self. I have no desire to be the songwriter, the conductor, or to control the whole choir and orchestra. Reading the Scriptures, especially the Hebrew prophets, the Psalms, the Wisdom books and, above all, the Gospels and New Testament writings touches into this inner longing, strengthens it and enables it to begin to flow into every aspect of human life, especially into those aspects I had never noticed before – as, for example, the meaning of peace, a simple word which can so easily and painlessly slide over the surface of our minds, leaving no trace. When the word 'peace' pierces the surface of our consciousness, then it can feel like a shifting of our inner tectonic plates. Our inner reaction is panic and our instinct is to escape at any cost from extinction. Our attention is diverted from God and God's promises and becomes totally focused on our own protection, without a thought of what our escape may be doing to other individuals or nations. We are caught up again in the spiral of violence; our efforts to defend ourselves become the very means of our own destruction.

I believe God is our rock, our refuge and our salvation, an all-inclusive God from whom no one is excluded. I believe that Jesus, as Paul describes him, image of the unseen God, became one of us in Jesus of Nazareth, not because we were sinners, but because God is love and wants to be with us in every detail of our lives. As St Athanasius expressed it in the third century, 'God became a human being so that human beings might become God'. In John's Gospel, Jesus' final prayer to his Father, when at supper with his disciples, is: 'May they all be one. Father, may they be one in us, as you are in me and I am in you … With me in them and you in me, may they be so completely one that the world will realize that it was you who sent me and that I have loved them as much as you loved me' (Jn 17.21-23).

Love is not a thing, not a thought, not an abstraction. Love can only exist in relationship. The very life of God, as explained in Christianity, is a relationship between three Divine Persons in a life of such intimate sharing that no one Person has anything which is not equally shared with the other two. In asserting that Jesus died for our sins, and also asserting that Jesus is God, we must also be asserting that God the Father and God the Holy Spirit also share fully in this life-giving gift. If this assertion seems to be false, at least it avoids the prevalent misunderstanding that Jesus died on our behalf in order to satisfy God the Father's insistence that Jesus should pay, with death through crucifixion, the ransom the Father demanded for the redemption of humankind and of all creation. This belief that the whole Trinity is involved in Jesus' gift of himself enables us to begin to understand in a new way the reality of God's presence to each of us in every moment of our lives. God's eternal presence means that God is always fully present in every moment; God is not time-bound – God is. Nor is God space-bound. God is the God of compassion. Consequently, there is no place within our own lives, no height or depth, no length or breadth of our inner states of fear, or terror, of light or of darkness, where God is not, always closer to us than we are to ourselves and always beckoning us to take the leap of entrusting our whole being to the God for whom our hearts are created.

Exercises

- You might like to try writing a letter to René Girard after having read this chapter, letting him know your own reactions to it, the questions it raises for you. The point of this suggestion is to enable you to explore your own reactions and the questions the exercise can open up for you. May you enjoy the exercise.

    (*Girard wrote many books and articles. A most useful summary of his work is to be found in* The Girard Reader, *edited by James G. Williams, a Crossroad Herder book, the Crossroad Publishing Company.*)

7

'What can we little people do?'

'What can we little people do?' is a question put to me by a Croat
in 1988 when I was on a Peace pilgrimage to Jerusalem by way of
Yugoslavia. Tito was still the dictator and holding the impoverished
and divided country together. After his death a very long and bloody
war broke out in the Balkans. The war is now over, but the tensions
remain. I frequently remember the Croat's question. This final chapter
on Peace is a response to the question, 'What can we little people do?'.

It is not an answer. It is a response. Mysteries cannot be made to
disappear by our answers. Peace is a mystery but our responses can
enable us to get in touch with the mystery.

Frequent responses to questions of peace and violence

The following responses are quoted because they all avoid the question
of violence within ourselves. Until this question is addressed, our
efforts to achieve peace will not only be ineffective, they will themselves
contribute to the spread and intensity of violence in our world.

As I have already said, the Roman Emperors' dictum, 'To preserve
peace, prepare for war', is a principle which has been followed until our
own day, endorsed by the majority of religious people of all Christian
denominations, of people of other faiths and by atheistic humanists.
Within all these categories there have always been minorities who have
resisted this advice, often at the risk/cost of their own lives.

'The life of man is nasty, brutish and short [...] The condition of
man is a condition of war of everyone against everyone' (Thomas
Hobbes [1588–1679], *Leviathan*). This pessimistic assumption of

Thomas Hobbes was also the assumption which lay behind the USA's decision to retain the nuclear deterrent. It was that human greed was a fact of life, innate and unchangeable: to ensure national defence we need to discover a weapon so devastating than no nation could dare to risk attacking us. The implication that follows from this remark is that ultimately, violence can only be remedied by violence. That is also the hidden assumption that lies behind the Just War theory.

Over 60 years after the Hiroshima and Nagasaki bombing it is commonly claimed that the nuclear deterrent has brought peace to the nations. It is true that nuclear war has not broken out between the nations; it is totally false that the nuclear threat has brought peace.

The nuclear threat is the most devastating form of terrorism: it is cosmic terrorism, a human creation, threatening the survival of all organic life on our planet. The source of the violence is in our human minds and hearts. Deepening our understanding of the process which can lead us into omnicidal destruction is the most urgent task facing each and every one of us. It is the first step towards freedom from fear and to entering into the wonder of life.

There have been many wars and millions of casualties throughout the world in the last 60 years, wars encouraged by the superpowers, who have supplied the arms which enable dictators to control their own people and to subject them to the slow war of grinding poverty in marginalized countries in order to increase their national income.

The world's leaders acknowledge that terrorism is the greatest threat to world peace; they also believe that terrorism is best answered by counter-terrorism. Some examples:

'Terror is the greatest twenty-first century threat.' (Tony Blair 2003)
'The greatest threat this world faces is the danger of extremists and terrorists armed with weapons of mass destruction.' (George Bush 2005)
'Terrorism is the greatest threat to world peace.' (Vladimir Putin 2000)
'Terrorism is the greatest threat facing free democracies in the twenty-first century.' (Angela Merkel 2006)

In themselves, none of those quotations reveal any awareness of the reality that nuclear deterrence is, in fact, the most terrifying threat of all and that as long as it is held by one nation, or group of nations, it will lead to the increase and spread of terrorism in every country.

Before considering 'What can we little people contribute to peace in our world?', we need to look at some of the major underlying causes of the terrorism which threatens our survival today.

Climate change

This is happening today at an unprecedented pace in human history, already causing massive displacement of peoples, the frequency of natural disasters, flooding, drought, food shortages, widespread social unrest. The damaging effects of these events afflict most devastatingly the poor, the oppressed, women and children. *(I am not asserting here that climate change, in itself, is the cause of the spread of terrorism. The cause lies in the human response to this fear.)*

The marginalization of the majority of peoples

The world has become much wealthier in recent decades than ever before and this prosperity boom has increased the gap between rich and poor. Within the same organization today, the earnings of some employees can be hundreds of times greater than the earnings of the lowest paid. This is a major cause of social unrest, leading to violence as the rich grow richer and the poor become more impoverished. The situation is worsened by the almost universal policy of settling all violence by greater violence. The weak, the desperate, the struggling are named terrorists; those in power can always afford to exercise superior forms of terrorism and call it peace. This is not a new phenomenon in human history. The ancient Roman historian Tacitus, observing the controlling methods of powerful warlords in Britain, commented: 'They create a desert: they call it peace.'

Competition over resources

If everyone lived at the current USA rate of living, it is reckoned that we would need five more Planets Earth to sustain us. If everyone lived at our present rate of European living, we would need 2.1 planets to sustain the human race.

I am using statistics here which I first gathered about eight years ago and I know that today's statistics can be considered out of date tomorrow, but disregard of all statistics is a very crude way of renouncing our own responsibility for anything which is not centred on our own vision of our own wellbeing.

The underlying assumption in such an attitude to life might be described 'The world exists to praise, reverence and serve me/our group's interests', which suggests a somewhat restricted vision of the Universe! So treat these statistics as provisional, but they are indicators of modern forms of enslavement for the majority of the human race, a misfortune which we prefer to ignore, attributing the blame to our favourite scapegoats.

To return to a few more statistics. Here are some figures for what was spent on security in the USA in 2005: 48 billion dollars were spent on homeland security and 2.6 billion dollars were spent in fighting AIDS worldwide. Again in the USA, in 2001, 2,500 people were killed in terrorist attacks, 3,500 died from malnutrition, 14,000 died from AIDS, there were 30,000 suicides, 42,000 died in traffic accidents, and there were 30,000 firearm deaths.

Global militarization

From the late 1940s until the 1980s, it was reckoned that the Warsaw Pact countries plus NATO spent one trillion dollars annually on rearmament. The fatal casualties in worldwide conflicts were around 25 million and 75 million were seriously injured. Most of the casualties were in Vietnam, Korea, Afghanistan, results of the Cold War conflict with the Soviet Union, justified on both sides as struggles for freedom and liberation but, in fact, about access to oil.

After the collapse of Soviet Russia and the end of the Cold War, global militarization continues, the new enemy is 'terrorism' and the arms dealers are thriving. Many more countries now possess nuclear defence systems. The UK's nuclear defence system is totally dependent on US support. We are updating our nuclear defence system, which is now a first-strike weapon, designed to be used when our leaders decide that for the protection of our sovereignty and national values we must destroy the nuclear bases of our enemies.

So, 'What can we little people do?'

This is both the most threatening and, at the same time, the most valuable question we can ask ourselves. We shall discover within ourselves a deep reluctance to face the question. It is in facing it that we shall discover that the threat we fear is, in fact, an invitation to accept the treasure that is within us. The treasure is not just a personal gift; it is also for the benefit of everyone else: we are all intrinsically linked and dependent on each other.

We can grow in our realization that:

- **our most valuable source of learning lies in our own experience.**
  That is why I hope that the most valuable thing this book has to offer is to enable readers to discover this for themselves by doing the exercises offered at the end of each chapter. The exercises may evoke very strongly felt negative emotions of anger, resentment, fear, bitterness etc. Before throwing the book out of the window, pause and ask yourself why you are reacting in this violent way. The answer is because the exercises we have been doing have touched into our self-preservation defences, built up over the years, leading us to counter violence with violence – a habit so deeply ingrained that we are no longer capable of recognizing it. We are, in fact, on the track of something which is fundamental to our freedom. Our reactions are not the real threats to our existence: they are invitations to become more alive and free, more compassionate and forgiving; they are helping us to unearth our real selves, a discovery that is accompanied by a growing sense of peace, joy and fulfilment in living compassionately.

- **the source of our violence does not lie in the existence of hostile external powers.**
  The source lies within each of us, in our ways of thinking and behaving, in our minds and hearts. Our violence is not natural; it is the result of our education which we have so appropriated that we consider our way of being, of reacting and behaving to be normal, sane, righteous, sensible and responsible. We no longer recognize the violence we are doing to ourselves and to others.

- **often our normal language is also very violent.**
  This has been expressed in the phrase, 'The most violent word in our language is "should"'. I do not know the original author of that much-quoted saying, but I think it is dangerously and harmfully misleading, besides being itself an example of violent language, by attempting to eradicate a commonly used word from our language. I have also read others who advocate the elimination of all words from our language which the writers consider violent, for example: 'right', 'wrong', 'good', 'bad', 'selfish', 'unselfish', 'terrorist'. I dislike these suggestions because I think they are themselves violent. Perhaps I can best explain this reaction more clearly by using the word 'ought', a frequently used and a very necessary word. This is not quibbling about words: it is getting us to the heart of the matter of the nature of peace.

  'This is the way you ought to behave' is, in itself, an ambiguous phrase. Where is the 'ought' coming from, from within me or from without? To return to the violin-playing example, if I want to become a violinist I ought to practise the violin daily. I do so. In practising daily, am I doing so because my teacher has told me to do so, or because I love violin-playing? If I am practising out of a sense of duty, I may play every note correctly, but I shall never be a life-giving violinist because I play out of duty, to be approved of, not because I am in love with music. The all-important question is: 'Do I live my life totally dependent on the approval of others, or do I live because I feel drawn to live in this way in the depth of my being?' The only person who can answer this question is yourself!

- **we can learn about Non Violent Communication.**
  My own immediate reaction on hearing about Non Violent Communication (NVC) many decades ago was to dismiss it as being too glib, too smooth, unrealistic and out of touch with the real world. It was many years later, having been given the opportunity to work with people across the Christian denominations, with people of other faiths and of no professed faith, with people of different cultures in different parts of the world, and with vast numbers of Christians who had given up churchgoing because the experience no longer spoke to

their own concerns in day-to-day living, that through this experience I began to recognize the importance and the value of NVC in every aspect of human life. NVC is not glib and superficial, a refusal to face 'the real world': it is a process which enables us to see our world differently. As our vision of life changes, our reactions to events begin to change. We move from a world of conformity, monotony, restrictedness and loneliness into a world of unlimited opportunity, creativity and at-home-ness. NVC does not supply us with knowledge: it offers us questions which only we can answer, and the answers enable us to see the world differently and react to it differently. This is the way we can begin to live more fully and communicate peace and compassion to others.

There are two basic questions which lie at the heart of NVC. The first is 'What is alive in me?', and the second is 'How do I communicate this aliveness to others?' Underlying both questions is the assumption that we are created for one another and not, as Thomas Hobbes stated, as enemies of one another.

From infancy, most of us have been brought up to categorize all that we experience in judgemental form. This form is not only ineffective, it is positively damaging. To communicate our aliveness to others we must avoid being judgemental. An Indian philosopher, Jiddhu Krishnamurti has written: 'The highest form of human intelligence is the ability to observe without judging.' We can all practise this art without having any desire to be considered the most intelligent of mortals! When we do communicate our feelings to another, we must make it clear to them that the reason for these feelings does not come from them: the source of our feelings is within our own minds and hearts. The other has evoked those feelings in us, but they are our feelings, not the other person's, so the other cannot be judged.

People who are in touch with their own needs do not make good slaves. That is why we are brought up to believe that attending to our own needs is an act of selfishness. This complaint is a subtle form of enslavement. It can prevent us from ever consulting our own unique self: we ignore it for peace's sake.

The object of Non Violent Communication is to enable us to live out of compassion for others, not out of fear of failing to comply with authority's requests, or to receive rewards. Such a desire is not popular with those in control. NVC is costly: as a way of life, it demands everything. It

was through NVC that I came to realize the wisdom and depth of Jesus'
Gospel teaching in a way I had never experienced it before.

How are we to learn how to communicate with others non-violently?
We must learn to listen. Listen for what? For what is alive in them. How
can I do this without being judgemental? How can I observe without
judging/condemning the other? Non Violent Communication (NVC)
offers answers:

- Tell the other what you do not like about their behaviour. This is
  information about yourself, not an accusation of them.

- Tell them of your felt reaction. This is information about
  yourself. They are not responsible for your feelings, although
  their behaviour has evoked these feelings and brought them
  into your consciousness.

- Tell them what needs of yours were not being met by this
  behaviour. In doing this you are communicating *your* needs:
  you are not accusing them.

- What request are you making of them? This request is an
  invitation, not a command. If it is ignored, or rejected, you will
  not withdraw your compassion, your desire for the good of the
  other.

This process is not an instant remedy to finding peace in conflict – it
requires continual practice. Slowly it begins to change the way we
see things, the way we see other people. We begin to meet ourselves
in them, begin to see them as another self, begin to understand the
meaning of 'Love your neighbour as yourself', not as a command,
but as a deep need/longing in ourselves which brings us to life, a life
we begin to delight in bringing to others. We begin to appreciate the
meaning of phrases we had heard before, but never appreciated – for
example, 'Love is the discovery of yourself in others and delight in the
recognition'. The process is slow: it demands not less than everything,
but it is 'the pearl of great price' which Jesus speaks of in the Gospels
and which we are all invited to discover. It already exists; in religious
language it is called 'The Kingdom of God'.

As an example of how Non Violent Communication can bring the
Jewish/Christian Scriptures to life in us, here is an example from St
Paul's letter to the Colossians in which he writes of Christ as head of
all creation:

> He is the image of the unseen God and the first-born of all creation,
> for in him were created all things in heaven and on earth: everything
> visible, everything invisible, Thrones, Dominations, Sovereignties,
> Powers, all things were created through him and for him. (Col.
> 1.15-16)

I always liked the sound of this passage without asking what possible
meaning the words have in my own experience. When I began looking
at the nature of peace and violence, a meaning became clear which
linked in with my own experience: the experience of dominating
systems in our own world now, which affect every aspect of our human
life. Millennia of conditioning in a culture of blame, fault-finding,
punishment and reward have trained us to believe that our ideal in
life must lie in becoming nice, harmless, subservient, generous people.
The ideal woman ought not to have needs. The ideal man must give
his life for King and Country. Those who fall short, which includes
all of us, must be punished – this is called retributive justice. Those
who comply do violence to themselves, but they also damage others,
because violence is, of its nature, infectious and spreads like wildfire.
The Thrones and Powers, Dominations and Sovereignties of which
St Paul writes exist and thrive in all those individuals and gangs who
struggle to control the lives of others through threats and punishments
in order to enforce conformity to an imposed system. Such systems
are to be found in all layers of society, from local gangs, terrorists of
all kinds, to government officials, multinational executives, church and
religious authorities, militant atheists.

The answer is not to get rid of all structures: we need structures to
sustain life. We need to recognize the source of this destructiveness and
then work non-violently to restore compassion, truth and restorative
justice. This has shown me the wisdom of Jesus' words, the meaning
of 'the kingdom of God', the meaning of 'Your faith has saved you,
go in peace' in a new, enlivening and delighting way. The words have
not changed anything: the facts are still as obdurate as before. What is
changing is the way I am seeing these same facts. They are no longer
threats; they are invitations not only to me, but to all humankind. That
is why the Hebrew prophets and Jesus keep telling us to 'wake up',
'repent' (which means 'change your minds and hearts') and 'believe'
(which means entrust yourself) in the Gospel (which means the Good
News).

What is it that we are being asked to believe? In the reality of God in whom we all live and move and have our being. This God reveals Godself in the reality of our own human experience. God is not an external object. God is not the sum of all creation. God is. 'I am who I am', and in this God all creation exists. This God is more intimate to us than we are to ourselves. This God is continuously drawing us into the unity which is God's own life. Our life is an invitation to us to enter into this unity, an invitation for which we were created and for which our hearts long. We get inklings of this reality when our hearts are opened and we find ourselves called out of ourselves, beyond ourselves into something infinitely greater than our own egocentredness, into a life of wonder, surprise and delight at the fact that we are where we are and on a journey, led by our restless hearts, which St Augustine of Hippo described 1,500 years ago: 'Lord, you have created me for yourself and my heart is restless until it rests in you.'

This is the conclusion of Part 2 on Peace, and introduces the final Part 3 of *Cry of Wonder*, entitled 'Holiness'. This is not a separate subject from Parts 1 and 2: it is a development of all that we have been considering, so that we can recognise Holiness in what we call 'our ordinary, everyday life', in our own unique experience. What we begin to recognize is real but extraordinary, a reality which beckons us out beyond ourselves into a unity and peace within ourselves, with all humankind and with God who had us in mind before time began and who will always be beckoning us.

Exercise

- One true answer that any of us can make to the question asked in this chapter, 'what can we little people do?' is 'little or nothing', if we think in terms of numbers, in terms of quantity. If, however, we think in terms of quality, our answer is 'infinitely more than we can think or imagine'. Write your own comment on this statement, then see what it tells you about yourself. If you can keep in touch with your own felt experience, your effort cannot fail.

Part Three

Holiness

Identity and holiness

This chapter is an introduction to Part 3 of *Cry of Wonder*. Part 3 is not introducing a new topic: it is developing the themes of Unity and Peace that we have already considered by focusing on how we can become aware of connections. How, in our own experience, can we allow Unity and Peace to move from our heads to our hearts, from thinking about to living, from telling to witnessing?

I was going to call this third section of the book 'Spirituality', but have changed it to 'Holiness', because 'Spirituality' has become such a popular and misused word in recent years that writing about it is like writing on water. The root problem is not the word spirituality itself; the problem is in the general and growing dislocation between the language we use and the reality in which we live, a dislocation which signifies a deep split in the core of our being, a split between the virtual and the real.

In the 1970s there was much talk about identity within Christian circles and within society in general. After many years of pondering this subject of identity, I remember a moment of clarity and of relief when I admitted to myself that I did not know my identity beyond the phrase 'I am a human being'. Identity cards can be very useful, but no matter how accurate they may be, and however lengthy, they cannot express the uniqueness of every individual human being. Having records of our own unique fingerprints, eye prints, unique DNA, which can distinguish us from every other human being, are signs of our uniqueness. They give information about us – they do not tell us who we are. This failure is a blessing, not a curse: it is leading us beyond ourselves. The ancient Greeks had a word for this process; they called it 'ecstasy'! The Greek word means to take a stand outside of yourself.

To say 'I am a human being' means that I am essentially a related being. I have no identity which is not a relationship. How can this truth, which we considered in Parts 1 and 2 on 'Unity' and 'Peace', take hold on us in such a way that it can begin to transform us by setting us free from the narrow boundaries of our thinking, which trap us into ever-narrowing circles of violence? This setting free restores to us our sense of wonder and delight. It restores us to life, to hope, and it is infectious, because we are all one. It is also costly, demanding not less than everything, but it is a cost we are glad to pay, because it is the answer to our deepest longings.

As a Christian, I do not believe God is an object outside us. God is the source of our being. God is in all things. God's centre is everywhere: God's presence has no boundaries. As the psalmist expresses it in Psalm 138 v. 7: 'Where could I flee from your presence? If I climb the heavens, you are there, there too, if I lie in Sheol. If I flew to the point of sunrise, or westwards across the sea, your right hand would still be guiding me, your right hand holding me.'

How can we open ourselves to this encounter?

Many decades ago I read a book in which the author explained that stillness was the highest form of prayer, a prayer without thought, without imagining, without words or memories. Being an ambitious youth at the time, I thought this invitation to do nothing to reach the highest form of prayer was worth trying. Half an hour later, feeling cross, exhausted and frustrated, I abandoned this highest form of prayer. It was as though, through my effort to be still, I had invited every thought, memory, feeling and imagining that I had ever experienced to flood into my consciousness. The harder I tried, the greater the torrents of distractions that filled my consciousness. One very valuable lesson I learned from that experience was 'never try too hard to pray'!

The reason for being still and silent in prayer is to enable us to become more consciously in touch with God, who is always greater than anything we can think or imagine, but who is constantly within us and around us, the God of every pulse beat, communicating with us through every breath we breathe, God present in every one of the trillions of cells in our bodies with their miraculous transport and communications systems, which enable us to transform what we eat and drink to become our developing bodies, to think, reflect, react to our surroundings and, especially, teach us how to relate to each other and so find God.

'Be still' is a teaching in all major world religions and among many people who profess to have no religion.

Here is one simple way of being still:
This is a more detailed version of what I have already given in the preamble on pages ix–xiv.

Sit with your feet flat on the ground. Your back straight but not rigid, your body relaxed.

Concentrate your attention on what you can feel in your body. *(Don't think, just focus your attention on what you can feel in your body. If you get no further than your big toe, you are doing well!)*

If you feel an itch or discomfort, hear noises or have interesting thoughts, acknowledge what is happening but return to your physical feelings.

Once you feel more relaxed – but do not be in any hurry – you might like to turn this exercise into more explicit prayer, repeating slowly to yourself, for example, 'In God I live and move and have my being'. This is a way of meeting God in our awareness of our own body, in our own surroundings.

It is good to begin prayer with a stillness exercise, however short. If you never move on from stillness you are still praying well. In Christian belief it is God's Spirit who prays in us. Through stillness we can become more aware of this truth and join ourselves more wholeheartedly with God.

Before you begin this exercise, decide how long you are going to spend on it. Start, for example, with five minutes. You may go on for longer, if you like, but do not abandon the attempt before you have completed the five minutes. When you have completed the time you have set yourself, then spend a few moments reflecting on the experience. During the stillness period itself, you are totally concentrated on what you are physically feeling at the moment; consequently you avoid reflection. In the reflection period, just note how you are *now feeling*. Was it for you tense or relaxing, enjoyable or sad, peaceful or agitated?

Just note these reactions: do not judge them. The categories of right and wrong, true and false do not apply to feelings in themselves; they apply only to the way we react to them. We shall be looking at this point in more detail later.

If you disliked your attempt at being still, or if you found it in any way difficult or unattractive, do not consider your reaction to be a sign of failure. Such reactions are very promising signs: signs of life and of your growing self-awareness. The value of this reflection period is that it can encourage you to repeat the exercise frequently. Doing the exercise will also activate your sense of wonder, together with your sense of humour.

Here is an image which I have already mentioned, but I repeat it here, because it can be very helpful in coping with what are so often called 'distractions'. 'Distractions' are not signs of failure – they are signs of life. The image is to enable you to make full use of the 'distractions'. They are like scattered diamonds.

Imagine you are standing on the midpoint of a bridge that spans a wide river busy with barges sailing up and down. This image represents our mind as we try to be still. The barges represent the many thoughts, memories, images, actions and reactions, hurts and delights which flow into our consciousness. We cannot stop the flow without ceasing to be silent. What we can do is focus our attention on the barges, while remaining still on the bridge. We do not jump off the bridge to travel with any of the barges: we observe them without engaging with them.

I owe the idea of this image to Fr Tony de Melo sj in his book *Sadhana*. The version I give here is an adapted version, which I have learned after many years of working with individuals and groups from different cultures.

This image reveals the purpose of the stillness exercises. The purpose is to develop the art of being still, yet alert, in a very busy and complex life. It enables us to observe what is happening without being judgemental. This is easy to write about and talk about. To live always with this attitude, observing without being judgemental, is something we all find difficult, even impossible. Facing into this difficulty/impossibility we are on the threshold of the 'Cry of Wonder'. By refusing to acknowledge the difficulty we encounter, we are turning the key which encloses us in our prison of security.

Another helpful exercise to try is this breathing exercise:
In this exercise the focus of your attention is on the physical feeling of breathing in and out. Adopt whatever posture you find most helpful,

allowing you to be both relaxed and alert. Without attempting to change your natural rhythm of breathing, observe the physical experience of breathing in and the physical experience of breathing out. You may find it easier to focus first on the in-breaths, then on the out-breaths. When the 'barges' start moving on the river of your thoughts, observe them from the bridge, but do not jump off the bridge to examine them. Keep the exercise going for whatever time you have decided to give it, but do not shorten the time. The reason for this advice is that when you feel the being still is becoming a struggle for you, it is usually a sign that you are breaking into a deeper layer of consciousness. If you always give up when anything begins to be difficult, you will never break through to deeper layers of consciousness. However, sudden tragedies can befall us which hurl us into new layers of consciousness. They can also hurl us into deep prayer of desperation without any preparatory stillness exercises!

You can also turn this exercise into a deep form of prayer by letting your in-breath be an expression of your inner longing, your basic desire. Don't try to analyse what is happening, just appreciate your in-breath. Where does it come from? That is why God is also called 'The Spirit'. In every breath you breathe, the Spirit, who holds all creation in being, is giving you life. The Spirit is the Spirit of God drawing you into unity and peace with all creation. Now speak with God as your heart prompts you.

Stillness through walking
This seems to be a contradiction: in fact, it is a very common Hindu and Buddhist practice. It consists in slow walking, focusing your attention on the physical sensation you experience as you go. As in the sitting exercises, let your attention focus on different parts of your body. As thoughts, memories, images come to mind, observe them, but do not engage with them – let the barges pass! When you have finished the exercise, give a few moments, as in the previous exercises, to a brief reflection in which you note your mood after doing the exercise, but do not attempt to analyse. All these instructions are given to enable you to learn from your own body, your own experience, which is the most valuable source on which you can draw in your search for meaning in life. In walking it can be very helpful to have some word or short phrase which you can repeat as you go in time with your steps.

These stillness exercises I have described are frequently recommended as a useful method of preparing to pray. They are very useful, but considering them in this way, as a means to something which is more important, can blind us to their innate value. They are of value in themselves. The truth of this statement can only be learned by doing the exercises, not by talking about them. The reason for all this emphasis on *felt* reactions is, I repeat, because our emotions and feelings are far more intelligent than our conscious minds. They may be compared to signals inviting us to give attention to what has given rise to this felt reaction. They are inviting us to enter a deeper layer of our consciousness, where we can become aware of connections of which we were previously unaware. All our inner felt reactions are interconnected with our basic desire.

When you begin to experience their value, you will be drawn to practise them frequently in whatever way you find helpful. As a Christian, I do not believe that prayer is only possible for us if we follow certain rules given by religious authorities. I believe God is in all things. I believe that in these stillness exercises, I am becoming more aware of the reality of God listening to me and so enabling me to let the Spirit of God pray through me. Prayer is about letting God be God to us and through us in every detail of our lives. Prayer is about attitude, not particular actions. Formal prayer, as in doing a stillness exercise, is a means of enabling us to live this attitude in the way we are in the world. God is there all the time, delighting in our being.

These exercises in being still are not a luxury for the leisured classes: they are essential in human life. There is no situation, however apparently chaotic, in which being still cannot be practised in some form.

Whether or not you are a religious believer, when you begin to reflect on the 'why' questions of life, then it is very helpful to have a conversation with yourself. I heard the story of a fellow Jesuit, who fell off a ladder while reaching for a book on the top shelf of the library. Landing on the floor with the ladder on top of him, he was heard to be muttering repeatedly, 'O God, why did you make me such a bloody fool?' Such intimate conversations with God do not have to be preceded with a stillness exercise! But to have such intimate conversations with God is the purpose of all methods of prayer. It is in having these conversations that we can learn how to pray.

There are as many ways of praying as there are human beings
How am I to pray? The way you find most helpful at present. Your way of praying will vary over time. What was helpful in childhood may not

be helpful in adolescence. Middle-age prayer is unlikely to be the same in old age, but there are some general signs which indicate a healthy development. The signs are in our way of living, our way of perceiving, our way of reacting to crises and traumas, to rejection and accusation, to wealth and poverty, honour and insult, success and failure.

Prayer is a way of being, not a specialized activity for the chosen few. Prayer, as it develops, becomes simpler, quieter, less wordy, more childlike. These are not changes that we devise: we discover they are happening.

In Christian understanding there is a sense in which we can all say, 'Prayer is impossible for me'. If we think of prayer as something we perform and offer to a distant God, then it is impossible because we are already living in God. The Spirit who lived in Jesus and raised him from the dead now lives in us and prays in us. We are never alone. We may be totally unaware of this presence in our conscious minds, but its presence is influencing all our decisions, whether we are conscious of it or not. In prayer, whatever form it takes, we are begging to become aware of the reality in which we are being held.

So when you find the 'why' questions of life are knocking at the door of your consciousness, let them in, hold them before God and hear from deep within your being these words being said: 'Don't be afraid. I am with you', and talk simply from your heart as your heart directs you.

Another sign that our prayer is coming from the Spirit of God praying within us is our growing awareness of our essential relatedness. Our awareness begins to break free from its egocentricity and begins to find itself in its relationship with the rest of creation. This experience was well expressed over 2,000 years ago in the writings of the Roman poet Terence (c. 190–159BC): '*Homo sum; nil humani a me alienum puto*', 'I am a human being; I consider nothing human to be foreign to me'. Another way of expressing this truth, linking it with Unity and Peace, is 'I am at home wherever I am' – a truth which is at the heart of Holiness, too.

The Review of the Day

I end this chapter by introducing a daily prayer, the Review of the Day, which will already be familiar to many readers. This method of prayer has a variety of names: Examination of Conscience, Examen, Examination of Consciousness. It is a suitable prayer towards the end of the day, but it can be made at any time and in any place.

I repeat it here, because although I know it is a most valuable gift for enabling us to live fully and to share that fullness with others, I also know that it, like any other form of prayer, can be so presented that it can nurture our egocentricity, leading us to make our sinfulness the central truth of our lives. I believe that it was awareness of this danger which led Martin Buber, the Jewish mystical writer of *I and Thou*, to declare 'Nothing so masks the face of God as religion' – a remark I at first considered a dangerous exaggeration. Fifty years later, experience has brought me to recognize the truth of this spiritual writer and most religious man. When religion is reduced to a system of conformity to certain regulations, then that system becomes an idol, robs us of our humanity, which is God living intimately within us. As the Hebrew prophets remind us, we become what we worship and we lose our humanity.

In Ignatius Loyola's Spiritual Exercises, almost every subject he offers for prayer is called 'a repetition' – an unfortunate word, because it suggests going back over the same material you have already done. Repetition has a much more important meaning: it means continue with whatever held your attention in the last prayer session. Repetition leads to further discovery and a deepening awareness of all your felt reactions connecting with your basic desire. By this means you are delving more deeply into the source of all your desire, the desire to be at one with God, with yourself and with all creation.

As you become more familiar with the Review of the Day, you will discover your own best way of doing it and it will become clearer to you that this exercise is about a way of living out your own basic desire in life. The Review of the Day does not give answers to your problems, but it does help you to deepen your hope that 'all manner of things will be well' and that you can never be alone because your heart knows that the Heart of the Universe has promised, 'Don't be afraid. I am with you always'.

The subject matter of the prayer is the events of your day, for that is where God is for you. Other people can tell you about God, but for you God can only be found in your experience. This kind of prayer can be called 'earthing our prayer' because it is earthed in our own daily experience and God is in every moment of it. The time recommended for this prayer is about 15 minutes, but there is no need for a stop watch!

The first half of the prayer consists in thanksgiving to God for the gifts of the day. The second part of the prayer is our response to the gifts God is offering us, talking with God as a friend speaks with a friend.

As with all prayer, it is useful to begin by being still for a few moments, conscious that we are in the presence of God and begging God that our whole being should be taken up in this act of surrender to God's invitation to find ourselves in Godself.

'O God, Grant that my whole being may accept your invitation.'

You can make this prayer with integrity when you are also aware of your lamentable performance so far. You are transforming your lamentable performance into a recognition of your need before God. In this way you are living out the first of the beatitudes, which can be translated, 'Blissfully happy are those who know their needs, God is with them.'

Now recall the day, looking at the moments you have enjoyed, appreciated, valued. Avoid, like the plague, any moralizing at this point.

In saying this I am not declaring that morality has no place in Christian life: it has a very important place. Then why exclude any deliberate moralizing at this point? Because we switch our attention from God's love and compassion as the core of our lives to our personal failures and so I let my personal sinfulness become the focus of my attention, not the goodness and overwhelming generosity of God. This attitude is, in itself, sinful: because it is not allowing God to be God; it is projecting onto God my own sinful tendencies and so masking the face of God.

Recall those moments for which you are grateful: observe then without making judgements. In this way we can slowly become aware of how many such moments there were, far more than we realized at the time. Apparently trivial moments become precious, like the sight I had today of a tiny child in bright, diminutive wellington boots and a huge smile on his face as he stamped his way through the puddles, delighting in the present moment.

The psalms are full of these moments of delight in which all nature shares. The psalms want to declare these moments, to sing and to dance to them, to invite everything in creation to join in.

The gratitude this appreciation elicits in us is a most precious aspect of our being. It is a way of being which affects every part of us, imbuing us with love, enabling us to live more fully and freely and securely, directing our energies outwards so that serving becomes more instinctive and preferable to a life of self-protection against the fears which haunt us.

'A true sacrifice to God is a grateful heart', declares the psalmist. A common Eucharistic prayer, introducing a hymn of praise to God, begins with these very solemn words: 'It is our duty and it leads to our salvation that we should always and everywhere ...' If asked at this point to complete the sentence, many of us, as a result of our religious upbringing, would complete the sentence with 'avoid sin at all costs, always and everywhere', and expect to be congratulated on our right answer. The Church's own answer in the official liturgy is 'that we should thank you always and everywhere'. We all need to thank God for those wonderful words and let them be the theme tune of all our days. As gratitude begins to take hold on us, we begin to see life very differently, respond differently, decide differently and so begin to create a new future for ourselves and for those we encounter.

In all kinds of prayer that you find helpful, always ensure that it includes familiar conversation with God. This does not have to be reserved for the end of your prayer time: your whole prayer time can become a conversation. This familiar conversation with God is something which comes very naturally to children, but if we are not accustomed to it, we are likely to find it difficult at first. This leads to another general truth about all prayer: **Prayer is learned by praying**.

If you never feel drawn to pray in any other way than thanksgiving, then do not think you are failing in some way. If the spirit of God, which leads all your prayer, wants you to pray differently, you will be led into it gently, by attraction. Meanwhile, always pray as you can: not as you can't.

Prayer for Enlightenment

This is the second part of the Review of the Day: it is a further development of the first part, not a new method of prayer. It is a deepening of the gratitude theme. In the first part, our attention was on those events we appreciated, valued and enjoyed. In this second part we look at all the other events which may have been difficult, annoying, disturbing, frustrating, painful. God is in all things. Where is God to be found in our inner turmoil, our fears, our failures, our uncertainties?

It is in God's light that we see light, so the first request in this second part of this prayer is: 'O God, enlighten my mind and heart so that I may know you and come to know myself.' In praying for enlightenment, we are praying to know the desires and attitudes which underlie our moods and emotions so that we may always choose the course of action which brings life to us and to others, and avoid the destructive.

The next step is to look at our own predominant moods and feelings during the day, but without judging them. This is the only way to learn from our own experience, and it is only in and through our own experience that we can find God, now holding us in being.

Moods and feelings, in themselves, are neither right nor wrong, true nor false. The categories of right and wrong, true and false, sinful or not sinful belong not to the moods and feelings in themselves, but in the way we respond to them. Our moods and feelings are very intelligent, important and valuable signals, inviting our attention to the life-giving direction we are being invited to take and warning us against the life-threatening directions. If we give attention to these feelings and emotions, then our hearts react with joy and peace to what is life-giving, but with anxiety and uneasiness to what is destructive.

We shall be considering these points in greater detail in the following chapters, because they affect every aspect of human life. Here I am giving you an outline of the method, so that you can practise it regularly on your own. The later chapters in Part 3 on Holiness will be showing in more detail that spirituality and prayer are not compartments of life, suitable for some but not for others: they are concerned with every aspect of the journey of life in which we are all engaged.

All our moods and emotions are the result of our desires. In this Review of the Day, we are observing this fact, then asking ourselves this all-important question: Are my desires all centred round me and my kingdom? Are my comfort, my success, my status, my reputation, my financial security, my health, my primary concern? Do I desire all creation to praise, reverence and serve me? Or do I desire to live in unity and in peace with others, whoever they may be, and to be at one with this God of all creation, who is inviting me to share in God's love and compassion for all creation?

Talk over the day with God, thanking God for all the gifts of today, acknowledging your own failures, then hurl yourself into the arms of this God who loves you and invites you to be like a child, lying peacefully in its mother's arms.

One last thought with which to end this chapter; it is a quotation from a very ancient theologian: 'Sin is forgetfulness of God's goodness.'

2

Holiness in the here and now

This chapter offers a few fundamental points on the meaning of Holiness: they are based on the teaching of the Hebrew Scriptures, the Gospels and the writings of the New Testament.

In the Hebrew Scriptures, God tells Israel: 'Be holy, as I the Lord your God am holy.' What then follows are many pages of detailed instructions on how we are to behave in our relationships with each other and with the situations we encounter in our daily experience of life. Jesus of Nazareth sums up all these regulations in one short phrase: 'Love the Lord your God with all your heart and all your soul and love your neighbour as yourself.' That, he declares, is the essence of the Law and the prophets. We may have heard these words thousands of times, but here we are going to look at some of their practical implications.

In Jesus' teaching of his followers, whether his own inner circle called 'apostles' (which means 'those who are sent'), or in the 72 followers who are called 'disciples' (which means 'the learners'), or in teaching the vast crowds who gathered to hear him, he gives no detailed instruction about a future Church – the word is mentioned only in St Matthew's Gospel, where it appears three times. He does have much to say about the nature of authority:

The rulers of the pagans lord it over their subjects and their important people love their authority to be felt. With you, it must not be like this. The greatest among you must be the least of all, and the first among you must be the servant of all, for the Son of Man came not to be served, but to serve and to give his life in the service of others.

As we have already seen, the core of this teaching on the use of authority is to be found in the account of Jesus' temptations in the desert in the Synoptic Gospels, in Matthew, Mark and Luke. Further instruction on the dangers of control and domination are to be found in St Matthew Ch. 23, a scorching criticism of dominating chief priests, Scribes and Pharisees, the Jewish religious authorities in Jesus' lifetime. These passages were included in the official canon of Scripture centuries after those authorities were no longer active in Palestine; they were written for the early Christian communities where the writers were aware of these pharisaic attitudes continuing among Christian leaders.

God is the Holy One

Here is Isaiah's vision of Holiness in Isa. ch. 6, vv. 1–10:

> In the year of King Uzziah's death (740BC) I saw the Lord Yahweh seated on a high throne; his train filled the sanctuary; above him stood seraphs, each one with six wings; two to cover its face, two to cover its feet and two for flying. And they cried out to one another in this way.
> 'Holy, holy, holy is Yahweh Sabaoth
> His glory fills the whole earth.'
> The foundations of the threshold shook with the voice of the one who cried out, and the Temple was filled with smoke. I said,
> 'What a wretched state I am in! I am lost,
> For I am a man of unclean lips
> and I live among a people of unclean lips.
> and my eyes have looked at the King, Yahweh Sabaoth.'
> Then one of the seraphs flew to me, holding in his hand a live coal which he had taken from the altar with a pair of tongs.
> With this he touched my mouth and said:
> 'See now, this has touched your lips,
> Your sin is taken away, your iniquity is purged.'
> Then I heard the voice of the Lord saying:
> 'Whom shall I send? Who will become our messenger?'
> I answered, 'Here I am, send me.'

In this passage, the effect on the prophet Isaiah at this revelation of the Holy One is to make him aware of his own need for purification. The Lord of all creation takes notice of Isaiah's distress and purifies his lips by desperate means, which do not destroy him, but enable him to answer the invitation which follows with 'Send me'.

This passage communicates many things about the nature of God. God is the God of all creation, a God who listens to the prayers of the helpless and weak and heals them. And it is through this inner healing that Isaiah is enabled to utter from the core of his being, 'Send me'.

What has this passage to say to our fragmented selves? It tells us that this mysterious God is a God who brings healing. The healing is not an impersonal magic potion: it is the very Spirit of God, who lived in Jesus and raised him from the dead, as St Paul keeps telling us, so that we can let God take us over, leading Paul to write in his letter to the Galatians, 'I live now not with my own life, but with the life of Christ who lives in me'. And what is the nature of this life I am called to live in my own unique way? It is not a life of conformity to a set of rules, rites and regulations: it is a life of freedom in and with the Spirit of God. But what will be the pattern of this life?

I like to think that it was in answer to such a question that Jesus gave us the parable of the Final Judgement in Chapter 25 of Matthew's Gospel. Here is an abbreviated version:

> All the nations of the world will be assembled before the Son of Man (the Messiah who is to come) and he will separate the people from one another as a shepherd separates sheep from goats. The sheep will be on his right, the goats on his left. Then he will say to those on his right, 'Come, you whom my Father has blessed, take for your heritage the kingdom prepared for you since the foundation of the world. For I was hungry and you gave me food; naked and you clothed me, sick and you visited me, in prison and you came to see me.' Then the virtuous will say to him in reply, 'Lord, when did we see you hungry and feed you; or thirsty and give you drink? When did we see you a stranger and make you welcome; naked and clothed you; sick or in prison and go to see you?' And the King will answer, 'I tell you solemnly, in so far as you did this to one of these people of mine, you did it to me.'

What is astonishing, at first sight, with our split spirituality way of seeing things, is that in this answer Jesus makes no mention of religion, spirituality, religious rites and services. We can then reach the totally false conclusion that Jesus is dismissing all forms of religion and spirituality, which is the reaction of millions of people in the developed nations today. The truth is that Jesus does not see things in this split way. We live in God's presence always and everywhere. Everything is sacred. All our manner of being, which is directed to the love and service of others, is giving praise to God. Where holiness dwells in a human being there is no split between our words and the reality of our behaviour. God identifies God's very Self with every single person, religious believers and with those who profess no religion. There is no escaping from this reality unless we choose non-reality, annihilation.

What is it that blocks us from this awareness, what is it in us that leads us to use religion as a way of hiding from the face of God?

When Jesus taught us how to pray, he gave us the 'Our Father'. There are many translations and versions of this prayer, but here is a traditional formulation:

> Our Father, who art in heaven, hallowed be Thy name, Thy kingdom come, Thy will be done on earth as it is in heaven. Give us this day our daily bread, and forgive us our trespasses as we forgive those who trespass against us, and lead us not into temptation, but deliver us from evil. Amen.

It is a wonderful prayer, but here I want to comment only on the phrase 'Thy will be done', because the common misunderstanding of its meaning is key to our understanding why there is such a massive secession from church allegiance in developed countries today and why religion is considered unnecessary in today's world. But the phrase can also lead us to a new way of understanding, which can show us why it is that we are so locked into injustice and violence today.

The phrase 'Thy will be done' is the source of our freedom. If our words are expressions of the reality in which we are living, then 'Thy will be done' expresses our total abandonment to God. In fact, the words have been so communicated to us that they become very bad news; they no longer attract, they repel, and God is relegated to the outer ether.

Let me illustrate this truth with a modern parable, an imaginary fiction expressing a truth which is true for all times.

A modern parable

A Catholic couple go to a priest who gives marriage instructions for all engaged couples and which they are obliged to attend. The priest is very open-minded and suggests to the couple that they should formulate their own marriage vows, which they will declare to all who come to the wedding. On the wedding day itself, the bride walks down the aisle of the church with her father as the Wedding March is played. At the altar steps the father gives his daughter to his son-in-law, who is standing at the foot of the altar where the priest celebrant awaits them. When the organist has completed his recital, the celebrant welcomes the bride and groom, their families and friends to the ceremony, then invites the groom to express his marriage vows to his beloved. Having cleared his throat loudly, he then declares his love. 'I love you very much my dear, but do realize that after this ceremony I shall no longer have any interest in what you might want or desire. Our future together lies in your hands. If you promise to be true to our marriage vows in which you pledge yourself to total obedience to my will for the rest of your life, then we shall have a very happy marriage: if you do not live in this way, our marriage will be very unhappy for both of us in this life. Not only that, but after death you will be sentenced to eternal damnation.' Having expressed his love so movingly, the celebrant then turns to the bride and asks her: 'And will you accept this man to be your husband for the rest of your life?' Hopefully, if she has not already stomped out of the church in fury, she will reply loudly and clearly 'Certainly not', before leaving her husband and the church behind her, never to return.

I know this parable seems absurd, but the point it is making is not absurd: it is tragic. In the teaching of religion, the image of God communicated to so many is of God the judge, God whose main interest in us is in the sins we commit, and whose main preoccupation is in deciding the appropriate punishments. I base these statements on decades of work giving one-to-one retreats to a wide variety of people of different religious affiliations and of none. In this kind of work, if people can be encouraged to speak about their own inner struggles, observing their felt reactions without passing judgement on themselves, they are enabled to reach deeper layers of their consciousness and so become consciously aware of their own past conditioning to conform – a conditioning which is still affecting them in the present, leading them to build up defences against the threats their fears arouse in them. The result of this is that we can end up so dominated by our fears that our conscious lives become centred on our self-preservation, blinding us to the wonder of life and to the invitation to join it, a life of self-giving in love, the invitation our hearts can respond to if we can learn to listen.

For the rest of this chapter, I offer some ways with which you can experiment on your own, ways of discovering the wonder of your being and in particular of the wonder of desire.

Take some scrap paper – you may need quite a lot – and start scribbling your answer to this question: 'What do you long for in life?' Just write, scribble whatever comes to mind. Do not censor your own writing. You are not being asked, 'what should I want': you are being asked what it is you really do desire. One person, to whom I gave this question, answered: 'To burn down churches.' That was her first step in a most amazing journey: she was beginning to get in touch with herself and with life.

Do not be surprised if you find this exercise difficult at first. Another answer I got from a person to whom I had recommended this exercise was: 'No one has ever asked me that question in my life, nor have I asked it of myself.' This, too, was a first step for that person in a journey out of darkness into freedom and joy. So, keep returning to this question, and just scribble. What you have written is for your eyes only. There is no need to show it to anyone else and you can tear up or burn whatever you have written. What is important is that you should catch a glimpse of the wonder of your being, because it is that glimpse which will begin to show you both God and yourself.

When you feel you have scribbled enough, then read over what you have written and try to find for yourself, what are my priorities in this list, what is the fundamental desire, the root desire from which all the other desires arise? The answer does not usually come in an instant: it is a lifelong process and it is our heart that directs us, not some external authority figure, however wise and expert they may appear to be. We need guides in life, we need experts, but we need them to enable us to make our own unique way through life, not to turn us into replicas of themselves. Hence the wise saying of von Hügel: 'Where your heart is, let your brain be also.'

In reading over your list of needs and desires, it is also useful to note how many of them are incompatible. Examples of incompatibility might be my desire always to be popular versus my desire to be transparently honest at all times, my desire to be generous and my desire to have a secure bank balance, my desire to be understood and my unwillingness to listen to those who bore me, my desire to be healthy and my affliction with an incurable illness. You can do all this with your own list of incompatible desires and needs. What soon becomes very clear is my need to have some clear priority in life which can guide me through these perplexities. Here you are coming to the heart of the matter. May this question never leave you! Keep asking it of yourself. It is the question which begins to open the closed doors of our perception, the doors which begin to reveal the wonder of our being and lead to our transformation.

Among all its other benefits, pursuit of this question begins to show that the incompatibility of our desires is not due to the faults and failures of other people, or the action of external malignant forces: the fault lies in our way of perceiving our experience. This is where the roots of our violence lie. It is in acknowledging these roots that our journey into peace and unity must begin. Much more important than that recognition is our need to know the attractiveness and power of our own fundamental desire in our lives. We can live for decades without becoming aware of it, because our upbringing has so convinced us of our essential sinfulness and frailty that we cannot think beyond our own self-preservation. What can deliver us from this overpowering fear in which we are imprisoned?

The essence of freedom is that we should be able to follow and shape our lives by the deepest desire of our being. Our danger is that we should so be conditioned by our own fears that we lose all trust in ourselves and hand over our lives to the experts, to those who know best, or to what we call 'common sense', and so live securely and contentedly within this framework. No matter how hard we try, there is within us an eternal restlessness, a longing which we cannot describe or define clearly, yet which will not allow us to rest in any such framework of certainty. This state is not a punishment, it is an invitation; it is not an affliction, it is a gift. It is called freedom.

Freedom is not the same as liberty – a distinction which is frequently ignored. Here is a very striking quotation. It is an excerpt from Franz Jägerstatter, an Austrian farmer, who was executed in Berlin on 9 August 1943 for refusing to serve in Hitler's army. From his prison in Berlin he wrote, with his hands shackled: 'Even if I write these words with my hands in chains, I still find it much better than if my will were in chains.' He had no liberty, but the dominating power of the Nazi regime could not take away his freedom.

To grow in freedom we need to practise what is called 'detachment' or 'indifference' or 'self-denial' – unfortunate, negative-sounding words which have nothing of the exuberance and power of the word 'freedom'. 'Detachment', 'indifference' and 'self-denial' describe the inner disposition of the free person. But in human beings, the only inner disposition which can overcome our false attachments is through a stronger attachment. That is why fear can never rid us of our false attachments. And that is why in all religious teaching and preaching, and in the inner life of all of us, our attention must always be focused on the attractiveness of God who is love, compassion and forgiveness and is constantly drawing us into this way of being, which is for the benefit of all.

Today, in all religions and among people of no professed religion, pilgrimage has come back into fashion – an ancient custom which goes back to the origins of Christianity, when Christians called themselves 'People of the Way' and Jesus, in John's Gospel, describes himself as 'The Way'. A long time ago I read an article written by two sociologists who claimed that in undertaking a pilgrimage, people are doing more than they realize. Consciously, they may want to go to visit the birthplace or workplace of some famous person, or to visit some particular church, or to be touched by the relics of some ancient saint, or they just want some form of diversion, or even of escape from a difficult situation. Chaucer's *Canterbury Tales* illustrates something of the variety of forms pilgrimage can take and the variety of people who are attracted by it, not always for the noblest of motives. I have had the opportunity to do two long pilgrimages on foot: one from Weybridge, near London, to Rome; then 12 years later, a longer pilgrimage from Ayrshire, my birthplace in Scotland, to Jerusalem. The reason I found the sociologists' article on pilgrimage so attractive was because it helped me to a clearer understanding of my own pilgrimage experience.

The sociologists claimed that those who go on pilgrimage are people who are in search of some meaning in their lives. The pilgrimage is a means of enabling them to do this, but this intention is not necessarily in their conscious minds when they set out – it only becomes clear on later reflection. This was certainly true in my own experience. It is an inner search, but it cannot normally be done from an armchair. Consequently pilgrims choose a place, a destination, or even just choose to wander wherever the mood takes them. This decision influences every other decision till the pilgrimage ends. This fact becomes more obvious on a walking pilgrimage than on a flight, or bus journey.

On reflection later, I saw clearly that every step of my way followed from the decision to walk to Jerusalem, how much I carried, the direction and distance I followed each day, where I stayed and for how long, etc. I then began to realize how important this reflection discovery was. In the journey through life, what was it that corresponded to Rome or Jerusalem? It was this question which showed me the importance of desire in my life, especially the search for my basic desire, the question we are focusing on in this chapter. On a walking pilgrimage, especially, the luggage question is continuous and I must make daily decisions about it, otherwise my feet will cease to collaborate. The general question which arises affects every aspect of our lifestyle. Is my luggage for the journey through life, or do I journey for the sake of my luggage? I can then see clearly that this is a fundamental and most practical question, not just for the duration of the pilgrimage but for every detail of my life, and of every human life. Do I live for my possessions, or do I have possessions in order that I, and every human being, should be enabled to live? The answer is not an answer which comes from logic: it is an answer which comes from observation of my own inner disposition. All our moods and inner feelings are responses to our desires. Is it true, for example, that approximately one billion people are destined to live at starvation level in our world, not because there is no food available for them, but because of our distribution system, which enables the rich to grow richer and condemns the poor to starvation? Do these facts tear us apart inside, or do we devise ways of escaping from the problem by ignoring our inner feelings, or by pretending they do not exist? In this way we can live at peace and consider ourselves righteous as we continue to pursue and approve a style of living which is plundering the earth to the detriment of millions who are already living, and creating conditions which will make human life impossible for future generations.

Here is a very simple way in which we can raise our awareness on these questions:

Write your own Faith Autobiography

Do not be put off by the solemn title. It is a very simple exercise. Ask yourself: 'What have been the key events in my life: the people, the places, incidents, discoveries, the life-giving events, the traumatic events, the threatening events and the joyful?'

Having asked yourself these questions, then scribble down whatever comes to mind without attempting any analysis or self-judgement. Having started on this exercise, you will probably find a chain reaction, as one memory leads you to another. Scribble them down, too. This exercise can profitably last for a lifetime!

What is the point of this exercise? It brings more of our past life to consciousness. Our past continuously affects our present, even although we have forgotten the events in our conscious minds. Jews and Christians constantly remember what they call 'The Passover', when God led Israel out of Egypt, through the wilderness and into the Promised Land. They do this to remind themselves of the truth in which they are now living: that this God is still with them, a God who remains faithful in spite of their infidelity. And through this habit of remembering the goodness of God in the past, they come to learn more about the nature of God in the present.

Their knowledge of God is always developing. The ruthless God, who wipes out Israel's enemies, is very different from the God who is described in the Book of Wisdom, the God who overlooks our sins so that we can repent, the God of whom St Paul writes to the Corinthians: 'For our sake God made the sinless one into sin, so that in him we might become the goodness of God' (2 Cor. 4.21). And this is the God now holding us in being. When we try to forget or to ignore this God, or try to turn God into a God in our own image, our inner moods and feelings, which are so much more intelligent than our conscious logical minds, are expressing their disapproval in what we experience as inner turmoil, fear and dread, a sense of hopelessness. These are not punishments from God; they are invitations to turn back to God, invitations to be healed and refashioned. That is why this kind of exercise is so useful and necessary. It is bringing us to the threshold of transformation, to the longing of our heart, a heart which is now much more conscious of our own close relationship in Christ with every other human being.

Another useful exercise is to write your own obituary notice as suggested in Chapter 3 of Part 2 on Peace

This may appear to be a very threatening exercise, but if you follow the guidelines given, you may find yourself enjoying the task.

The point of all this is to enable you to find and keep reminding yourself of your deepest desire. That is the meaning of 'Doing God's Will'; it is about searching for that way of life which resonates with the core of your being, what St Augustine of Hippo described in his Confessions over 1,500 years ago: 'Lord, you created me for yourself, and my heart is restless until it rests in you.' 'Lord, let me find your love, laughter and compassion in the core of my being.' That is one expression which speaks to me. At the same time I realize that I am light years away from living out that desire, but that does not quench the desire: it leaves me hopeful and grateful.

In all that I have written so far in this book, I have made little mention of the source which has guided me through life, the Spiritual Exercises of Ignatius Loyola. In the following chapter I shall give a brief account of these Spiritual Exercises and why, in spite of all the difficulties I have had in my experience of being given these Exercises as a duty to be done, the experience has taught me that these same Exercises, in their essence, are a means of enabling the pilgrim to make their own discoveries of the gift of life which has been given to them, not as a reward for good conduct, but because it is of the nature of God to love.

Exercises

- In reading this chapter, did you experience any predominant felt reaction? Make a brief note of the feeling and of what gave rise to it.

- Get started on your own faith autobiography and then your obituary.

3

Holiness reveals our split spirituality

I have written eight books, all of them, including *Cry of Wonder*, based on the Spiritual Exercises of Ignatius Loyola. When I began writing this final Part 3, I was going to call it 'Ignatian Spirituality', but soon abandoned the title in favour of 'Holiness'.

There has been a renewed interest in Ignatius of Loyola's Spiritual Exercises in the last 60 years. In the documents of Vatican II, all Religious Orders and Congregations within the Catholic Church were encouraged to renew themselves by returning to their original foundation documents, to the inspiration out of which they have grown. Jesuits returned to the study of the Exercises and uncovered the fact that the Spiritual Exercises were written by Ignatius as a guidebook for those giving them to others individually and not to groups. This has been a most welcome and encouraging development, but it has also produced a stream of books and articles that reinforce – under the claim that they are 'Ignatian' – the split spirituality that Ignatius was trying to heal.

I chose the word 'Holiness', also misunderstood in our day, but in its biblical roots, in the prophetic tradition, in the Psalms, in the Gospels and New Testament writings and in the Christian Mystical tradition, holiness is very earthed in human experience. God urges in Leviticus, 'Be holy as I the Lord your God am holy'. This is then followed by pages of regulations about our behaviour towards one another in every area of life. The word 'Holiness' directs our attention to God, the living source of all that exists, but it also directs us to the reality of God in our everyday experience. Split spirituality is pernicious, because it focuses attention on our sinfulness and diverts our attention from the goodness and generosity of God. We are so accustomed to interpreting the inspired word of God in this way that we are no longer aware of the misuse. Consequently, to say 'God gives God's very self to us out of love' becomes suspect and can make us feel uneasy, whereas 'God died for our sins' becomes a reassuring affirmation of our orthodoxy. Keep repeating these two phrases to yourself and notice your felt reactions. It is only in our own experience that we can find God. While I believe this statement is universally true for humankind, I also know that it needs qualification.

The qualification is this: that the experience which raises our awareness of the reality of God in all things arises out of the *direction* of the minuscule steps we take in our journey through life. God is not a proposition to be studied: God is the source of all creation, 'the love which moves the sun and other stars', as Dante expressed it. That love moves our hearts, too, and is continuously drawing us into God's own unity and love.

Why do I bring in Ignatius of Loyola at this stage? Because in listening to my own experience, I know how many decades it has taken for me to begin to see connections between events. What I am discovering continuously are glimpses of the mystery of God and, in this light, seeing my own life in a totally different way. I am no longer the centre of my interest because I know I am part of something far greater and more attractive than myself, that I live in a pattern of relationships, in a state of becoming what my heart directs me towards – letting God be the God of love to me and through me. I want to record this in some way, simply because I find it life-giving and want to share it.

This outline of Ignatius' life is very sketchy, but it is a necessary background to understanding why he has so many insights which can help us to understand many of the major problems facing us today.

Inigo Lopez – his name before he became known as Ignatius Loyola – was a Basque nobleman, who lived from 1491 to 1556. In 1534 he founded the Society of Jesus, a Roman Catholic Religious Order of men, known as 'The Companions of Jesus' and later as 'The Jesuits'.

Brought up as a youth in the Spanish court, he emerged in his twenties a very ambitious man who, in his own words, 'was filled with a great and vain desire for fame'. He was not a professional soldier as we understand the term today, but he was a good swordsman, ready to serve in wars at the bidding of his own leaders. In his late twenties he was seriously injured in the battle of Pamplona in northern Spain, where the Spaniards were besieged by vastly superior French troops.

Inigo and his troops refused to surrender until a cannon ball came over the parapet, wounding Inigo in both knees. The French troops carried him back to his birthplace, Loyola Castle, where he lay for many months in great pain waiting for his knees to heal. His agony was prolonged by his own request that a broken knee should be reset and a protruding bone should be sawn off, lest his leg should be unsightly for the rest of his life.

It was during this period of immobile convalescence, in the room in which he had been born, that he was nursed back to health. He whiled away his time in daydreams and it was through these daydreams that he was drawn into a new and transformed vision of his life and to a deep longing to live his life in the service of God.

His first set of daydreams centred on the royal lady whom he would marry and so launch himself into a life of fame. He could lose himself in these daydreams for hours at a time. After his conversion, this daydreaming and his imaginative tendency were to play an essential part in his spiritual development, affecting every detail of his life.

He became bored with this daydream and asked for novels. Novels were scarce in those days and Loyola Castle had none, but they found him two books to read: *A Life of Christ* by Ludolf of Saxony and *Lives of the Saints*. In his boredom he read them, then he began daydreaming again, but this time his daydreams were centred on Inigo outdoing all the other saints in their austerities, prayers, fasting and healing ministry. In his daydreams he assured himself that if Dominic could be a great saint, he could surpass him, and all other saints, in sanctity!

For a time he alternated between the two sets of daydreams; then he noticed something which was to transform his life and which was to lead him later to start composing his Spiritual Exercises. He noticed a qualitative difference in the after-effects of the daydreams. While both sets were pleasant at the time, he noticed that his dreams about marrying the royal lady left him bored, empty and sad, while the dreams of outdoing the saints left him hopeful, happy and strengthened. This was his first lesson in discernment, in spotting the difference between the creative and the destructive movements within us and around us. Having noticed this difference he decided that he must set about becoming a great saint!

I love this story for the picture it gives of God's attitude to God's beloved people.

Inigo is still full of self-centred ambition, enamoured of honour and fame. God does not admonish him, declaring that before he dare plan to be a great saint, he should first do some serious penance for the sinfulness of his own past and present life. God draws and teaches Ignatius through his desires and Ignatius responds as best he can, although he is still immersed in his own sinfulness. His path to recovery is coming about gradually through following his deepest desire. That lesson is still necessary for us 500 years later.

Ignatius' spirituality is very earthed. God can only be found in and through our everyday experience. It is an all-inclusive spirituality, open to all people and to every aspect of our humanity. Today, how often do the liturgies you attend, the sermons, the lectures on spirituality/ religion ever touch earth?

Ignatian spirituality enables us to find God in other types of spirituality. In Roman Catholicism we have groups so devoted to Benedictine, Dominican, Franciscan, Carthusian, Cistercian or Jesuit spirituality, as they understand it, that they refuse to look at any other. They are still less inclined to look at Orthodox spirituality, and would consider interest in other faiths to be a form of heresy.

Ignatius, and all the initiators of schools of spirituality, would encourage their followers to follow whatever increases their faith, hope and love for God and for creation. This is the God we must follow, for God is in all things for all of us. Like every other spirituality, followers of Ignatius must beware of our universal tendency to idolatry, replacing the one Creator God with our own particular image of God.

'Discernment' is the key word which sums up the essential characteristics of Ignatian spirituality. Discernment is characteristic of all the traditional spiritualities, not only in Christianity, but also in other major world religions. Ignatius' method is unique in that he develops his spirituality by focusing on decision-making – an occupation in which, as human beings, we are all constantly engaged. The word is derived from the root Latin word '*discernere*', meaning to separate out.

Applied to life in general, what is it that we have to separate out? What is it that brings us to life and what is it that deadens, and how do we learn how to spot the difference? In his Spiritual Exercises Ignatius does not present us with a theoretical treatise on the subject. He presents exercises, which we must do ourselves, then learn the answer to these questions in our own experience. In what follows I shall offer a few key texts from his exercises, so that you can experiment for yourselves. Ignatius began writing his book shortly after his conversion at Loyola. The final version was published 20 years later! You can practise and reflect on these Exercises on your own. For the early Jesuits, it was in learning to trust and be open with their retreat-giver that they began to notice the Exercises' life-giving powers, introducing them to inner freedom and the deep longings of their hearts.

The First Principle and Foundation

The first key text is called 'The Principle and Foundation.' Here is a version which I wrote in my book *God of Surprises*, in which I try to translate the original into language which is more suited to the twenty-first century. It is also a way of making connections between the themes of this book.

> Before the world was made we were chosen to live in love in God's presence by praising, reverencing and serving God in and through creation.
>
> As everything on the face of the earth exists to help us to do this, we must appreciate and relish everything that helps us and rid ourselves of all that is destructive to our living in love in God's presence.
>
> Therefore we must be so poised (detached/indifferent) that we do not cling to any created thing as though it were our ultimate good, but remain open to the possibility that love may demand of us poverty rather than riches, sickness rather than health, dishonour rather than honour, a short life rather that a long one, because God alone is our security, refuge and strength.

We can become so detached from any created thing only if we have a stronger attachment; therefore our one dominating desire and fundamental choice must be 'to live in love in God's presence'. I add the following comments.

It follows from this that all things on the face of the earth must be kind because God's self-giving is in every event. Creativity and destructiveness have their origin in the human mind.

Attachments in themselves are essential in human life if we really are related beings. The words 'detached/indifferent' are unfortunate, suggesting an 'I could not care less' attitude. A much better word is 'freedom', meaning being free to act and to respond to circumstances with my whole being and in harmony with my deepest desire. Freedom includes single-mindedness, complete openness, being totally engaged in whatever I am doing, which is always done through love and service of others, which is to be in harmony with the reality of God who is in all things. How do I learn to distinguish the attachments which are turning me away from God from those which are leading me in the path of God?

Ignatius introduces this question in what is called 'The First Week of the Exercises'.

This does not mean seven days: it may last much longer, it may be shorter; all depends on the inner movements of the pilgrim. The guidelines I give here are those of which I was almost totally ignorant during my 17 years of Jesuit training. The reason I do this is because I am still encountering the consequences of that ignorance in myself and also in others working in spirituality who have not yet begun to acknowledge their own ignorance of themselves. They are still giving the Exercises in instructional mode, talking about them instead of enabling their pilgrims to experience them for themselves. Why do we tend to do this, delivering spiritual information to others in a way which restricts and cramps them rather than sets them free?

In the first part of the Exercises, Ignatius considers personal sin, in which he includes the phrase: 'I will look on myself as a sore and abscess from which have issued such great sins and iniquities and such vile poison.' This passage I particularly disliked because it re-echoed so much of what I had heard and read of matter being bad and spirit being all uncontaminated goodness. Ignatius presents these loathsome findings about himself to God in prayer and ends this section with 'a cry of wonder', then reflects on how all creation has sustained and nurtured him throughout his life. He also reflects how God is still inviting him into unity with all creation and with God's own life.

The result of this meditation is that it liberates us from a disordered attachment to our own self-preservation, freeing us from that self-preservation tendency which separates us from our own deepest self, from others and from God.

Freedom is about being and relating as our whole being wants to do – to allow God to be the God of love and service to me and through me. In the depths of our being, we do not desire to be models of conformity. Really free people are people who resist to the death all those external forces which imprison us in fear of our own wellbeing.

In giving the Spiritual Exercises, the early Jesuits learned how to give them through their own experience. They adapted their methods to the needs of their pilgrims. They gave the full Exercises to relatively few people. The majority who came to them made only the 'First Week'. I do not believe this was because Ignatius thought they were incapable of going further. I believe his reason was that after having done the first part, they would be capable of continuing on their own journey through life with all its hazards because they were now convinced, through their own experience, that God is always for them and closer to each than they are to themselves.

In the next chapter, I shall introduce another key meditation of the Spiritual Exercises, commonly called 'The Kingdom'. It is like a second Principle and Foundation, introducing the pilgrim to the next stage of meditations and contemplations on the life of Christ from infancy until Passion week. If you have read this book so far and done some of the exercises recommended at the end of each chapter, you will realize that you have already engaged in this Kingdom exercise and will be engaged in it for the rest of your life. It will enable you to make connections between what we have already considered – connections of which you may not have been aware when you began focusing on Unity and Peace.

Exercise

- Continue with your faith autobiography and your own obituary.

4

In the split is our call to glory

All the chapters in Part 3 on Holiness are emphasizing our need for an 'earthed' spirituality with its roots in our own everyday experience as distinct from a split spirituality, which looks down on earthy matters and presents us with a heavenly world, which has shaken itself free of material contamination and which we shall enjoy fully in the next heavenly world of eternal bliss, provided we do what we are told by our civil and religious authorities. Earlier in this book we have been looking at the meaning of 'Unity' – that it involves all humankind without exception, and at 'Peace' – that it concerns all aspects of human life. In Part 3 on Holiness, we are looking at Ignatius Loyola's sixteenth-century Spiritual Exercises as one way of seeing our world, the Universe, ourselves and our God. It is a book of invitation, not of threat. It is written to encourage us all to wonder and to dream, because all of us are caught up in something far greater than our logical minds can ever grasp or imagine. We all live enfolded within the goodness of God.

In this chapter we shall look at two of the key meditations in the Spiritual Exercises.

The Call of the King Meditation

To explore the phrase from the Our Father, 'Thy Kingdom come', Ignatius Loyola offered the parable of a temporal king. This would have been intelligible and familiar to his contemporaries: today the concept of king is more at home in fairyland. I give it here because the outdated parable contains essential elements to inspire, motivate and draw humankind in all ages.

Do not let the details of Ignatius' imaginary king preoccupy you. The details are only a starting point. You may devise your own imaginary leader, a person whom you admire and would like to imitate but is light years away from being anything like a king. This character invites you to collaborate in a project to initiate a new way of seeing and reacting to our world. It is a way of unity for all humankind, a way of living at peace with all creation, a lifestyle which brings joy to the core of your inner being.

In the parable Ignatius imagines a king 'whom all Christian princes and people reverence and obey'. The king addresses his people, telling them that it is his will to conquer the whole land of the infidels. This includes all who are not Christian – he is re-echoing the Crusade appeal, accepted in Ignatius' time, but repented of in today's Roman Catholic Church. The words which are important for us today are in his appeal to his followers. They must be prepared to have the same food, drink and clothing as their leader. They must also work with him during the day and the night so that they may later share in his victory as they have shared in the labour.

Having heard this call made to them personally, they are then invited to consider what response they would like to make to this invitation, and how they would think of any knight who refused such an invitation. This is the first part of the parable. At this point there is no commitment, no decision asked of the pilgrim.

In the second part of the parable, it is then applied to the call which is, in fact, being addressed by God to each one of us. God's call is universal. It is not reserved to a particular nation, a particular group, but to every individual: 'My will is to conquer the whole world and all my enemies and thus enter the kingdom of my Father. Whoever wishes to come with me must labour with me, so that following me in pain, they may also follow me in glory.' Then he adds: 'Reflect on this invitation that all those who have judgement and reason will offer themselves whole heartedly for the task.' Notice that there is still no exhortation to reach a decision at this point. So far, the purpose of this exercise is to prepare the pilgrim to consider wider horizons, to stretch their imagination and make them more aware of their own inner feelings. This is an essential feature of his spirituality – to enable people to discover for themselves, while also allowing them to be themselves.

To proceed in this way is incompatible with enforcing conformity to any project which is contrary to the deepest desire of the individual.

The final point Ignatius makes in this parable of the Kingdom distils the essence of his message into a few brief sentences. All that follows in the book of the Exercises is an elaboration and a deepening of these few sentences.

The final point he makes is addressed to those who 'feel prompted to distinguish themselves in the service of their eternal king and lord of the Universe'. They not only feel drawn to offer themselves to labour with their Lord. They want to go further, to do more, and so he states: 'They will work against their human sensitivities, against their carnal and worldly love. They will make offerings of greater worth and moment.' Those words, as they stand, are open to ambiguous interpretations today – interpretations which mask the essential point that this way of living is not something imposed, but followed rigorously because it is desired passionately. In other words, it is desire which leads, a desire for freedom to be at one with oneself, with all humankind and all creation, and with God, who is the heart of it all.

As I grow in awareness of the potential within me to be totally self-centred, then I realize that I must cling to my deeper longing to find the inner freedom which can allow me to be what I most want to be, able to choose that way of life where I know my fears for my own survival can never be the dominant desire of my life.

Acting against 'carnal and worldly love' does not mean I must conduct a constant war against everything that attracts me and gives me pleasure. Failure to understand this has impoverished the lives of many most generous people. Our human life is a gift from God, freely given and to be enjoyed. There was a Jewish writer who stated that at the Final Judgement of all humankind, God will ask us one question, and one question only: 'Did you enjoy my creation?' If our answer is 'Certainly not, I was far too busy acting against my carnal and worldly love', then we are in trouble!

This emphasis on desire runs through every part of the Spiritual Exercises. Religious instruction can so emphasize sin in general, and my own sin in particular, that it blinds and deafens me to the reality of God's continuous self-giving to us in love. The Hebrew prophets are forever warning us against the dangers of idolatry, including the phrase, 'we become what we worship'. If we allow our fear of sin to predominate in our lives, then we become what we worship, lose our regard for other people and treat them inhumanly. Could it be that fear of idolatry underlies the phenomenon of massive secession from church-going today, not only from churchgoing, but also from all manner of religious belief? This is a question we need to ponder carefully. Instead of condemning those who have given up church membership or church attendance, could it be that they might be acting in a way which is true to their inner self, a refusal to conform to pressures which, they feel, are dehumanizing them?

The attractiveness of God has been so neglected and the sinfulness of human beings so overemphasized that we have ended up by taking measures for our own preservation which are, in fact, violent and destructive. The most obvious example of this is in what are called national nuclear defence policies. To those who have them, they are the most obvious way of ensuring our national protection. To hold contrary views is considered treachery. The views favouring nuclear defence are also held with uncompromising certainty by its proponents. Dedication to this cause has all the hallmarks of idolatry. Argument on the issue only emphasizes its futility. What can we do in face of this? We need to give our attention to the roots of violence. These roots are in the workings of our own human minds. Once we can acknowledge this, we can begin to become aware of our own violence in our everyday life.

In his Spiritual Exercises, Ignatius gets to the heart of the matter of the roots of violence. He knows they lie in each individual. He does not tirade against the wickedness of others. He invites and encourages us to face up to our own hidden violence, but he does so gently, without threats or coercion.

Ignatius ends his Kingdom parable with a final prayer. He does not tell the pilgrim what to do. Its object is to clarify for ourselves what we might desire to do if we engage seriously with the invitation God now offers to us. The rest of his Exercises are to enable us to surrender totally to God in every aspect of our lives.

Here is his final prayer in the Kingdom parable (Ganss translation):

'Eternal Lord of all things, I make my offering with your favour and help. I make it in the presence of your infinite goodness, of your glorious mother and of all the holy men and women of your heavenly court.

'I wish and desire, and it is my deliberate decision, provided only that it is for your greater service and praise, to imitate you in bearing all injuries and affronts, and any poverty, actual as well as spiritual, if your most holy majesty desires to choose and receive me into such a life and state.'

The wording may not appeal to you, but notice what underlies the words and express them in your own way. Whenever we address God, we do not do so alone, for God is in every breath we breathe, the origin and source of all human desire. Consequently, we always have a mass of supporters, living and dead, who are wishing us well. We need to remind ourselves constantly of this truth, especially when we feel overwhelmed by loneliness and a sense of emptiness and meaninglessness in our lives.

'Actual poverty' means lack of personal ownership of material goods: spiritual poverty means an inner detachment from these goods, whether I possess them or not. It also includes acknowledgement of our emptiness before God, leading to a deeper sense of our total dependence on God. Another way to explain Ignatius' meaning of spiritual poverty is to say that in asking for this gift, we are asking for such an inner longing to be at one with God that it overcomes all counter-attachments to our personal preservation, to health and wealth, honour and status. These attachments are not wrong in themselves, but our particular attachment to any one of them may blind and deafen us to our essential relationship with God, which must include our relationship with ourselves and with other people, whoever they are.

A key word which emerges from this Kingdom parable is a favourite word in the teaching of Jesus Christ: the word 'Remember'. It means putting together our disconnected selves, torn apart by our conflicting desires, which do violence to ourselves and to those around us. It is a lifelong task of submitting ourselves in every detail of our lives so that our creator God may take over, continuing God's self-giving in us and through us, building God's kingdom of unity, peace and love.

The Two Standards Meditation

This meditation from Ignatius' Spiritual Exercises is presented here because it explores a reality which every human being encounters, whether they profess a religious belief, or not. It also takes us deeper into the heart of the matter – which is, finding God in all things.

I once gave an individual eight-day retreat to a woman, Sarah Hipperson, who lived for 19 years at Greenham Common, an area of Buckinghamshire which stored nuclear missiles, a defence against Soviet Russia during the Cold War.

On hearing of this new base, Sarah, a qualified lawyer who had been a lifelong opponent of nuclear defence, went into action. She was a married woman with a large, grown-up family. She was a magistrate of court, entitled to act as a judge and to sentence offenders on minor legal charges. Sarah took up residence in the Peace Camp set up just outside the fence surrounding RAF Greenham Common Airbase.

In the summer months women came in thousands from all parts of Britain and were joined by thousands more from Europe and America, people of all faiths and of no professed faith. While the majority of protesters stayed for limited periods, Sarah decided to stay until the missiles were removed.

Living conditions for the women were harsher than anything the ancient fathers and mothers of early Christianity had to endure in the desert, where the weather was warm and predictable. The Greenham women were forbidden shelter of any kind. Their only protection from wind and rain was sheltering under 'benders', tree branches covered with tarpaulin. They were also raided frequently, not only by American military from within the base, but also by unfriendly natives, who could tolerate the proximity of nuclear weapons designed to vaporize innocent men, women and children in Soviet Russia, but could not tolerate having unwashed women in their neighbourhood, contaminating their shopping centres! The reason they were unwashed was because they were forbidden to have running water or toilets in their camps. Their bender shelters were easily removed by the military, the local police and unfriendly neighbours, but also easily replaced by the campers from the woodlands around. They collected water in buckets from local wells and streams.

Sarah lived under these conditions for almost 20 years. At night, she used to emerge from her tarpaulin shelter with a pair of wire-cutters, cut her way through the perimeter, find the building where the weapons were stored. She then sat down and started singing hymns until the guards arrested her. Sentences, at first, were short, a week or two. Whenever she was arrested, she fasted. On one occasion she fasted for a whole month and decided afterwards that she would never again attempt such a fast. Both prisoners and warders looked forward to her visits! With other women, she also arose at night when they knew the military vehicles would be going out on manoeuvres. They lay on the ground in front of them until forcibly removed by the military. As she had a legal background, she took the Ministry of Defence to court on several occasions, some of which she won, conducting her own defence, and improving living conditions for the protesters.

When the nuclear weapons were eventually withdrawn, she asked me if she could make an eight-day individually given retreat. When I asked her why she was making this request, she answered: 'Because I want to put my spiritual life in order.' On hearing this I wished I had a life like hers to put in order.

Why this lengthy preamble to Ignatius' meditation on the Two Standards? The reason is because her story enabled me to understand and appreciate Ignatius' method in a new way which I have followed ever since.

I did not intend giving Sarah a cut-down version of the Spiritual Exercises. I wanted to help her to discover for herself. Without giving her any preliminary instructions, or showing her the text, I recommended that she spend one day simply recalling her Greenham experience, noting her inner experiences of peace, disturbance, of light and of darkness. At the end of the day, I listened to her account, only interrupting now and again to play back to her what I had heard in order to check that I had understood. Later, I gave her a copy of Ignatius' Two Standards and she had no difficulty in understanding them: the points Ignatius was making coincided with what she had experienced. She felt joyful, because she had begun to see that what she had previously considered to be faults on her part were, in fact, valuable insights which she had ignored or resisted because they upset her peaceful feeling.

One brief example – one of the aspects of Greenham which she found most difficult – was the opposition she encountered among the campers themselves. Some wanted the whole Greenham movement to be directed towards winning rights for women, rather than to the clearing of nuclear weapons from Greenham. Sarah resisted this move, became very unpopular with many, lost friends and felt isolated. She experienced an inner revulsion of her whole being and was very upset. The notion of spirituality in which she had been educated had convinced her that if she were moving in the direction of God, everything should be sweetness and light. That is why at the end of her heroic 20 years, she felt the need to put her life in order. In fact, what she needed to re-think was her notion of spirituality and the meaning of Jesus' passion, death and resurrection in our lives. He, too, had suffered rejection, even by those closest to him and by the established authorities within Judaism who condemned him as a blasphemer, and by the civil authorities who allowed his death by crucifixion between two thieves. Dying, he had called out: 'God, my God, why have you forsaken me?' His last recorded words were: 'Into thy hands I commend my spirit.'

In attempting to present, in writing, Ignatius' Two Standards meditation in shortened form but with texts from his original version, I have constantly been trying to explain the meaning behind the original text, a procedure which has bored me and is likely to bore the reader as well. Consequently I shall now attempt another method. I shall explain what I now understand as the essence of his spirituality in my own words. Readers can test this against their own experience, then later read the original text, if they feel so drawn.

The Two Standards meditation may be compared to a lens which enables us to discover a new way of looking at all our experience of life, so that we can begin to understand the significance of our inner life and its connexion with our felt experience. This is a transformative experience, affecting every aspect of life.

Ignatius imagines the whole human world divided into two separate groups: those who are dedicated to the following of Christ and those who are dedicated to anti-Christ. He calls the anti-Christ leader Lucifer, which means 'the Light-bearer', because the work of the evil one masquerades under the appearance of light. In the meditation he reveals more of the nature of this destructive force, which affects all human beings, and compares it with the nature of Christ. He pictures Lucifer 'sitting on a smoky throne in the middle of Babylon'. Lucifer summons countless demons, 'some to one city, some to another, and so covering the whole world, excepting no province, place, state or individual'.

Ignatius uses his imagination to encourage the pilgrim to use their own. He also uses it here to emphasize the global reality of this division. Do not allow yourself to be distracted by details of his visual imagination, but find your own and test them against your own experience.

He then imagines the kind of address Lucifer might make to his followers. He tells them to set up snares and chains; how first he should tempt people to covet riches (as he usually does, at least in most cases), so that they may more easily come to vain honour from the world, and finally to surging pride. In this way, the first step is riches, the second is honour, and the third is pride; and 'from these three steps the enemy entices them to all the other vices'.

Another name he has for Lucifer is 'the enemy of our human nature', not 'of our souls', thus avoiding the dangerous split in our spirituality. Note, too, how he does not condemn riches and honour in themselves, but the way we relate to these things. Awareness of this distinction lies at the heart of Christian discernment, which we shall consider in a later chapter. We can easily misinterpret pride by identifying it with outer signs of haughtiness, affectation, strutting around like a peacock. Pride is an attitude, a worldview, which puts me firmly in the centre of the Universe, round which the whole Universe revolves. This is not the conscious attitude of the proud person, but the attitude lies at the heart of all their everyday decisions and determines them. Their outward actions betray the reality of their own inner life.

We become so preoccupied with our own survival that we have no energy to concern ourselves with other people's concerns. We can see this on the macro scale when we look at the fact of world hunger, leading to a death rate of 20 per cent of the world's population every year, not because there is not enough food, but because our humanly devised distribution systems put monetary gain before human welfare. Similarly our fear of violence leads us to devise a defence system which threatens the survival of the entire human race. Even if a nuclear war were never to break out, the money spent by the world's nations on nuclear and other methods of defence is already destroying our respect and reverence for human life. Worse still is the dehumanizing effect this attitude already has on all of us, in all aspects of our lives, learning to regard other people as objects to be used for our own protection. This attitude creates a fear-filled society.

Ignatius then gives God's address to his followers. In contrast to Lucifer's smoky throne in Babylon, Jesus is on a plain near Jerusalem, 'in an area which is lowly, beautiful and desirable'. Notice his constant emphasis on the attractiveness of Jesus, whose approach is always courteous and gentle, not threatening or terrifying. He then imagines how Jesus would, like Lucifer, send his followers throughout the world, to spread his teaching among every state and condition. His concern is humankind, not limited to particular people or groups.

Jesus' followers are to help all people by attracting them, first, to the most perfect spiritual poverty and also, should God wish so to choose them for it, for actual poverty; and secondly, by attracting them to a desire of reproaches and contempt, since from these results humility.

So the steps Jesus recommends, according to Ignatius, are: 'First poverty in opposition to riches; the second, reproaches or contempt in opposition to honour from the world; and the third, humility in opposition to pride. Then from these three steps they should encourage people to all the other virtues.'

Ignatius emphasizes the attractiveness of Jesus' teaching. This emphasis is vital because it engages our hearts and we can respond with genuine enthusiasm, not out of a sense of duty. Spiritual poverty denotes an inner willingness to surrender our lives totally to the love and service of God, so that our whole lives are in harmony with the love of God, a God in love with God's creation. Growth in spiritual poverty can usefully be compared to a journey/pilgrimage. It is an attitude which permeates every feature of our lives. Practice in spiritual poverty is a lifelong process and it consists in tiny steps. The important characteristic of the steps lies not in their length, speed, walking style etc. but in the direction of each step. Is each step drawing us more closely into harmony with God's will for us, which is that we should be at one with Godself allowing the spirit of love and generosity so to possess us, that the deepest longing of our heart is that we should be at one with God's love and service of all humankind and of all creation?

It is only in the power of God that this attitude is possible. As long as we allow fear to reign over us or make self-preservation the object of our lives, we are acting against our deepest desire. As we come to realize this, we also become aware of our own fragility, and this can be very painful. Our pain is not a sign of failure – it is a sign of success. It can throw us back in desperation, forcing us to ask the question: 'Where is my rock, my refuge, my strength?' We are on the threshold of the answer to our longing, and it evokes a 'Cry of Wonder'. This is not a one-off happening. It is entry into a new way of living and of being – a slow dawning on us of the reality of God in every breath we breathe, however faltering.

In the following chapter we shall look more closely at Discernment, which lies at the heart of the Spiritual Exercises, but it also lies at the heart of our lives.

Exercise

• Just note anything in the contents of this chapter that speaks to your own experience of life.

5

Discerning the split

Figure 1

This image came to me many decades ago, after I watched a popular TV programme called *One Man and his Dog*. Each shepherd had his own dog, and they were all provided with a small flock of sheep. They had to drive their sheep over a hilly cross-country route dotted with various obstacles, running streams, narrow openings into fields, through small gaps in dense hedgerows, ending up in a small enclosure with an open gate. The first shepherd to complete the demanding circular route in record time was the winner.

I began to see some fascinating parallels between shepherding and the work I was then engaged in, giving individual retreats, reflected on the similarities and found them – and still find them – very helpful in every aspect of life.

The Visual Aid includes the shepherd. Over 2,500 years ago the Jewish psalm writer had been struck by the same comparison! 'The Lord is my shepherd, I shall not want.' In my imagining, the sheep represent our many conflicting desires, inclinations and appetites, which divide us and pull us apart. The sheep dog represents 'the fine point of the soul', our deepest desire. To get in touch with this image, you might draw your own sheep and give them a name. This exercise may keep you usefully occupied for a very long time!

It was a very experienced shepherd who informed me that the whole operation of shepherding depends on one factor, and one factor only. If this factor is missing, the shepherd may be a fine outstanding person of irreproachable character and abundantly gifted, and his/her dog may be a champion Crufts winner, but if the pair of them do not relate well, their shepherding will be totally ineffective! This was a most enlightening comment for me and it has relevance for all our everyday activities and for the decisions which underlie them.

It is also useful to reflect and notice that our most noisy, urgent and insistent desires are usually the most superficial. Our deepest desires are quiet, although affecting every aspect of our lives. A most telling example of this characteristic of desire is to be found in St Mark's Gospel ch. 5, vv. 1–20, in which Jesus heals the raving demoniac (see 'Unity', Chapter 3). A simple but essential lesson which comes out of this story and is applicable to all our ways of praying is: Always pray out of your deepest desire. Never let your attention become so fixed on your lamentable performance that you have no energy left for wonder, gratitude and joy. The story of the demoniac emphasizes the truth that there is no situation of hopelessness which is greater than God's love and compassion. Through his encounter with Jesus, the demoniac becomes aware of his deepest desire and can therefore carry out in his life what Jesus is asking: 'Go, Tell ...'

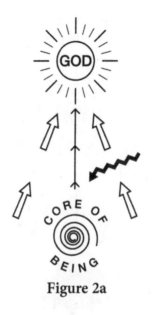

Figure 2a

This illustrates our felt experience when the core of our being is directed to God. The white arrows represent our inner movements which are in harmony with whatever we are doing, however earthy our actions may be. I may be trying to clear a blocked toilet, an act of service to the household which demands all my attention. It is the doing of a task which is our service of God, not the fact that I pepper my activity with prayers, an activity which may distract me from tightening the necessary nuts and bolts!

I may, for example, be totally engaged in living in a situation which is very demanding, but I enjoy what I am doing and am grateful to be doing it. Then the thought occurs to me, 'you will never be able to keep this up', a thought which afflicted Ignatius after his conversion and decision to abandon himself totally to God's service. This thought which takes us away from our deepest desire is represented by the black arrow, a reminder that we live in a world of creative and destructive forces. If this thought does not seem to match your own experience, then please wait before dismissing the thought of destructive forces. Awareness of a destructive force of any kind is not an affliction: it is a gift, an essential part of being human. Our acknowledgement of this can be an invitation to keep returning to our basic desire, so that we can recover our sense of direction, handing over our fears about the future to God, the source of any good I may be able to do and whose power is always greater and closer to me than I can think or imagine.

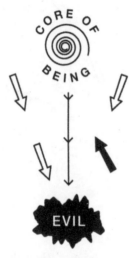

Figure 2b

This represents the core of our being if it is totally turned away from God. The figure is not asserting that any human being has ever reached this state: it is a state which is a possibility for any one of us, because God has given us freedom, and God is always faithful.

The white arrows represent our own desires, actions and reactions in pursuit of our own self-aggrandizement, whatever form that may take. Such decisions and the actions which follow will bring us self-assurance, pleasure, delight and certainty because they are in harmony with what we consider to be our deepest desire. The black arrow depicts a contrary movement arising from a deeper level of my consciousness, which pierces the security I have built around myself, shaking my self-confidence. This black arrow represents a shaft of grace. I may forget about it, distract myself from attending to it: what I cannot do is destroy it, because God is faithful and will never desert us. The black arrow signifies salvation. It can always be ignored: it can never be destroyed, thank God!

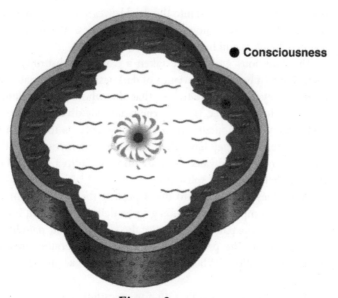

Figure 3

This represents my memory of a well I had discovered on a cross-country walk. It was a well springing up from ground level near the edge of the ruins of an ancient monastery in North Wales. About 25 years later I returned to the spot, found the well and the ruins, but it bore little resemblance to the memory I still had in my mind. This did not disturb me, because the image which had formed in my mind, however different from the original, was instigated by the well itself, and it still affects the way I understand the work I do in giving, and training others to give, the Spiritual Exercises individually. This lesson is not limited to retreat-giving: it reveals something of the nature of my own consciousness and its limitations.

It was months after my discovery of the well that I imagined the little grains of sand, which I could see being bounced around by the movement of the water, to be conscious of what was happening. They were very happy in the bright sunlight, grateful for the force of the water and the pleasure it gave them. They then began to feel sorry for other grains, which were constantly grumbling and did not appear to appreciate or value themselves or their situation. They also felt an inner urge to declare their message to those who seemed limited to bewailing their own existence. Then, through the movement of the water, the happy grains were moved into the dead leaves and the mud at the edge of the well. They were now saying to themselves: 'We are in darkness, trapped, helpless and hopeless.'

The conscious grains have taken a leap into absurdity. They are interpreting a passing experience of darkness as the ultimate meaning of life. They have failed to see that the whole well, including the unfailing flow of water, is their true reality. By divinizing their bright moments and demonizing their dark moments, as though they were separate realities, they have chosen the dark moments to be the only true power which prevails. They are now caught in a very real danger, namely, their own split spirituality.

What they have failed to do is present their own plight to God in prayer. Complain about it, beg to be delivered from it, but do not refuse to face the pain of it, because the answer to our pain lies within the pain itself. The pain forces us back in desperation to the ever-recurring question: 'Where ultimately is my rock, my refuge and my strength?'

It is through persisting with this question that we can begin to break through our own self-imprisoning walls of our own self-preservation certainties and touch into the depths of our heart, where God is. This is not an abstract escape route of our own manufacture. It is a felt and indestructible experience, a cry of wonder that in the depths of my darkness, God is always there. I shall be afflicted again with these moods of despair – it is part of life – but having experienced once the cry of wonder and constantly practised it and delighted in this new way of seeing life and everything in it as gift, I can slowly begin to see that all these traumas are not life-threatening, but life-promising, because they are bringing to consciousness the truth of my existence, which is to be drawn more deeply in the life of God, living in love and service of others.

This leads us to our final Visual Aid. I owe this illustration to my Jesuit colleague, Fr Gerald O'Mahony, which he gives in his book *At The Still Point – Making Use of our Moods* (Eagle Books, Guildford 1993).

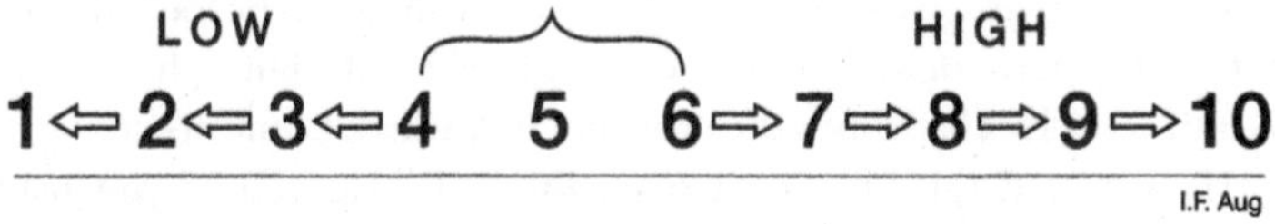

LOW   HIGH

1⇐2⇐3⇐4   5   6⇒7⇒8⇒9⇒10

I.F. Aug

Figure 4

Although, as human beings, we are all unique, we all experience shifting moods of light and darkness. No amount of writing or discussion can change that fact. What we can do is change the way we interpret these moods and so learn to see them as invitations to continue on our journey with hope through life, learning to let God's Spirit transform us.

On a scale of 1–10, numbers 1–3 represent our extremes of passivity on the left-hand side and numbers 7–10 represent our extremes of hyperactivity on the right-hand side. At both these extremes we are out of harmony both with ourselves and with God. As we move towards numbers 4–6, we are returning to be more in touch with ourselves and with God.

On any given day our moods and feelings are many and varied. The value of this scale is to alert us when we notice our predominant moods and feelings are at either extreme. This can enable us to react to the moods in a constructive and creative way: if we are being overactive, then deliberately slow down; if we are being passive and lethargic in responding to our situation, then deliberately step up the pace of life, but at both extremes avoid doing violence to ourselves.

One final reflection on Figure 4. When we do feel we are enveloped in darkness, trapped in annihilating doubt, there are a few simple questions we can ask ourselves before sinking deeper into what, on later reflection, we can see was a home-made melodrama. Am I overworking, not allowing myself sufficient sleep, food, physical exercise? Am I avoiding companionship with those around me? By acting against these tendencies I am, in fact, turning back to my true direction in life. Similarly, bestirring ourselves to act against our tendency to extreme passivity, giving attention to others, learning to listen to what they have to say and how they say it – just being with them. Acting in this way, we are already turning back to God, and will discover that we have moved to the spaces between 4–6.

Briefly, our excessive downswings and upswings can be looked upon not as afflictions, or signs of our essential inferiority, but as invitations to hurl ourselves back into the arms of God, which is our home.

Having read this chapter, I hope this will help you as you read, reflect and pray on the guidelines which follow in Chapter 6.

6

Guidelines for discernment

The substance of this chapter derives from a section of the Spiritual Exercises of Ignatius Loyola. He began writing these Spiritual Exercises very shortly after his conversion experience. His first set of daydreams, as he lay in bed waiting for his damaged knees to mend, of marrying the royal lady and so pursuing a life of fame and glory, enjoyable at the time, had left him bored, empty and sad. The second set of daydreams about outdoing all the saints of the past in his dedication to a life of austerity and hardship, dedicated to following Christ totally for the sake of his Kingdom, left him afterwards joyful, grateful and hopeful. His guidelines came out of his own felt experience. He had no theological or spiritual qualifications. He was an ill-instructed layman, with a strong streak of the fictional Don Quixote in him and also a strong streak of violence. He is not attempting a treatise on spirituality: he is writing from his own very raw, felt experience.

One of the dangers of fame is that the real person is soon forgotten and idealized accounts are given. These mask the truth and also leave later generations with misleading notions of holiness – notions which take no account of personal experience, but praise a model of holiness so sublime and perfect that any ordinary mortal becomes convinced that they can never attain to it. Much damage has been done and is still being done by modern writers who convince others that anything 'earthy' is bound to be contaminated and therefore unworthy of their notice. In their dedication to these models they seem to be blissfully unaware of the meaning of the Incarnation, as though enfleshing human beings in corruptible bodies was an unfortunate slip-up in God's work on creation!

Ignatius was a Christian and a humanist. His spirituality has been described as 'finding God in all things'. His guidelines on discernment, on recognizing the presence of God in all that happens, assume a source of knowledge in all of us which cannot be reduced to logical ways of thinking. God is always greater and God continues to operate through people who are illiterate, who would not recognize a syllogism if they saw one, yet have a mysterious, insightful wisdom and can spot the action of God in what is described officially as 'criminal behaviour'.

What I offer here is an abbreviated version of Ignatius' first fourteen guidelines for discernment. My excerpts are not a translation of the original. I have written them in a terminology which I have found more intelligible to our own times. Ignatius introduces his own guidelines with a caution: 'They can help, at least to some extent, in the practice of discernment'. They are not magic formulae which can give clear answers to all our problems. I hope that what I write can help 'to some very small extent'. Listening to your own experience is what can help you most.

Guidelines for distinguishing the creative from the destructive in our own experience

First Guideline
If the core of our being is directed to God, then the decisions we make in harmony with that fundamental desire will resonate in our moods and feelings, bringing some measure of peace, strength and tranquillity. The destructive forces, outside and within us, will oppose this decision that brought us peace, causing agitation, sadness and inner turmoil.

As God is in all things, these guidelines apply to all human beings, whatever their religious beliefs or lack of them. Earlier in this book, I mentioned the encounters I had with a group of communists on the subject of 'Catholics, Communists and Politics'. The man who turned the meeting into a reflection on God was a hardline Marxist and militant atheist! He was passionately involved on behalf of oppressed peoples and considered religion to be the opium of the people, belief in God being the source of all oppression. The Catholics present assured him that this God was not the source of their faith. We all discovered, through this encounter, that we had much more agreement on essential values in human life than differences, and appreciated the huge contribution that he had made. Discernment is about recognizing the Spirit of God active in all situations and in all places.

Notice, too, the mention of 'moods and feelings bringing some measure of peace, strength and tranquillity'. Our nearness or distance from God is never to be measured simply by the intensity of our feelings of attraction or repulsion. At the core of Christian belief is the belief that God, who is love and compassion, is everywhere, and God's boundaries are nowhere.

God is not the problem; the problem lies in how we have been conditioned to mistrust our own experience, the deep longings and desires of our own hearts. When we act and react in ways which run counter to our deepest desire, then our wise body sends out distress signals. Ignoring these distress signals habitually narrows our horizons, imprisons us in a strait-jacket of self-concern and dependence on external authority figures.

Let us suppose that I have committed myself to a particular way of life, or to a course of action, convinced that this is God's will for me – then later, I am assailed by doubts about the rightness of that decision. A way of acknowledging that doubt is to ask ourselves the question: 'If I could wave a magic wand, in what other situation would I prefer to be?' I have met this kind of doubt in my own life, but also in the lives of countless others, actively involved in peace, justice and integrity of creation work, to whom I have given individual retreats. The answer almost always given is: 'I prefer to stay where I am. If I were to withdraw from this commitment I could no longer live in peace with myself.' This kind of answer echoes the Hebrew prophets in their complaints before God, especially Jeremiah:

> The word of Yahweh has meant for me
> Insult and derision all day long.
> I used to say, 'I will not think about him.
> I will not speak his name any more.'
> Then there seemed to me to be a fire burning in my heart,
> imprisoned in my bones.
> The effort to restrain it wearied me,
> I could not bear it. (Jer. 20.8-9)

I have met many admirable Jeremiahs among people of different religious traditions and of none. What binds them together is a passion for justice, peace and integrity for all humankind. This passion is also called 'enthusiasm', a word which in its Greek origin means 'God within'.

Second Guideline
If the core of our being is turned away from God, any decisions we make which are in harmony with that fundamental aversion will comfort and console us, while the creative forces outside and within us will trouble us with stings of conscience.

The white arrows which appeared in Figure 2a on page 292 represent our inner reactions to our moods, the decisions we make, the actions we perform, which are in harmony with the core of our being, our longing to let God be the God of love and compassion in every detail of our lives. The black arrow represents the moods, feelings and thoughts which come into our consciousness and are opposed to this fundamental desire. We live in a world of creative and destructive forces. What we are presently engaged with is the source of the destructive forces. What we have seen is that those forces are in every individual. How are we to recognize them at work in ourselves? We have no difficulty in finding the sources of destruction in forces outside us. The task of our lives, the greatest challenge we shall ever have to face, is to face the possibility that the only possible course for me is to trace the source of destruction within me, acknowledge the truth of it and respond with all my being in total surrender to God. This is what our hearts long for. The more I can respond to this drawing of God, the more my whole being rejoices, is at peace and in harmony with my deepest desire. What I am describing is a lifelong journey. It is on behalf of all human beings, because God is always nearer to us than we are to ourselves and God's love for us is indestructible. The moods, feelings and thoughts which plunge us into darkness are the very ones which can enlighten us, if we can acknowledge them. They are signs of progress, not of failure.

Third Guideline
Creative moods and feelings are to be distinguished from destructive, not by their pleasantness or painfulness, but by their effect. If going with the mood or feeling leads to an increase of faith, hope and love, then it is creative; if it leads to a decrease of faith, hope and love, then it is destructive.

'Ignore your feelings' was advice commonly given to children by parents and teachers and to Christian congregations by preachers. I had an abundance of this instruction. Experience has shown me that such advice is as crassly stupid as advising motorists to ignore traffic lights.

This guideline is a warning against simplistic judgements which declare that whatever pleases us is good and whatever displeases us must be bad.

Faith can be described as the gift of seeing that all creation is an effective sign of the reality of God. It is the gift of being 'at home' wherever I may find myself, because God is in all things and all things are in God. Creation itself is not God, but a manifestation of God.

Here are two simple examples:

(i) I have lost someone very close to me and the experience is very painful. This pain can push me towards despair, or it can force me to ask a further question: 'Where can I find an ultimate security?' The reaction towards despair is destructive for myself and others. Staying with the question can enable me to recover awareness of a deeper layer of consciousness, which enables me to recover awareness of a deeper layer within me, a level of wonder and desire, a new vision of the depth of mystery of my being, of an inner longing which I know is not of my creation, is not an escape into fantasy, but a finding of myself. I have had the privilege of sharing these moments with people, who constantly say 'I came on this retreat to find God and I have found myself' – echoing St Augustine's words of 1,500 years ago, when he found himself praying to God, 'That I may know you, that I may know myself'.

(ii) I am on bad terms with someone who then fails in a particular venture. News of the failure pleases me greatly. Allowing this dislike to influence the way I respond to this person strengthens the hate virus, and the hate virus, when we allow it to influence us, results in a decrease of faith, hope and love.

Fourth Guideline
Moods and inner feelings, whether pleasant or unpleasant, which are drawing us towards God are called Consolation: painful moods and inner feelings which are drawing us away from God are called Desolation.

This guideline is of fundamental importance in discernment; it guards us against over-simplification. Desolation, as described here, always feels unpleasant. We do not enjoy anxiety, inner turmoil, feeling bored and dead within. But such feelings, if we can look at them and acknowledge them, can be a sign of life and of health. The negative feelings are the expression of our deepest desire, a signal of its opposition to the course of action we are taking and which is now breaking through to our conscious mind.

Finally, if someone really were to turn away from God in the core of their being, they may live carefree lives for years, but every now and again they will have a pang of regret, because God never gives up on anyone, and God's love is indestructible. No person, no situation is ever hopeless.

Fifth Guideline
In desolation we should never go back on a decision made in time of consolation, because the thoughts and judgements springing from desolation are the opposite of those coming from consolation. It is, however, useful to act against the desolation. We should also examine the cause of our desolation.

This guideline does not forbid us from ever changing a decision which we took in consolation. Nor does it ban us from taking any decision in time of desolation. I met one person addicted both to smoking and black coffee drinking, who was settling into a deep depression when he decided he would try anything to jump out of the state, so he gave up both addictions and improved. The guideline only forbids going back on a decision made in time of consolation, while you are in the grip of desolation. When the desolation lifts, you may then go back to discern whether you should remain with your decision.

The final sentence of this guideline can help us avoid years of self-imposed misery! It is simply telling us, when feeling trapped in misery, to look at some very earthy points: are we eating, sleeping, taking enough physical exercise, overworking or being indolent, allowing ourselves enough recreation time? Common-sense questions, and however we respond to them, do it gently, avoiding any form of violence. If we fail to do this we can fall into a lifetime of self-constructed spiritual melodrama!

In my experience of listening to hundreds of individuals of different and of no professed faith, the most common sources of desolation I have found are first, lingering guilt and second, the inability to forgive oneself or anyone else.

Guilt is a healthy reaction to our own wrongdoing. Never to experience any conscious guilt after wrongdoing indicates psychopathic tendencies.

Lingering guilt persists long after the offence has been acknowledged and repented of. It hovers over everything in our past, seems to permeate our being, yet cannot be identified. This is a dire affliction. One exercise which can help is to imagine oneself in prayer before the dying Jesus on the cross. Tell him exactly how hopeless you are feeling. 'Dear Lord, I believe your death on the cross was your final act of love for us all, but do realize that you have met your match in me.' See how long you can keep saying this! Then reflect on what you have said. You have uncovered the absurdity of your own exclusive focus on your own failures, as though they are the most important event in human life.

Another remedy for our inability to forgive is to imagine we are sitting with the person(s) we cannot forgive and Jesus is also sitting with us. Tell your enemies how hurt you feel about what they have done to you and why you cannot forgive them. Then turn to Jesus and see, in imagination, how he might reply.

Sixth Guideline
In desolation, remember two things: i) The desolation will pass; ii) If we can keep the focus of our attention on God's goodness, even if we have no felt experience of God's presence, God will teach us through the desolation. It is as though God is banishing our false securities, revealing God's self to our inner emptiness in order that God may fill and possess it.

The fact that I have no felt experience of God's presence is not a sign of God's absence. This guideline points us back to the core of our Christian faith. If we are to find God and know God's peace and freedom, we must not allow our security to rest in any person, or group, or on any created thing.

Seventh Guideline
In consolation, make the most of it! Acknowledge it as a gift, freely given, to remind you of the state in which you are living permanently and which no power can ever take from you. You are living permanently enfolded within the goodness of God, who is continuously drawing you into God's own life. Let this truth be the anchor of your hope in all future desolation.

As we reflect in this way upon 'felt' consolation, we come to a deepening awareness of the transcendent within us, that we are caught up in something most attractive and much greater than ourselves.

Eighth Guideline
We must face the fears that haunt us.

Every fear we experience can become an invitation to acquire a deeper awareness of the presence of God at the core of our being. This is not a piece of knowledge: it is a real experience, but words can never contain it. An 'Ah!' of wonder is the response. If we can acknowledge our inner fears before God, they can turn out to be our greatest allies. They can hurl us into the lap of God, our rock, refuge and strength. Remember the poem of Francis Thompson, 'The Hound of Heaven':

> All which thy child's mistake
> Fancies as lost, I have stored for thee at home:
> Rise, clasp my hand and come!

Remember also the phrase 'hardening of the oughteries' from Dr Frank Lake. We need to befriend not only our fears, but also our hates and everything that repels us. By 'befriend', I mean acknowledge their existence openly in prayer before God and let God's creative Spirit hover over the chaos, as in the first Creation story in the book of Genesis. Keep doing this and let this phrase guide you through all the vagaries of your life.

'Oughteries' and Orthodoxy: I have already written on this distinction. I just call it to mind in this final guideline because it is a vital distinction in all our discernment. If God's will were not to bear any relationship to our deepest desire, then all our talk about the attractiveness of God, God's unfailing love, compassion etc., would be without meaning or, as St Paul might write, 'like gongs booming or cymbals clashing'. If this were the truth of things, then we would be forced to find our security in some authority external to ourselves. It is this attitude that Martin Buber had in mind when he wrote, in *I and Thou*: 'Nothing so masks the face of God as Religion.' This is an attitude which is widely prevalent today among fundamentalist Christians, who condemn all who do not conform to their own ideas on religion. The same attitude prevails among atheistic humanist fundamentalists. The ideal for all such fundamentalists is a society of people who conform to whatever the current authorities may impose.

They will become the backbone of any totalitarian state. We have to choose. We cannot surrender our freedom to any person, or group, nation or religion.

In the following and final chapter of this book, I shall write on 'Keeping the Vision Alive'.

Exercises

- After reading these guidelines, make a note of any word or phrase which attracts your attention, whether the felt reaction is pleasant or unpleasant. Very frequently, the unpleasant reactions turn out to be the most helpful, provided we give them attention.

- Write your own guidelines and review and revise them periodically.

- On Figure 1 (see page 291), give names to the sheep which form your flock. The names denote your own inner tendencies. All of them are gifts and potentially creative, depending on how you choose to relate to them.

7

On keeping the vision alive

A theme which has run through every part of this book is the importance of desire in our lives.

Why is desire so important? Because it is desire that determines the
course of our life and every detail of it, whether we are conscious of
its influence or not. This is true for every human being. Desire is not
some predetermined fate which befalls us. It is desire which enables
us to have a say in the direction our life takes. Desire draws us in and
through the events we experience; it also warns us when we are doing
violence to ourselves. Desire is continuously drawing us out beyond
ourselves. The ancient Greek word for this phenomenon is *'ekstasis'*,
from which we have the word 'ecstasy', which means literally 'taking a
stand outside ourselves', becoming aware of the reality in which we are
all living in a way which stretches our minds and hearts beyond all the
boundaries which formerly confined us. That is why it is so important
to keep asking ourselves: 'What is the basic desire of my life?'

This chapter sums up and binds together the themes of this book by
giving the answer to this basic question provided by Ignatius Loyola in
his Spiritual Exercises. You will not be surprised to hear that his answer
is that only you can discover this answer in your own experience.
The exercises offered at the end of every chapter of the book are steps
that can enable you to do this. At the end of this chapter I shall give
Ignatius Loyola's own answer in his final contemplation of his Spiritual
Exercises.

As I have said, the event which changed my attitude to his Spiritual
Exercises and turned my boredom with them into enthusiasm was the
recovery of an amazing fact about them – a fact unknown by most
Jesuits for four centuries after Ignatius' death. The great recovery

was the fact that in the 1960s, after Vatican II had urged all Religious Orders and Congregations to recover their original charism leading to their foundation, the Jesuits discovered that the book of the Spiritual Exercises was originally written as a handbook for retreat-givers only, to enable them to lead people through the Exercises individually. The reasoning behind this was the belief that we are all unique and different and that there is no uniform way of forming people spiritually. The first ministry of the early Jesuits was in the giving of the Spiritual Exercises to individuals. They preached and taught as well wherever the need was greatest. They did not accept parishes or bishoprics so that they could be mobile and able to minister wherever the need was greatest. In the first 50 years of their existence, their missionary work spread from Europe and became worldwide, adapting their methods to the needs of the people they encountered, work which still continues today.

I was very caught up with this reintroduction of the individual retreat and have been engaged in it ever since. I saw the transforming effect of the individually given retreat on the lives of so many people, religious believers of all kinds and of people who professed to have no religious affiliation. I discovered a rich spirituality in so many who did not recognize their own giftedness. I shall always be grateful for the insights I was given through these people.

Fifty years later, I feel saddened, but not deluded. I still know that the individual retreat can enliven and transform all kinds of people. My sadness is that I do not see the promise of those earlier decades being realized in the churches or in society today. Yes, there are individuals and groups who are living heroic and selfless lives and are witnesses to God's love, justice and care of creation, but I also see a Catholic Church beset with problems of its own making and I see it taking measures to remedy the situation which, in fact, are worsening it. There is a massive failure of confidence and a desperate power struggle to retain control.

How are we to engage in this global problem? We must start with ourselves, with our own experience; there is no alternative. There is a massive resistance in all of us to facing this task. We blame others for all our crises, have far more trust in the power of control and of violence than in the power of peace. Consequently, we continue to act violently without realizing we are doing so.

The way of unity, the way of peace is not a useless dream. It is already happening in our world. I have seen this indomitable goodness and generosity, hope and trust in the human spirit through decades of encountering people individually through the Spiritual Exercises, given in a variety of forms to people who have neither the time nor the money to afford expensive courses. It is the most desperate people who have taught me most. They are all different in the details of their lives, but there is a common pattern which most of them manifest. In their desperation and withering loneliness, they find themselves crying out, 'God help me. I am perishing'. On reflection later they discover that in that moment of self-abandonment to God, they did recover their ability to cope without crumbling. This self-abandonment is a lifelong process. It is never completed, we have never arrived, but God has become more attractive and the conviction that God is with us in all our situations becomes like a spring of water welling up within us.

In Ignatius' own lifetime, there were many criticisms in the universities and from many eminent clerics within the Catholic Church against the Spiritual Exercises. Briefly, the substance of the criticism was that Ignatius' method of letting people discover for themselves was undermining the authority of the Church. The retreat-giver was no longer in control. In light of my own experience, I wonder if that same fear may not account for the mysterious loss of the individually given retreat for 400 years, and may not also account for the widespread unease within the Catholic Church of today? I know this is a massive question, but the crises it is addressing are also massive and life-threatening.

Where are we to find an anchor for our lives? Is it to be found in some form of external authority to which we can surrender our lives with confidence? This is the danger the Old Testament prophets called idolatry.

I end this book with Ignatius Loyola's answer to this problem. He gives it in his final contemplation in the book of the Exercises, which is called 'a contemplation to attain the love of God'. It is a reminder to keep with us always because it is focused on the goodness of God who is now holding us in being. I give it here in abbreviated form.

He begins with two brief statements on the nature of love:

Love ought to find expression in deeds rather than in words.
Love consists in mutual communication. That is to say the lover gives and communicates to the loved one what they have, or are able to give; and in turn the one loved does the same for the lover. Thus

the one who possesses knowledge will give it to the one without it, similarly with wealth and honour. Each gives to the other.

He then applies this to the relationship between God and ourselves. Then he gives a petition:

To ask for what I want, for an interior knowledge of all the good I have received and am receiving so that full of gratitude I may be able to serve God in everything.

What he is asking for is something towards which my whole life is directed, not something I shall possess. The petition is that we should become increasingly at one with God.

Ignatius then gives four points to consider:

Then consider the gifts you have received, all that you have valued, appreciated, cherished. These earthy things are gifts from God, tokens of God's self-giving to you in love. In light of this, how do you want to reply?

And he offers a prayer you can make after each of these points:

'Take Lord and receive all my liberty, my memory, my under-standing and my entire will, all that I have and possess. You gave it all to me, to you I return it. All is yours. Dispose of it entirely according to your will. Give me only the love of you, together with your grace, for that is enough for me.'

The second point: See how God dwells in creatures; in the elements giving them being; in the plants giving them growth; in the animals giving them sensation; and in humankind granting them the gift of understanding; and so how God dwells also in me, giving me being, life and sensation and causing me to understand. To see too, how God makes a temple of me, as I have been created in the likeness and image of God's Divine Majesty. And in light of this to reflect on myself and repeat, 'Take Lord and receive'.

The third point: To consider how God works and labours on my behalf in all created things on the face of the earth: that is, God acts in the manner of a person at work; in the heavens, elements, plants, fruit and cattle, giving being, conserving life, granting growth and sensation, etc. Then to reflect within myself and repeat, 'Take Lord and receive'.

The fourth point: To see how all that is good and every gift descends from on high. Thus my limited power descends from the supreme and infinite power above, and similarly with justice, goodness, pity, mercy, etc., as rays descend from the sun and waters from a fountain. Then to reflect on myself and repeat, 'Take Lord and receive', and finish with the 'Our Father'.

The earthiness of his spirituality is very clear in this final summary. Ignatius must look down now in amazement at our modern split spirituality, with the battles which go on about science and religion. Ignatius would have delighted in the wonderful scientific and technological advances of our day.

Ignatius Loyola's final contemplation at the end of his book of the Exercises is far more than a final prayer at the end of a retreat. It is a way of summing up the whole nature of the spiritual journey in which we are all engaged, a way of keeping the vision alive. The daily Review of the Day, Examen, etc., is a condensed version of the final exercise to attain the love of God.

I dedicate this book in gratitude to all those people to whom I have ministered through the individually given retreat in the last 60 years, for all they have taught me about the attractiveness of God and the mystery in which God holds all creation. The act of writing has been a great joy and I have a growing sense of the support of so many, living and dead.

And a final request to the reader. Please remember me in your prayers, however vaguely, and I shall remember you similarly in mine. God's postal service transcends both space and time! 'Alleluia!' – a Hebrew word meaning 'Praise the Lord!'

Acknowledgements

I acknowledge the source of this book which is in the countless people, of all Christian denominations, of other faiths and of no professed faith, who have opened their hearts to me. I do not know their names, but I do know they have revealed to me a God of Unity for all creation, a God who offers Peace in conflict for all human beings, a God who offers God's very Self to us, because God is our Love and our Peace.

In particular, I want to acknowledge and thank those individuals and groups who, in recent months, have ensured the final editing and production of this book, a task which is beyond my competence owing to age and the development of incurable pancreatic cancer.

I thank Maggie McCarthy, LSU, with whom I have collaborated for many years for her support and her work in preparing the text of *Cry of Wonder* for publication. Thanks too, to Chris Townsend and family for their invaluable support in producing this book. Thanks to Robin Baird-Smith, my publisher at Bloomsbury for his constant support and encouragement.

I give my thanks to the staff and community at Campion Hall, Oxford, who welcomed me and enabled me, unemployed, to write *Cry of Wonder*.

My thanks to Sarah Hipperson and my nephew, Gerry S. M. Hughes, for agreeing to my recounting and reflecting on their stories.

I acknowledge with gratitude the many friends who continue to support me with their ability to listen, to love and to laugh in and through the Spirit of God.